VORWORT

False Friends sind eine notwendige Begleiterscheinung des Fremdsprachenlernens. Es handelt sich um einen Fehlertyp, der auf allen Ebenen der fremdsprachlichen Kompetenz auftritt. Es ist ein weitverbreiteter Irrtum, daß False Friends nur im Englisch des Lernanfängers vorkommen. Auch bei fortgeschrittenen Englischkenntnissen fallen Fehler im False Friends-Bereich mit erstaunlicher Regelmäßigkeit an. Zwei Beispiele aus dem Bereich der Adjektive mögen dies verdeutlichen: Dem deutschen False Friends-Partner "*dick*" stehen im Englischen als Entsprechungen "*thick*" oder "*fat*" gegenüber. Insofern handelt es sich um einen einfachen False Friend. Andererseits dürfte der deutsche Sprachbenutzer bei der Wiedergabe von Wendungen wie "ein *dicker* Fehler" = "a *bad* (a *serious* or *grave*) mistake", "eine *dicke* Eiche" = "a *stout* oak" oder "im *dicksten* (= starker, dichter) Feierabendverkehr" = "in *heavy* rush-hour traffic" leicht in Schwierigkeiten geraten. Aber auch umgekehrt hat der Lernende bei Verbindungen wie "eine *belegte* Stimme" = "a *thick* voice", "*dichter* Nebel" = "*thick* fog", "*dickflüssige* Farbe" = "*thick* paint" oder "*dichtes* Haar" = "*thick* hair" nicht unbedingt bessere Karten.

Englischlernende durchschauen sehr schnell ein False Friends-Paar wie "*selbstbewußt*" und "*self-conscious*", das nicht, wie viele annehmen, "*selbstbewußt*", sondern "*befangen*" (oder "*gehemmt*", "*verlegen*") entspricht. Anders verhält es sich in den folgenden Gebrauchssituationen: Wenn etwa der Arbeitskollege "*zu selbstbewußt*" auftritt, ist "*self-assertive*" das treffende Adjektiv zur Kennzeichnung eines solchen Verhaltens. Sollten Sie aber meinen, Ihre Freundin könnte ein wenig "*selbstbewußter*" sein, so liegen Sie mit "*(be) more self-assured*" goldrichtig. Leider gebrauchen hier viele "*self-confident*", das die richtige Lösung für "*selbstbewußt*" in fast allen anderen Fällen ist. Übrigens können Sie "*befangen*" im juristischen Sinn keinesfalls mit "*self-conscious*" wiedergeben, sondern nur mit Adjektiven wie "*prejudiced*" oder "*partial*". Selbst – zugegebenermaßen – leichtere False Friends können sich beim aktiven Sprachgebrauch als ausgesprochene Stolpersteine erweisen.

Das vorliegende Buch und der Nachfolgeband "More False Friends" (rororo sprachen 9172) sind nach vier Schwierigkeitskategorien gegliedert: im ersten stehen die EASY FALSE FRIENDS und NOT SO EASY FALSE FRIENDS im Mittelpunkt, im zweiten Band werden die DIFFICULT FALSE FRIENDS und PARTICULARLY DIFFICULT FALSE FRIENDS behandelt.

Gerne benutze ich die Gelegenheit, einigen *native speakers* zu danken, die an diesem Buch in verschiedenen Stadien seiner Entstehung beratend beteiligt waren:
Peter Bews, B. A., der die erste Manuskriptfassung mit Sachkenntnis und manchen Anregungen begleitete.
Dr. J. Tudor Morris, M. A., der landeskundliche Detailfragen sachgerecht klärte und eine frühe Teilfassung dieses Buchs mit erfrischenden Kommentaren förderte.
Christina Lausevic, B. Sc., P. G. C. E., die der Durchsicht des Manuskripts ihre fachlich fundierte Sachkenntnis angedeihen ließ.
C. Ross Martin, B. A., der sich mit bewundernswerter Geduld für Fragen des sprachlichen Feinschliffs zur Verfügung stellte.
Ihnen, aber auch einigen ungenannten Personen, die mir mit ihrem Sachverstand weiterhalfen, bin ich zu Dank verpflichtet. Außerdem erfuhr ich bei der Abklärung von deutschen Bedeutungen im Gebrauchskontext Unterstützung durch die Sprachberatungsstelle der Dudenredaktion (Bibliographisches Institut). Allen sei an dieser Stelle nochmals aufrichtig gedankt.

Die Dialoge wurden original für dieses Buch geschrieben. Eine Reihe von Ideen hierzu stammt aus englischsprachigen Zeitungsberichten der Jahre 1987 bis 1991.

Heidelberg, Ostern 1991 — Hartmut Breitkreuz

ERRORS

Hartmut Breitkreuz

False Friends

Stolpersteine des deutsch-englischen Wortschatzes

Zeichnungen
Mathias Hütter

rororo

Rowohlt

Originalausgabe
Veröffentlicht im Rowohlt Taschenbuch Verlag GmbH,
Reinbek bei Hamburg, Oktober 1991

Umschlagillustration Gerd Huss
Umschlagtypographie Büro Hamburg/Peter Wippermann
Satz Times und Helvetica (Linotronic 500)
Gesamtherstellung Clausen & Bosse, Leck
Printed in Germany
1480-ISBN 3 499 18492 3

For Helga, Beate and Elke – my True Friends

God keep you from … **False Friends.**

W. Shakespeare: **Richard III**, 1_{15-16}

INHALT

VORWORT 9

Gebrauchshinweise:
LERNEN IM FALSE FRIENDS-BEREICH –
LERNBEDINGUNGEN UND LERNTIPS 11

False Friends-Zeichen und -Typen 19

TEIL I: Stolpersteine des deutsch-englischen
Wortschatzes 21

EASY FALSE FRIENDS:
False Friends-Paare A–W 22

Tests 1–4: FALSE FRIENDS TRAPS 51
Lösungen 1–4: TRUE FRIENDS 52

TEIL II: Stolpersteine des deutsch-englischen
Wortschatzes 143

NOT SO EASY FALSE FRIENDS:
False Friends-Paare A–Z 144

Tests 5–8: FALSE FRIENDS TRAPS 177
Lösungen 5–8: TRUE FRIENDS 178

FINAL TEST I and Answer Sheet 272–274
FINAL TEST II and Answer Sheet 275–277

False Friends-Übersicht 278

Literaturhinweise 281

FALSE FRIENDS-INDEX 283

rororo sprachen
Herausgegeben von
Ludwig Moos

Falsche Freunde sind besonders tückisch. Die False Friends, jene Worte oder Wortpaare, die im Deutschen und Englischen gleich oder fast gleich aussehen und zudem in vielen Fällen täuschend ähnlich klingen, aber eine andere Bedeutung haben, sind zähe Begleiter. Ihrer Anwesenheit sind sich die meisten bewußt, wie die Beliebtheit des Gag-Englisch in der Art von "When do I *become* a beefsteak?" zeigt, doch ihre geschickteren Tarnungen durchschauen selbst sprachlich Fortgeschrittene oft nicht. Dieses Buch entlarvt die False Friends gründlich und hilft, sich ihrer mit Beispielen, Tests und griffigen Kommentaren auf immer zu entledigen.

Der Nachfolgeband "More False Friends" (rororo sprachen 9172) nimmt es mit den noch raffinierteren Vertretern dieser Spezies auf.

Prof. Hartmut Breitkreuz, M. A., lehrt auf dem Fachgebiet Englisch (Methodik und Didaktik des Fremdsprachenunterrichts und Angewandte Linguistik) an der Pädagogischen Hochschule Heidelberg.

LERNEN IM FALSE FRIENDS-BEREICH: LERNBEDINGUNGEN UND LERNTIPS

Die sprachliche Erscheinung der False Friends kann auf den ersten Blick als eine Art Sprachspielerei erscheinen. Bei näherem Hinsehen entpuppen sich die Falschen Freunde aber als ernstzunehmende Stolpersteine des deutsch-englischen Wortschatzes. Die hier behandelten False Friends-Paare dürfen zudem als ausgesprochen typisch für das Englisch des deutschen Fremdsprachenlerners gelten. Das sollte Grund genug sein, diesem besonderen Fehlerbereich mehr Aufmerksamkeit zuzuwenden.

Begriffsklärung

False Friends können als Wortpaare definiert werden, die durch fehlerhaften Sprachvergleich zwischen dem Deutschen als Muttersprache und dem Englischen als Fremdsprache entstehen. Bei diesem Vorgang folgt die Mehrzahl der False Friends-Paare der irreführenden Wirkung sprachlicher Ähnlichkeit wie in *Gift* ≠ *gift*. Eine kleinere Anzahl von False Friends unterliegt der täuschenden Wirkung sprachlicher Analogie wie in *selbstbewußt* ≠ *self-conscious*. Um im Beispiel zu bleiben: Die englischen Wörter *headline* (= *Schlagzeile*) und *heading* (= *Überschrift*) sind trotz ihrer Ähnlichkeit *keine* False Friends, denn es liegen hier weder sprachliche Ähnlichkeit noch eine sprachliche Analogiewirkung zwischen den deutschen und englischen Begriffspartnern vor.

Typen von False Friends

Je nach Ausgangspunkt der sprachlichen Beschäftigung ist generell zwischen False Friends des Fremdsprachenlerners, der falsch vom Deutschen auf ähnliche Wörter im Englischen schließt, und False Friends des Übersetzers zu unterscheiden, der bestimmte Wörter aus dem Englischen falsch ins Deutsche als Folge täuschender Ähnlichkeitswirkung überträgt.

Außerdem gibt es vier grundlegende False Friends-Typen, die der Englischlernende kennen sollte:

a) Rechtschreibbedingte False Friends wie in *Baracke ≠ barracks* (im Deutschen *r*, im Englischen *rr*)
b) Aussprachebedingte False Friends wie in *Technik* (Erstsilbenbetonung) und *technique* (Zweitsilbenbetonung)
c) Bedeutungsbedingte False Friends wie in *Schellfisch*, dem im Englischen nicht *shellfish*, sondern *haddock* entspricht
d) Mehrfach-False Friends (mehrfache Fehler-Kombination in einem False Friend).

Dieses Buch stellt die bedeutungsbedingten False Friends in den Mittelpunkt, die den auffälligsten und nach Meinung der Fachleute wichtigsten Fehlertyp unter den False Friends bilden. Aus diesem Grunde ist unter den bedeutungsbedingten False Friends zwischen vollen (totalen) False Friends wie *Tablett ≠ tablet* und halbwahren (partiellen) False Friends wie *borgen* ◑ *borrow* zu unterscheiden. Zwischen vollen oder echten False Friends-Paaren steht das Zeichen ≠ und zwischen halbwahren False Friends das Zeichen ◑.

Dem methodischen Aufbau jeder Lerneinheit (Unit) liegt jeweils ein False Friends-Paar zugrunde. Bei der Gegenüberstellung (Kontrastierung) von False Friends durchläuft der Lernvorgang vier Schritte:

Fehlerstufe: Bewußtmachung im False Friends-Dreieck

Ausgangspunkt im False Friends-Dreieck ist in der Regel der fehlerauslösende deutsche False Friends-Partner; das Adjektiv *ausgesprochen* dient als Beispiel. Dem deutschen Begriff stehen auf der Fehlerstufe meist zwei mögliche englische Entsprechungen im False Friends-Dreieck gegenüber. Hierbei kann der englische Begriffspartner *outspoken* zumindest von der Form her richtig sein, stellt sich aber von der Bedeutung her als falsch heraus; es handelt sich daher um einen False Friend. Bei dem anderen Begriffspartner *decided* (etc.) handelt es sich um die richtige Entsprechung, also den True Friend. Zur Bewußtmachung ergibt sich folgende Ausgangsform:

AUSGESPROCHEN ≠ outspoken

False Friend: outspoken

Fehlerauslösender deutscher Begriff: **AUSGESPROCHEN**

True Friend: decided (etc.)

In der fehlertherapeutisch angelegten Ausgangsform erscheint der False Friend *outspoken* auf der gepunkteten Linie und der True Friend *decided* (etc.) auf der durchgezogenen Linie. Das False Friends-Dreieck stellt zum Lernen eine Bewußtmachung dar, sich über den fehlerauslösenden deutschen Begriff, den ähnlichen (oder von der Form her gleichen) False Friend und die richtige Entsprechung, den True Friend, Klarheit zu verschaffen.

False Friends-Lernen auf der Korrekturstufe

Das Auseinanderhalten und Einprägen meist mehrerer Begriffe auf der Korrekturstufe bilden den entscheidenden Schritt auf dem Wege zur Bewußtmachung des Fehlerproblems. In einem Doppelschritt werden deutsch-englische und englisch-deutsche Bedeutungen in Anwendungsbeispielen gegenübergestellt. Gleichzeitig gilt es, die Kombinationsmöglichkeiten von False Friends mit anderen Begriffen zu erfassen.

Um im Beispiel zu bleiben: Dem deutschen Begriff *ausgesprochen* stehen auf der Korrekturstufe im heller unterlegten Feld die drei Adjektive *decided, marked, pronounced* gegenüber; *marked(ly)* ist bedeutungsmäßig meist negativ besetzt. In dem dunkel unterlegten Feld stehen die deutschen Entsprechungen für *outspoken*. Für dieses False Friends-Paar werden folgende Kombinationsmöglichkeiten kontrastiv angeboten:

ausgesprochen (Adjektiv)	(1)	**ausgesprochene** Vorliebe	**decided** preference
		ausgesprochene Abgeneigtheit	**marked** unwillingness
		ausgesprochener Akzent	**pronounced** accent
ausgesprochen (Adverb)	(2)	**ausgesprochen** gedrückt	**decidedly** gloomy
		ausgesprochen schlechtes Wetter	**extremely** bad weather
		ausgesprochen gemischte Gefühle	**markedly** mixed feelings

outspoken	(1) (be) an **outspoken** critic (be) **outspoken**	**offene** Kritik (üben) (sich) **freimütig** äußern
outspoken	(2) **outspoken** criticism **outspoken** views	**unverblümte** Kritik **ungeschminkte** Ansichten

Weitere Kombinationsmöglichkeiten lassen sich in diesem Fall finden; bei anderen False Friends können sie aber sehr begrenzt sein. Auf der Korrekturstufe hat dieses False Friends-Paar folgendes Aussehen:

AUSGESPROCHEN: (1) adj.: decided, marked, pronounced
(2) adv.: decidedly, extremely, markedly

Note: '**marked**' is mostly used in a negative sense.

(1) Mein Onkel hat eine **ausgesprochene** Vorliebe für englische Briefmarken aus dem letzten Jahrhundert.
My uncle has a **decided** preference for English stamps of the last century.
Es bestand **ausgesprochene** Abgeneigtheit, die Angelegenheit zu diskutieren.
There was a **marked** unwillingness to discuss the matter.
Der neue Rektor der Universität hat einen **ausgesprochen** schottischen Akzent.
The new Vice-Chancellor of the university has a **pronounced** Scottish accent.
(2) Die Stimmung der Labour-Abgeordneten war **ausgesprochen** gedrückt.
The mood of the Labour M. P.s was **decidedly** gloomy.
Ausgesprochen schlechtes Wetter unterbrach alle weiteren Segel-Wettbewerbe.
Extremely bad weather stopped all further sailing competitions.
Experten in Großbritannien betrachteten den neuen Haushalt mit **ausgesprochen** gemischten Gefühlen.
Experts in Britain viewed the new budget with **markedly** mixed feelings.

outspoken: (1) offen, freimütig
(2) unverblümt, ungeschminkt

(1) B. Andreatta was an **outspoken** critic of the Italian banks.
B. Andreatta übte **offene** Kritik an den italienischen Banken.
Many Russians are very **outspoken** nowadays about their country.
Viele Russen äußern sich heutzutage sehr **freimütig** über ihr Land.
(2) The **outspoken** criticism of the reporter surprised everyone.
Die **unverblümte** Kritik des Reporters überraschte alle.
One of the M. P.s echoed some of the Trade Secretary's more **outspoken** views.
Einer der Abgeordneten gab einige recht **ungeschminkte** Ansichten des Handelsministers wieder.

Zur besseren Unterscheidung ist der deutsche False Friends-Partner stets in großen, der englische False Friends-Partner in kleinen Buchstaben ausgedruckt. Die zugehörigen Anwendungsbeispiele folgen in kontrastiver Anlage erst deutsch-englisch, danach englisch-deutsch.

Kurz-Fehlertherapie im False Friends-Viereck
Aus Gründen der Lernerleichterung werden die bisherigen Vorgänge abschließend im False Friends-Viereck "auf einen Blick" gegenübergestellt. Die Vierergruppierung ergibt sich folgerichtig aus den beiden Blöcken der Korrekturstufe.
Für das False Friends-Paar *ausgesprochen ≠ outspoken* – um unser Beispiel wiederaufzunehmen – ergibt sich im False Friends-Viereck folgende Anordnung:

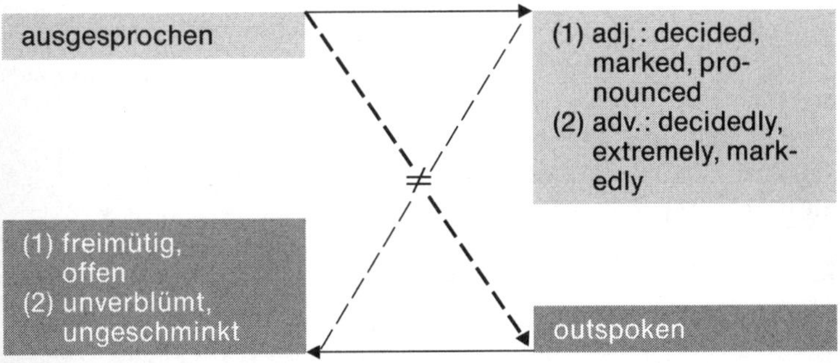

Die Kurz-Fehlertherapie im False Friends-Viereck sollte als Lernschritt in keinem Fall leichtfertig übergangen werden. Es geht um die richtige Bedeutungszuordnung, deren Anwendung im folgenden Übungsangebot ansteht.

Eigene Absicherung im Kontext

Der Schlußteil FALSE FRIENDS IN CONTEXT bildet ein erstes Übungsangebot in Lückentestform. In (teilweise) amüsanten oder nachdenklich stimmenden Dialogen, witzigen oder anekdotenhaften Begebenheiten, aber auch problemhaltigen Situationen kommt jeweils nur ein False Friends-Paar im Kontext zur Anwendung. Die Lernbelastung wird an einem Dialog, hier dem problemhaltigen Dialog *A Modern Village War*, verdeutlicht:

FALSE FRIENDS IN CONTEXT

A Modern Village War

Guardian Correspondent: Many people in Britain's industrial areas still live in ________ (1) unhealthy housing conditions.
Architect: I fully agree. That's where Prince Charles's "New Vision of Britain" starts from. His plan is for four new villages, where people both live and work.
Guardian Correspondent: That's where the problem began. People in the Dorchester area and even tenants of his own Duchy of Cornwall are against his scheme.
Architect: Prince Charles has been one of the most ________ (2) critics of architects in recent years. On the other hand, he also called the London Docklands a ________ (3) success for property developers.
Guardian Correspondent: I agree. Many angry families have recently protested in a series of public meetings against the new "live where you work" villages. The people of the Poundbury development don't want to be the Prince's guinea pigs.

SOLUTION

(1) **decidedly** unhealthy (2) outspoken (3) a **pronounced** succes

Einen Text mit wenigen Lücken (wie hier) kann auch der beruflich Beanspruchte ohne nennenswerten Zeitaufwand bewältigen; zudem stehen die Lösungen direkt unter dem Text.

Überprüfung des eigenen Lernfortschritts

Nach der Beschäftigung mit durchschnittlich 10 bis 12 False Friends ist jeweils ein Zwischentest eingeschaltet. Erstmals werden mehrere False Friends in Kontrastform angeboten, um die eigene Gebrauchssicherheit und den Lernfortschritt zu überprüfen.
Insgesamt stehen dem Lernenden 8 False Friends-Zwischentests (mit Lösungen) zur Verfügung. Diesen Lernfortschritts-Tests folgen am Schluß zwei Abschlußtests. Jede Einzelaufgabe verlangt in kontrastiver Form eine Doppellösung.

Tips zum Erlernen von False Friends

Vor der Beschäftigung mit einzelnen False Friends lohnt es sich, aus zeit- und lernökonomischen Gründen einigen “goldenen” Lerntips Aufmerksamkeit zu widmen.

Lerntip 1: Ähnlich geschriebene und teilweise auch ähnlich klingende Wörter im Deutschen und Englischen erweisen sich als hochgradig fehleranfällig.
In weit mehr als 90 Prozent der Fälle handelt es sich um False Friends. Lassen Sie sich nicht durch die täuschende Ähnlichkeit deutsch-englischer Wortpaare aufs Glatteis führen!

Lerntip 2: Stellen Sie stets die richtige Bedeutungsentsprechung zwischen den False Friends-Partnern her.
In diesem Buch kommt es nicht auf die äußere Gleichheit oder Ähnlichkeit von Wörtern an, sondern auf die richtige Entsprechung der Bedeutungen und deren verwendungsgerechte Kombination im Kontext.

Lerntip 3: Prüfen Sie, ob ein voller (totaler) oder ein halbwahrer (partieller) False Friend vorliegt.
Halbwahre False Friends bilden eine besonders fehleranfällige Gruppe. Das Tückische an diesem False Friends-Typ besteht darin, daß es bei *einem* False Friend teils bedeutungsverschiedene, teils bedeutungsgleiche Bereiche gibt. Aus diesem Grunde wird *Bank* im Englischen teils mit *bank* (= *Geldinstitut*) und teils mit *bench* (= *Sitzgelegenheit*) oder im Falle der Kirchen*bank* mit *pew* wiedergegeben.

Lerntip 4: Überprüfen Sie fehleranfällige deutsch-englische Wortpaare am False Friends-Viereck auf den richtigen Bedeutungsbezug.
Bei Verdacht auf Vorliegen eines Fehlers im False Friends-Bereich

prüfen Sie gleiche oder ähnliche deutsch-englische Wortpaare zunächst am False Friends-Dreieck und danach am False Friends-Viereck auf die richtige Zuordnung der Bedeutung. Wörterbücher helfen meist nicht weiter, wohl aber False Friends-Spezialwörterbücher.

Lerntip 5: False Friends, bei denen beim Gebrauch gleichzeitig Fehler in Schreibung, Aussprache und Bedeutung entstehen, sind Mehrfach-False Friends.
Es handelt sich um Mehrfach-Fehler bei einem False Friend (vergleiche das Beispiel *Baracke ≠ barracks* in dem Abschnitt "Typen von False Friends"). Solche False Friends müssen besonders geübt, um schnell "verlernt" zu werden.

Lerntip 6: False Friends tauchen auch in den Fachsprachen auf und führen meist ein zähes Eigenleben.
In fachsprachlichen Bezeichnungen vermutet der Lernende am wenigsten False Friends. Es handelt sich hier um einen berufsbezogenen Spezialtip, auf fachsprachliche False Friends zu achten. So kommen in diesem Buch folgende fachsprachliche False Friends vor: ein (elektrischer) *Ventilator* ist im Englischen nicht (electric) *ventilator*, sondern (electric) *fan*; zwar entspricht *Schlange* in der Regel *snake*, aber eine *grass snake* ist im Deutschen eine Ringel*natter*.
Nebenbei: Vielleicht können Sie mir den einen oder anderen fachsprachlichen False Friend, den Sie finden, mitteilen. Abschließend wünsche ich Ihnen für den richtigen Umgang mit False Friends den notwendigen (Lern-)Erfolg.

Hartmut Breitkreuz

False Friends-Zeichen und -Typen

False Friends-Zeichen	Zeichen-Erklärung	False Friends-Beispiele	False Friends-Typ
≠	ist nicht bedeutungsgleich, entspricht nicht	FLUR ≠ floor GIFT ≠ gift HELM ≠ helm VIKAR ≠ vicar	voller False Friend, totaler False Friend, echter False Friend
◑	ist nur teilweise bedeutungsgleich, entspricht nicht immer	BANK ◑ bank DICK ◑ thick RATE ◑ rate SALAT ◑ salad	teilweiser False Friend, partieller False Friend, unechter False Friend, 'halbwahrer' False Friend

TEIL I

EASY FALSE FRIENDS

ÄLTER ◑ older

older

ÄLTER
(verwandte Personen)

elder

ÄLTER(-e, -es, -er): elder (of relatives)

Note: It is more formally correct to speak of 'my **elder** sister' than to use 'older' (which is also in current use).

Heute rief mich meine **ältere** Schwester an.
My **elder** sister gave me a ring today.
Wer ist der **ältere** von beiden, Tim oder Harry?
Which is the **elder** of the two, Tim or Harry?

Note: ein älteres Ehepaar = an **elderly** couple
ein erfahrener Staatsmann = an **elder** statesman
T. S. Eliot's last play 'The **Elder** Statesman' was published in 1959.

but: ein schwarzer Holunder(baum) = a common **elder** tree

older: (1) älter (nicht-verwandte Personen)
(2) älter (von Dingen)

Note: 'Elder' cannot be used before 'than'. Always use '**older**' in this case.

(1) As you grow **older**, you begin to see things in perspective.
Wenn man **älter** wird, sieht man die Dinge mit mehr Abstand.
After the fight he looked at least five years **older**.
Nach dem Kampf sah er mindestens fünf Jahre **älter** aus.
Die Schauspielerin ist sechs Jahre **älter** als ich, aber sie sieht viel jünger aus.
The actress is six years **older** than me, but she looks much younger.
(2) The castle over there is **older** than you think.
Die Burg dort drüben ist **älter**, als du glaubst.

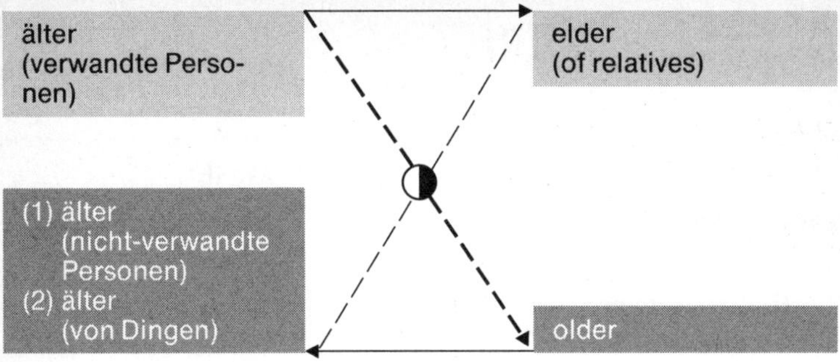

FALSE FRIENDS IN CONTEXT

Two Problems of a Different Order

Think Twice

Mr. Barnes, their teacher, was trying to teach the value of good behaviour to a class of youngsters.

Mr. Barnes: ... Of course, I'm a bit ________ (1) than you. But if your mother gave you two oranges and asked you to give one to your sister, would you give her the bigger one or the smaller one?

(Teacher waits a few seconds before pointing at Norman)

Norman: It depends. Do you mean my younger sister or my ______ (2) sister?

Teaching Bullies a Lesson

How many parents say good-bye to their child at the school gate to find out later it's been bullied by ________ (3) boys?

Little Richard Mack, for example, was seven when he died after being hit on the head by a golf ball. Some children said it was aimed at Richard by an ________ (4) school bully. Richard's father claims his son had been picked on before by an ________ (5) boy.

It's too late for little Richard, but there are hundreds of other youngsters suffering in silence.

SOLUTION

(1) older (2) elder (3) older (4) older (5)older

ANGEL ≠ angle

angle ['æŋgl]

ANGEL

fishing-rod

ANGEL: (1) fishing-rod, rod (AE fishing-pole)
(2) in combinations such as '**fishing**-licence'

(1) Hast du nicht eine bessere **Angel**? Damit fange ich nie einen Fisch.
Haven't you got a better **fishing-rod**? I'll never catch a fish with this one.
(2) Besorge dir zuerst einen **Angel**schein für die schottischen Seen, und kaufe dir dann das **Angel**gerät.
First get a **fishing**-licence for the Scottish lakes and then buy the **fishing**-tackle.
Plötzlich senkte sich die **Angel**spitze, und innerhalb von Sekunden lag er mit einem riesigen Fisch im Kampf.
Suddenly his **rod** tip dipped and within seconds he was tussling with the fish of a lifetime.

Note: **Angel**rolle = **fishing**-reel
but: der Angler = angler   angeln gehen = go fishing
das Angeln = angling
Angling is Britain's biggest participant sport.
More than one million people in Britain **go fishing** on rivers, lakes, reservoirs or at sea.

angle: (1) Winkel (math.); Blick-, Flugwinkel etc.
(2) Aspekt, Gesichtspunkt

(1) "Look, the first **angle** is an acute **angle**, the second is an obtuse **angle** and the third a right **angle**," the maths teacher explained.
"Schaut mal, der erste **Winkel** ist ein spitzer Winkel, der zweite ist ein stumpfer **Winkel** und der dritte ein rechter **Winkel**", erklärte der Mathematik-Lehrer.
If the police shoot at the kidnappers from this **angle**, they won't hit any of them when they leave the building.

Wenn die Polizei von diesem **Blickwinkel** auf die Kidnapper schießt, wird sie keinen von ihnen beim Verlassen des Gebäudes treffen.
Bonfire organizers were advised rockets should not exceed an overall **angle** of flight of 30 degrees.
Die Veranstalter von Feuerwerken wurden angewiesen, Raketen sollten einen Gesamt-Flug**winkel** von 30 Grad nicht überschreiten.
(2) You can see he is thinking of yet another **angle**.
Wie du siehst, denkt er noch an einen anderen **Aspekt**.
She always takes time to talk to the press to give them perhaps a new **angle**.
Sie nimmt sich stets Zeit, mit den Pressevertretern zu reden, um ihnen vielleicht einen neuen **Gesichtspunkt** zu liefern.
Note: tri**angle** = Dreieck
In the Eighties the bikini became little more than three tri**angles** held in place with string.

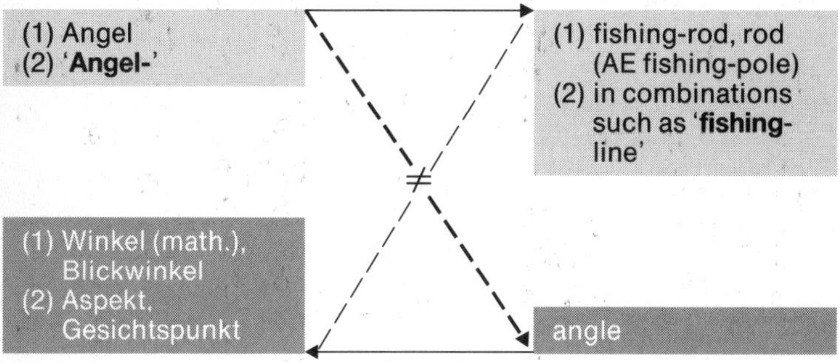

FALSE FRIENDS IN CONTEXT

Fisherman's Van Driven by Dog

What happened to angler Ray Harms and his dog at Portland Bill, Dorset, is true.
Angler: I parked my van at the top of the cliffs and left Muttley, my dog, inside to guard the van. Then I took my ________ (1) and clambered down to the beach fifty feet below.
Police Officer (trying to establish the facts): How long did you stay there?
Angler: About two hours. Then suddenly a big fish took the bait and began to pull.

Police Officer: Did you hold on to your ________ (2)?
Angler: I did, although the pull was strong. From my ________ (3). I could see I had hooked a giant eel, about five feet long – about the same length as my van.
Police Officer: What happened next?
Angler: The next thing I heard was a crunching noise behind me. Looking round I saw my van had crashed onto the beach, next to me.
Police Officer: Were you hurt?
Angler: Fortunately not, but when I saw what a mess my van was I dropped my ________ (4). The next thing I remember was my collie Muttley creeping out of the wreckage and coming to me with his tail between his legs. It was then that I went to pick up my ________ (5) and saw it had disappeared. The giant eel, a conger, had dragged it into the depths of the sea.
Police Officer: But how could your car have been moved?
Angler: The collie had accidentally released the handbrake, causing the van to roll off the clifftop and smash on the sand. Muttley knew he had done something stupid.
Police Officer: Can you show me your driving-licence and your ________ (6)-licence, please?

SOLUTION

(1) (fishing-)rod (2) (fishing-)rod (3) angle (4) (fishing-)rod (5) (fishing-)rod (6) **fishing**-licence

ALSO ≠ also

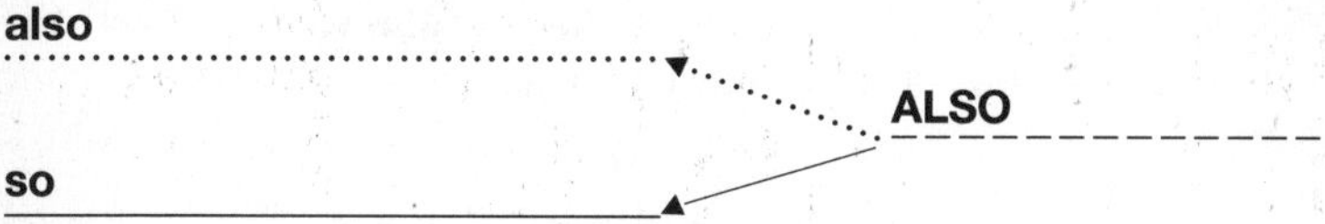

ALSO: (1) so; therefore (more formal)
(2) then (coll.)

(1) Unser Lehrer kam nicht zur letzten Stunde; **also** gingen wir nach Hause.
Our teacher didn't turn up for the last period, **so** we went home.
Er war zum dritten Mal nicht ausgezogen; **also** wurde der Gerichtsvollzieher herbeigerufen, um ihn herauszusetzen.
He failed to move out for the third time; **therefore** the bailiff was called in to evict him.
(2) **Also** ist es doch wahr? Wo warst du **also** den ganzen Nachmittag?
Is it true **then**? Where were you **then** all afternoon?
Warum **also** glauben die meisten deutschen Frauen, daß ihnen noch immer wirkliche Gleichberechtigung fehlt?
Why, **then**, do most German women feel that they still lack real equality?
Denkt **also** an den Mut des Schauspielers, der Jonathan spielt.
Consider the courage, **then**, of the actor who plays Jonathan.

also: (1) auch, ebenfalls
(2) außerdem, daneben

(1) Could you **also** come tonight?
Könntest du **auch** heute abend kommen?
What, he is a writer and **also** a politician?
Was, er ist Schriftsteller und **ebenfalls** Politiker?
Also aboard was the body of a three-month-old baby who had died of malaria.
Ebenfalls an Bord befand sich die Leiche eines drei Monate alten Babies, das an Malaria gestorben war.
(2) There were, **also**, two songs which had all the hallmarks of hits, one a love ballad and the other a gospel number.

Außerdem standen zwei Chansons, die deutliche Kennzeichen von Schlagern aufwiesen, auf dem Programm, eines eine Liebesballade und das andere eine Gospel-Nummer.
The new actress was young and beautiful, and **also** very talented.
Die neue Schauspielerin war jung und schön, und **daneben** sehr talentiert.

Note: not... either = **auch**... nicht (in negative sentences).
Her daughter hadn't returned from the weekend party and she had**n't** phoned **either**.

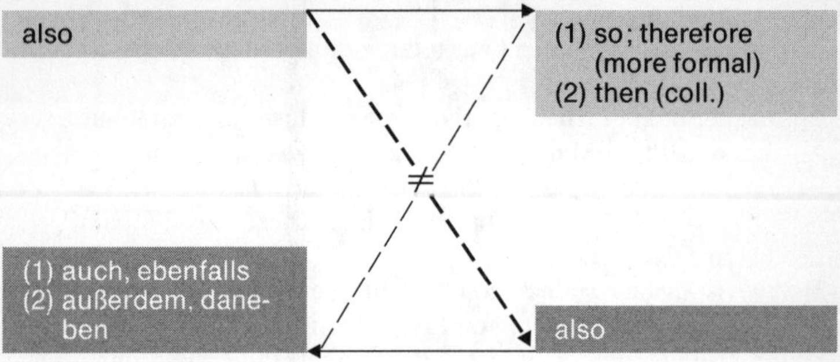

FALSE FRIENDS IN CONTEXT

Too Good to be True

I had written to a number of people. I ________ (1) wrote away to a male penfriend while I was in hospital. After a short time I ________ (2) received a letter in broken English, signed Belmonde.
________(3) I decided to visit him when I left hospital. Before I rang the bell, I thought of starting on a more personal note, "Why didn't you come and see me in hospital, ________ (4)?"
To my surprise the door was opened by a beautiful woman. She introduced herself as Belmonde. "Are you really Belmonde, ________ (5)?" I asked her in surprise.
She blushed a little and we fell in love almost at first sight. ________ (6) I popped the question within the hour. We have been married for more than thirty years!!

SOLUTION

(1) also (2) also (3) then (4) then (5) then (6) so; therefore

"Is it true then?"

BANK ◑ bank

bank

BANK

bench

(Sitz**bank** etc.)

BANK: (1) (Sitz**bank**) bench
(2) (Kirchen**bank**) pew

(1) Die grünen Plastik**bänke** im Park sehen besser aus als die alten, dachte die alte Dame bei sich.
The green plastic **benches** in the park look better than the old ones, thought the old lady to herself.
(2) Wie oft soll ich noch vor leeren (Kirchen-)**Bänken** predigen, fragte sich der Pfarrer.
How often do I have to preach to empty **pews**, wondered the vicar.

bank: (1) (Geldinstitut) Bank
(2) (Fluß-, See-) Ufer
(3) (Computer) Speicher

(1) The **banks** have raised interest rates by 1 per cent.
Die **Banken** haben die Zinsen um 1 Prozent erhöht.
(2) It was quiet here. The young man, who was unemployed, liked sitting on the **bank** of the River Derwent watching the ducks. On Sunday he would go fishing on the **bank** of the lake further south.
Es war ruhig hier. Der arbeitslose junge Mann saß gerne am **Ufer** des Derwent und beobachtete die Enten. Am Sonntag würde er am See**ufer** weiter südlich fischen gehen.
(3) "A computer is a memory **bank**," the programmer maintained.
"Ein Computer ist ein Gedächtnis**speicher**", behauptete der Programmierer.

Note: bottle **bank** = Container für Altglas
"All our bottles go to the bottle **bank** and all our paper is recycled," she emphasized.

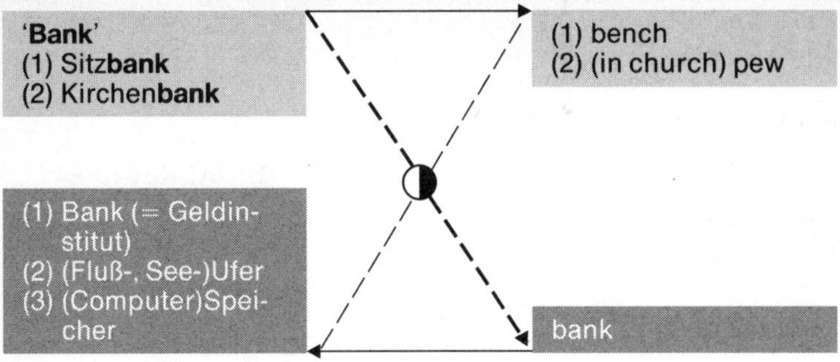

FALSE FRIENDS IN CONTEXT

Three Definitions: Same, but Different

First Definition: A ________ (1) is a place where they will lend you money provided you can prove that you don't need it.

Second Definition: A ________ (2) is a seat in a church where you can talk to God.

Third Definition: The ________ (3) of a river is a place for fishing and meditation.

SOLUTION

(1) bank (2) pew (3) bank

BARACKE(N) ≠ barracks

barracks [ˈbærəks]

BARACKE(N)

huts

BA**R**ACKE(N): (1) huts, shacks; shed
(2) (Elends**baracke**) shanty

(1) Es war Winter. Wie konnten die Gefangenen in den **Baracken** überleben? Es gab kein Gas und keine Kohlen.
It was winter. How could the prisoners survive in the **huts**? There was no gas and no coal.
Viele Brasilianer leben in ärmlichen **Baracken** ohne Wasser und ohne Elektrizität.
Many Brazilians live in poor **shacks** without water and without electricity.
“Trage die Sachen in die Werkzeug-**Baracke** da drüben”, sagte der Vorarbeiter.
“Carry the things to the tool **shed** over there,” the foreman told me.
(2) Mutter Teresa begann bald in einer **Baracken**-Vorstadt von Kalkutta zu helfen.
Mother Teresa soon started to help in a **shanty** town in Calcutta.

Note: Wellblech-**Baracke** = corrugated iron **hut**; Nissen **hut** (BE), Quonset **hut** (AE)
Bau**baracke** = contractor’s **hut**

barracks: Kaserne

Note: In BE the word ‘barracks’ is always used in the plural, although in both BE and AE ‘**one** barracks’ may be meant.

“Sorry, darling. But I’ll have to be back at the **barracks** by six in the morning.” She began to cry.
“Es tut mir leid, Liebling. Aber ich werde bis spätestens um 6 Uhr morgens in der **Kaserne** zurück sein müssen.” Sie begann zu weinen.

Prestwick Grammar School was an old brick building that looked just like a **barracks** from around the turn of the century.
Prestwick Grammar School war ein altes Backsteingebäude, das wie eine **Kaserne** um die Jahrhundertwende aussah.

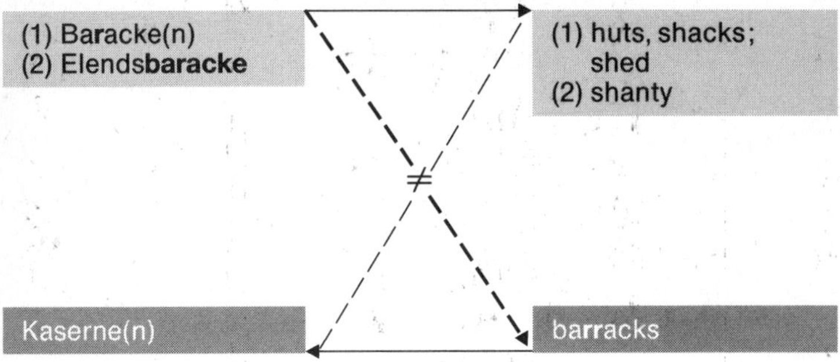

FALSE FRIENDS IN CONTEXT

Hunt for the Third Man

David: Did you hear the five o'clock news? Police are looking for the third member of an IRA gang which tried to blow up an army ________ (1) an hour ago.
Toby: Where was that?
David: I think the announcer said something about Tern Hill ________ (2).
Toby: What? But that's right here!
David: Yes. The IRA bombers had placed a getaway car and driver in one of the streets outside the ________ (3), but when the driver of the getaway car saw a lorry backing into the road, he jumped out of the car and fled into some wooden ________ (4) behind one of the terraced houses nearby.
Toby: Did the bombs go off?
David: No, but the police caught the two terrorists who planted the bombs and are now looking for the third man.
Toby: What about looking into our own ________ (5) in the garden first?

SOLUTION

(1) barracks (2) Tern Hill **Barracks** (3) barracks (4) wooden **huts/ shacks** (5) shed

"May I carry you over the threshold of my humble shack?"

BEKOMMEN ≠ become

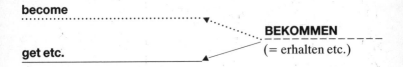

become

BEKOMMEN
(= erhalten etc.)

get etc.

BEKOMMEN:
(1) (erhalten) get (sth.), (empfangen) receive (sth.)
(2) (formal: erhalten) obtain (sth.)
(3) in idioms such as '**get** a bad name', '**get** cold feet'
(4) (bekommen) have
(5) in combinations such as '**have** a baby', '**have** visitors'
(6) (positiv: jdm. bekommen) agree with s.o.; do s.o. good
(7) (negativ: jdm. nicht bekommen) not agree with; can't eat/can't drink etc. sth.

(1) "Catherine, wir haben unser neues Auto **bekommen**. Wie wäre es mit einer Probefahrt nach Poole?"
"Catherine, we've **got** our new car. What about a test drive to Poole?"
Am nächsten Tag **bekam** Ian einen langen Brief von seiner Freundin.
Next day Ian **received** a long letter from his girlfriend.
(2) Sie können die notwendigen Informationen von der amerikanischen Botschaft **bekommen**.
You can **obtain** the necessary information from the American Embassy.
(3) Wenn du diese Methoden anwendest, wirst du einen schlechten Ruf **bekommen**.
If you use such methods, you'll **get** a bad name.
(4) Zu ihrem 80. Geburtstag **bekam** meine Großmutter ein Bach-Stück vorgespielt.
On her 80th birthday my grandmother **had** a piece by Bach played for her.
(5) "Hast du schon gehört? Unsere Nachbarin **bekommt** bald Zwillinge", erzählte ihm seine Frau.
"Have you heard? Our neighbour is going to **have** twins soon," his wife told him.

(6) Der Urlaub auf den Bahamas ist ihr **gut bekommen**.
Her holiday in the Bahamas **has done her good**.
Entgegen allen Erwartungen **bekam** ihm die Diät.
Contrary to expectation, the diet **agreed with** him.
(7) "Das Klima in Südspanien **bekommt** meinem Mann nicht. Deshalb fahren wir in diesem Sommer woanders hin", sagte Pat zu ihrer Freundin.
"The climate in the south of Spain **doesn't agree with** my husband. That's why we're going somewhere else this summer," Pat said to her friend.
"Ich weiß nicht warum. Aber Ziegenmilch **bekommt** mir **nicht**", klagte die junge Frau.
"I don't know why. But I **can't drink** any goat's milk," complained the young woman.

become: (1) (beruflich etc.) (etwas) werden, sich entwickeln zu
(2) (emotional, physical etc. change) werden (in combinations such as '**become** famous', '**become** angry', '**become** ill')
(3) (become of) werden aus

(1) Maud wants to **become** a pediatrician and Mark a pilot.
Maud möchte Kinderärztin **werden** und Mark Pilot.
By devoting all her time and energy a tennis player like Anke Huber can **become** the best player in the world.
Wenn sie alle ihre Zeit und Energie aufbietet, kann **sich** Anke Huber **zur** besten Tennisspielerin der Welt **entwickeln**.
(2) When I mentioned the company director's name, the receptionist suddenly **became** very friendly.
Als ich den Namen des Firmenchefs erwähnte, **wurde** die Empfangsdame plötzlich sehr freundlich.
You can **become** rich in the United States, if you work hard.
Du kannst in den Vereinigten Staaten reich **werden**, wenn du hart arbeitest.
(3) What will **become of** our plans to go to New Zealand?
Was **wird aus** unseren Plänen, nach Neuseeland zu reisen?

Note: When things or physical, mental conditions are worsening, '**go**' is used (instead of 'become').
go blind = blind **werden**
go bad = schlecht **werden**

go deaf = taub **werden**
go from bad to worse = sich (ständig) verschlechtern
go crazy/mad = verrückt **werden**
go wrong = schiefgehen etc.

but: Did the photos come out? = Sind die Fotos etwas **geworden**?
It'll be all right = Es wird schon **werden**.
He **became** interested in chess = Er begann sich für Schach zu interessieren.

Compare: **come** true = wahr **werden**
fall ill = krank **werden**
get dark = dunkel **werden**
turn pale = bleich **werden**

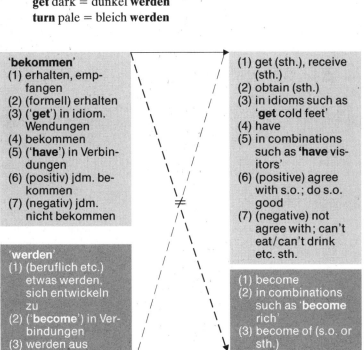

'bekommen'
(1) erhalten, empfangen
(2) (formell) erhalten
(3) ('**get**') in idiom. Wendungen
(4) bekommen
(5) ('**have**') in Verbindungen
(6) (positiv) jdm. bekommen
(7) (negativ) jdm. nicht bekommen

(1) get (sth.), receive (sth.)
(2) obtain (sth.)
(3) in idioms such as '**get** cold feet'
(4) have
(5) in combinations such as '**have** visitors'
(6) (positive) agree with s.o.; do s.o. good
(7) (negative) not agree with; can't eat/can't drink etc. sth.

'werden'
(1) (beruflich etc.) etwas werden, sich entwickeln zu
(2) ('**become**') in Verbindungen
(3) werden aus

(1) become
(2) in combinations such as '**become** rich'
(3) become of (s.o. or sth.)

A Future Nightmare: The Greenhouse Effect

U. N. Environmental Expert (at the end of his talk): . . . and about the year 2000 there'll be floods because of the greenhouse effect. Only if governments act now, can global warming be reversed.
Voice from the Audience: So what will ________ (1) of our world?
U. N. Environmental Expert: The warmth will melt the polar ice caps, raising the levels of oceans by up to three feet. Most low-lying countries, especially islands such as the Seychelles and the Maldives will disappear.
Another Voice from the Audience: What will ________ (2) of Britain?
U. N. Environmental Expert: Great parts of Britain could disappear. The London Docklands would ________ (3) a sunken city, the areas round Lincoln and Cambridge would be swamped and places like Doncaster would ________ (4) seaside towns.
Chairman from the Panel: Generally, there'll be crop failures and the new climate ________ (5) with us. Millions of people in Britain and other parts of the world will ________ (6) ill or even ________ (7) blind.

SOLUTION

(1) become (2) become (3) become (4) become (5) will not agree (with) (6) fall (ill) (7) go (blind)

BORGEN ◑ borrow

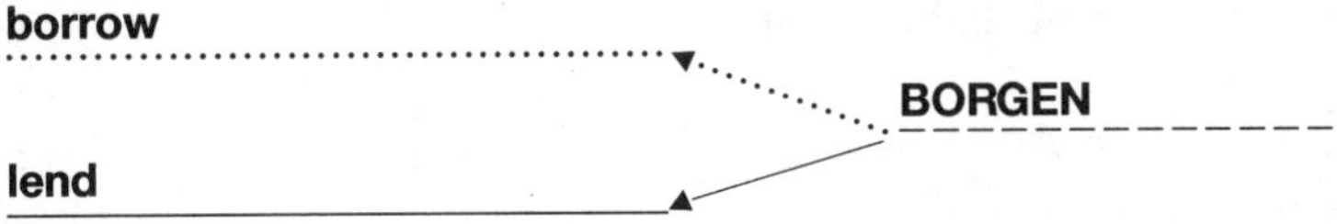

BORGEN: lend

Note: You (= A) **lend** something to somebody (= B) (A → B).

Kannst du mir dein Fahrrad **borgen**?
Can you **lend** me your bicycle?
“Glücklicherweise kannten wir Leute, die anboten, uns zinsloses Geld zu **borgen**”, erzählte sie mir.
“Fortunately we have had people who have offered to **lend** us money with no interest,” she told me.
Wir **borgen** Ihnen ab sofort ein Austauschgerät, da Sie einen neuen Fernseher für mehr als 300 Pfund gekauft haben.
We’ll **lend** you a replacement set right away, as you bought a new TV for over £300.

Note: (bankmäßig Geld) verleihen; beleihen = **lend**
“No other bank or building society **lends** more money than we do,” the Halifax Building Society leaflet said.
“On average we **lend** over £1 million on property every hour of every day,” it went on.

borrow: (1) (sich) etwas leihen
(2) (Bücher, Geld etc.) ausleihen

Note: You (= A) **borrow** something from someone (= B); you (= A) **borrow** things from people (= B) to return them (A ← B).

(1) Can I **borrow** your lorry for a day?
Kann ich mir deinen Lastwagen für einen Tag **leihen**?
(2) Peter, you’ll have to **borrow** the book from the University library.
Peter, du wirst das Buch wohl bei der Universitätsbibliothek **ausleihen** müssen.

"There's no lower limit to how much you can **borrow**," the bank manager told us.
"Es besteht keine untere Grenze, wieviel Sie **ausleihen** können", teilte uns der Bankdirektor mit.

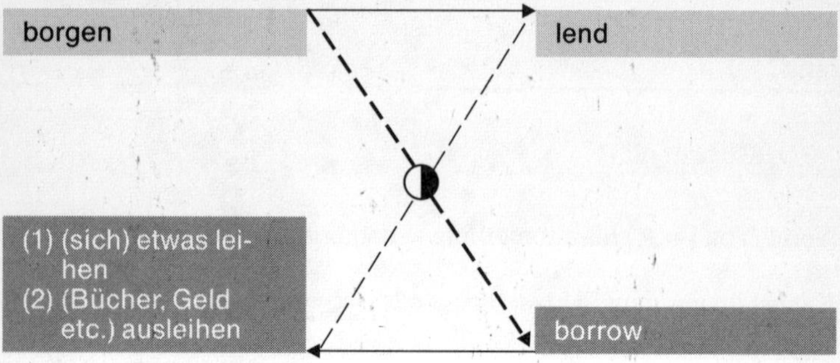

FALSE FRIENDS IN CONTEXT

Banking on Bankers . . .

Geoffrey had just ________ (1) a book on saving money from the library at the town hall. On the way out he met his friend, who looked at it and asked him, "Do you know what a banker is?" – "Not exactly," he replied. "Then listen. A banker is a man who ________ (2) you an umbrella when the sun is shining and wants it back the minute it starts to rain."

SOLUTION

(1) borrowed (2) lends

... and Banking on Friends

After a stag night Geoffrey found all his clothes had been stolen. He didn't know how to get home.
So the doorman ________ (3) him a pair of golf trousers and a polo-neck sweater to get him to the church where the vicar ________ (4) him a suit of his own but without the dog-collar.

SOLUTION

(3) lent (4) lent

"May I borrow some money?"

BRAUT ◑ bride

bride ·············→ **BRAUT**

fiancée [fɪ'ɑ̃:ŋseɪ] → (= Verlobte)

BRAUT: (Verlobte) fiancée

Dies ist Mary, meine **Braut**. Wir werden nach meinem Examen im Frühjahr heiraten.
This is Mary, my **fiancée**. We are going to get married after my exam in the spring.
“Ich machte ihr letzten Monat beim Essen einen Antrag”, sagte Frank, der seine **Braut** schon seit zwei Jahren kennt.
“I proposed to her last month over dinner,” said Frank, who has known his **fiancée** for two years.

Note: jilted **fiancée** = versetzte **Braut** (als Verlobte)
but: engagement = Verlobung
engagement party = Verlobungsfeier
engagement ring = Verlobungsring

bride (nur am Hochzeitstag oder unmittelbar davor bzw. danach):
(1) Braut
(2) `-**braut**` (in combinations)

(1) There were too many wedding guests. The happy **bride** was looking forward only to their honeymoon in Florida.
Es waren zu viele Hochzeitsgäste zugegen. Die glückliche **Braut** freute sich nur noch auf die Hochzeitsreise nach Florida.
(2) “Blow me,” Trevor murmured. The photo showed his would-be **bride** lying on the beach with another man.
“Das gibt's doch nicht”, murmelte Trevor. Das Foto zeigte seine angebliche **Braut** mit einem anderen Mann am Strand liegen.

Note: jilted **bride** = versetzte **Braut** (am Hochzeitstag)
would-be **bride** = angebliche **Braut**
bride-to-be = zukünftige **Braut**

but: newly married couple = **Braut**paar
wedding dress = **Braut**kleid

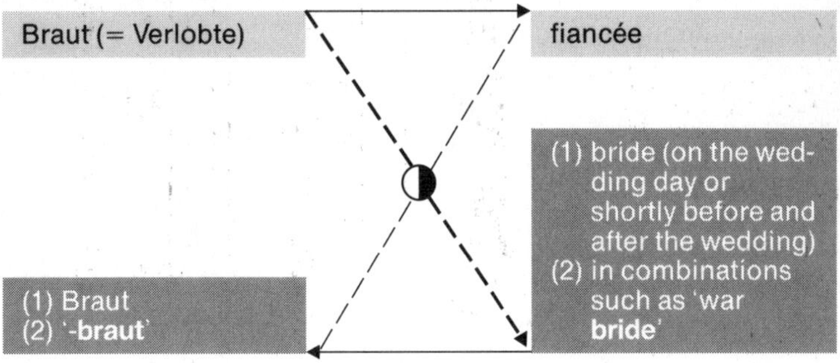

FALSE FRIENDS IN CONTEXT

Wedding Incidents

Her Aunt's Silver
It is their wedding day. The ________ (1) and groom are looking at their presents. Suddenly the ________ (2) stops and looks at one present for some time.
"Look, Harry, the knives and forks Aunt Chrissie bought us aren't real silver," said the ________ (3).
"But how can you tell so quickly that it isn't real silver?" asked the bridegroom in surprise. "Do you know anything about silver?"
"No," answered the ________ (4) with a meaningful smile, "but I know more about Aunt Chrissie than anyone else. By the way, she gave me what she said were silver spoons last year when I became your ________ (5)... I checked," Sally added, "and they weren't real silver."

Sally's Mistake
At the end of the wedding day Sally was so tired that Harry had to carry his ________ (6) into their hotel bedroom. To his surprise Sally whispered, "Thank you for a lovely day, Harry – see you in the morning!"

SOLUTION

(1) bride (2) bride (3) bride (4) bride (5) fiancée/bride-to-be (6) bride

"This is Jane, my bride-to-be or not-to-be ...."

BRAV ≠ brave

brave [breɪv]

BRAV
(= artig etc.)

well-behaved [ˌwelbɪˈheɪvd]

BRAV: (1) (artig) well-behaved, good
(2) (ehrlich, treu) honest, loyal
(3) (zaghaft, 'ohne Biß', ohne Schwung) uninspired; spiritless, toothless (sport)

(1) Die Kinder der Thompsons sind wirklich **brav**.
The Thompsons' children are really **well-behaved**.
"Auf Wiedersehen und seid **brav**", sagte ihre Mutter zu ihnen.
"Bye-bye and be **good**," her mother said to them.
(2) Trotz all der Anschuldigungen gegen ihren Mann hat sie **brav** zu ihm gehalten.
In spite of all the accusations against her husband, she remained **loyal** to him.
In Zeiten des Verlustes der Werte ist der Ruf nach dem **braven** Mann stets dagewesen.
In periods when values have lost importance, there has always been a call for the **honest** man.
(3) "Einige Spieler sind zu **brav** und ohne Initiative", kritisierte der Trainer die Mannschaft nach dem Spiel.
"Some players are too **uninspired** and lack initiative," the coach said, criticising his team after the match.
Lineker wurde zum Mannschaftskapitän ernannt, konnte aber an der **braven**, zusammenhanglosen Vorstellung wenig ändern.
Lineker was made team captain but could do little to prevent a **toothless** and disjointed performance.

brave: tapfer, mutig

"It never occurred to me that I was acting **bravely**," said the policeman after the fire. "The other policemen in my unit have been just as **brave**," he added.
"Ich dachte nie daran, daß ich **tapfer** handelte", sagte der Polizist nach dem Feuer. "Die anderen Polizisten in meiner Einheit waren genauso **tapfer**", fügte er hinzu.

It was a **brave** step of the government to accept even more Boat People.
Es war ein **mutiger** Schritt der Regierung, noch mehr Boat People (Vietnam-Flüchtlinge) aufzunehmen.

Note: be **brave** = mutig sein, Mut besitzen
"I **wasn't brave** enough to jump from the wall," the ten-year-old boy admitted afterwards.

but: gallantry medal = **Tapferkeits**medaille
gallantry award = **Tapferkeits**auszeichnung
"This brave man deserves some sort of **gallantry** award," demanded the passengers after the ship disaster.

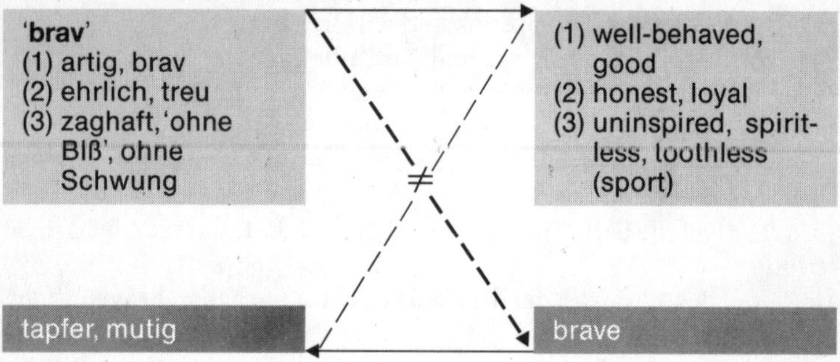

FALSE FRIENDS IN CONTEXT

Superdad to the Front

For the last two hours Mr. Henderson has been telling his son Tony about all his ________ (1) deeds in the Vietnam War.
Mr. Henderson: And that, my son, is the story of your ________ (2) father in the Vietnam War.
Tony, asking his father in a ________ (3) way: So what did they need all those other soldiers for then, Dad?

SOLUTION

(1) **brave** deeds (2) **brave** father (3) **spiritless** way

BRUST ◑ breast

breast [brest]

BRUST

chest

(Männer**brust**; **Brust**korb)

BRUST: (1) (Männer**brust**; **Brust**korb, **Brust**kasten) chest
(2) in combinations such as '**chest** complaints'

(1) Während eines Streits in einer Gaststätte zog ein Mann plötzlich ein Messer und stach seinem Gegner in die **Brust**.
During a pub row a man suddenly pulled a knife and stabbed his opponent in the **chest**.
Sie hatte sich die **Brust** (= den Brustkasten) verbinden lassen und laborierte an einer ziemlich schlimmen Knieverletzung herum.
She had her **chest** bandaged and was nursing a badly hurt knee.
(2) "Ihre **Brust**beschwerden kommen vom **Brust**muskel", erläuterte der Arzt.
"Your **chest** complaints come from your **chest**-muscle," explained the doctor.
Als die schwangere Frau vom Hubschrauber aus ihrem Haus geborgen wurde, hatte das Flutwasser **Brust**höhe erreicht.
When the pregnant woman was picked up by helicopter from her home, the floodwater had reached **chest** height.

Note: Arzneischrank, Hausapotheke = medicine **chest**
Facharzt für Lungenkrankheiten = **chest** specialist
but: (Eichen-)Truhe = (oak) **chest**
Kastanie(nbaum) = **chest**nut (tree) ['tʃesnʌt]
Kommode = **chest** of drawers

breast: (1) (Frauen-)Brust, Busen
(2) (kul.) Brust(stück) (von Tieren zum Verzehr)
(3) '**Brust-**' (in combinations)

(1) When he looked at her, he knew he liked her fine **breasts**.
Als er sie ansah, wußte er, daß er ihren schönen **Busen** liebte.
Her blouse was open, and she showed her well-formed **breasts** for a moment.

Ihre Bluse war offen, und sie zeigte einen Augenblick lang ihre wohlgeformten **Brüste**.
(2) When the waiter came, Mr. Thompson ordered a piece of chicken **breast**, whereas his wife had some smoked **breast** of goose on toast.
Als der Kellner kam, bestellte Herr Thompson ein Stück Hühner**brust**, während seine Frau geräucherte Gänse**brust** auf Toast nahm.
(3) Fortunately **breast** cancer in women can be successfully operated on if they see a doctor regularly.
Glücklicherweise kann **Brust**krebs bei Frauen erfolgreich operiert werden, wenn sie regelmäßig zum Arzt gehen.
Doing the crawl is much more strenuous for older people than doing the **breast** stroke.
Kraulschwimmen ist für ältere Leute viel anstrengender als **Brust**schwimmen.

Note: Since the Sixties **boobs** (always in the plural) is the word many women in Britain use for **breasts** (Howard, p. 32). It is a slightly slangy term used in conversation.
She had put on a lot of weight and her **boobs** were making her blouse too tight.

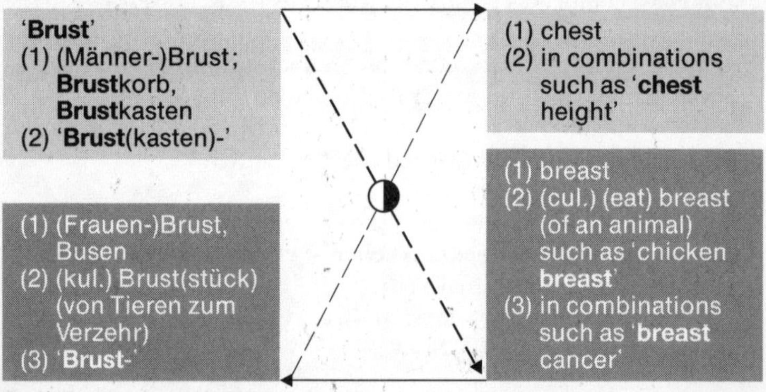
'Brust'
(1) (Männer-)Brust; Brustkorb, Brustkasten
(2) 'Brust(kasten)-'
(1) chest
(2) in combinations such as 'chest height'
(1) (Frauen-)Brust, Busen
(2) (kul.) Brust(stück) (von Tieren zum Verzehr)
(3) 'Brust-'
(1) breast
(2) (cul.) (eat) breast (of an animal) such as 'chicken breast'
(3) in combinations such as 'breast cancer'

FALSE FRIENDS IN CONTEXT

Film Review: Scandal at the Tory Club

The new film *Scandal* which opened at London's *Odeon* focuses on the Profumo affair in the Sixties. In it a beautiful girl, Christine Keeler, brings down the Minister of Defence John Profumo.
The main character appears twice stripped to her waist with her ________ (1) painted in gold. When a journalist wanted to interview her afterwards at a first night party in a London Tory club, she put him off, "Talk to your pharmacist if there's anything you'd like to get off your ________ (2)."

SOLUTION

(1) breasts (2) chest

"Yes, I'm having serious chest problems, doctor!"

FALSE FRIENDS TRAPS TEST 1

EASY FALSE FRIENDS

1.a. The Vietnamese Boat People had to live in ________ near a rubbish tip for months; several children and old people died (**Baracken ≠ barracks**).
1.b. The new recruits were promptly confined to ________ for the first three weeks. It was during this period that a bomb exploded in the rest-room in the heart of the ________ (**Baracken ≠ barracks**).
2.a. He was tired after six hours of sightseeing and was glad to find an empty ________ in St. James's Park (**Bank ◑ bank**).
2.b. Mary wanted to be alone, so she went into St. Mary's Church. All the ________ at the front were empty, so she sat down on one of them (**Bänke ◑ banks**).
3.a. Lord Miles once had to ________ a collar and tie from an usher to get into the House of Lords (**borgen ◑ borrow**).
3.b. "Why can't you ________ me three thousand pounds? It would open up a new career for me," he told his father (**borgen ◑ borrow**).
4.a. "When do I ________ my birthday present?" the little girl asked her mother when she woke up (**bekommen ≠ become**).
4.b. If you want to ________ a computer specialist, the best thing for you is to be trained by a big computer firm first (**bekommen ≠ become**).
5.a. "Today's ________ goes up the aisle in style," the presenter told the audience. "That is why Nia Parry was picked as BBC 1's '________ of the Year'" (**Braut ◑ bride**).
5.b. "My ________ and I have a lovely son and we're marrying next month," he told his friends (**Braut ◑ bride**).
6. "The child has been very ________ (**brav**) tonight," the babysitter said to the parents.
7. A young mother of three was hit in the ________ (**Brust**) by several bullets from an IRA killer.
8. When they came into the room you could hardly guess who the ________ (**älter**) brother was.
9. Was it untrue ________ (**also**)? Where did you stay ________ (**also**) last week?
10. Look at the photo over there. It's been taken at an unusual ________ (**Winkel**).

ANSWER SHEET: TRUE FRIENDS TEST 1

EASY FALSE FRIENDS

1.a. The Vietnamese Boat People had to live in **huts** near a rubbish tip; several children and old people died.
1.b. The new recruits were promptly confined to **barracks** for the first three weeks. It was during this period that a bomb exploded in the rest-room in the heart of the **barracks**.
2.a. He was tired after six hours of sightseeing and was glad to find an empty **bench** in St. James's Park.
2.b. Mary wanted to be alone, so she went into St. Mary's Church. All the **pews** at the front were empty, so she sat down on one of them.
3.a. Lord Miles once had to **borrow** a collar and tie from an usher to get into the House of Lords.
3.b. "Why can't you **lend** me three thousand pounds? It would open up a new career for me," he told his father.
4.a. "When do I **get** my birthday present?" the little girl asked her mother when she woke up.
4.b. If you want to **become** a computer specialist, the best thing for you is to be trained by a big computer firm first.
5.a. "Today's **bride** goes up the aisle in style," the presenter told the audience. "That is why Nia Parry was picked as BBC 1's '**Bride** of the Year'."
5.b. "My **fiancée** and I have a lovely son and we're marrying next month," he told his friends.
6. "The child has been very **well-behaved** tonight," the babysitter said to the parents.
7. A young mother of three was hit in the **chest** by several bullets from an IRA killer.
8. When they came into the room you could hardly guess who the **elder** brother was.
9. Was it untrue **then**? Where did you stay **then** last week?
10. Look at the photo over there. It's been taken at an unusual **angle**.

DICK ◑ thick

thick

DICK
(von Menschen etc.)

fat

DICK: (1) (von Menschen) fat, (füllig) stout, (pummelig) corpulent, (beleibt) portly (mostly of men)
(2) (von Haustieren, Insekten etc.) fat
(3) in combinations such as 'a **fat** cheque' (coll.)
(4) in combinations such as '**close** friends', '**high** praise', 'a **swollen** cheek'

(1) "Menschen, die zu **dick** sind, mag ich nicht", sagte Mabel zu ihrer Tochter.
"I don't like people who are too **fat**," Mabel said to her daughter.
Für ihr Alter ist unsere Nachbarin ziemlich **dick**.
For her age our neighbour is rather **stout**.
Um die Hüften war sie nicht gerade dünn; um ehrlich zu sein, recht **dick**.
She was not at all slim round the waist. To be honest, she was rather **corpulent**.
Wie immer war die alternde Schauspielerin auf Parties von einigen **dicken** alten Herren umlagert.
As always the ageing actress was surrounded at parties by several **portly** old gentlemen.
(2) Ohne Bewegung werden die meisten Hunde **dick** und faul.
Without exercise most dogs become **fat** and lazy.
Die Kellnerin schauderte, als sie eine **dicke** Made in der Pastete sah.
The waitress shuddered as she saw the **fat** maggot in the pie.
(3) Unser Chef hat stets eine **dicke** Brieftasche. Das kommt von dem **dicken** Gewinn unserer Firma in diesem Jahr.
Our boss always has a **fat** wallet. That's the result of our company's **fat** profits this year.
(4) Der Gewinn des Pokalfinales durch einen Dritt-Liga-Klub war eine faust**dicke** Überraschung.
The win of the cup final by a third division club was a **real** surprise.
Wir blieben im **dicksten** Feierabendverkehr stecken und verpaßten die Fähre.

We got stuck in **heavy** rush-hour traffic and missed the ferry boat.
"Er hat ein ganz **dickes** Lob verdient. Ohne ihn hätte die Mannschaft nicht gewonnen", betonte der Trainer.
"He deserves **high** praise. The team wouldn't have won without him," the coach pointed out.

Note: ein **dicker** Wagen = a big **fat** car
eine **dicke** Zigarre = a **fat** cigar
ein **dickes** Gehalt = a big **fat** salary (coll.)
eine **dicke** Provision = a **fat** commission (coll.)
but: ein **dicker** Fehler = a **bad** (**serious**, **grave**) mistake; a blunder
ein **dicker** Knöchel = a **swollen** ankle
eine **dicke** Rechnung = a **huge** bill
dicke Regentropfen = **heavy** drops of rain
Compare: Das **dicke** Ende kommt noch (nach).
The worst is yet to come.

thick: (1) (ice, paper, book etc.) dick
(2) (fog, hair etc.) dicht
(3) 'blöd', 'schwer von kapee' (koll.)

(1) As a child I used to go skating in winter when the ice was **thick** enough.
Als Kind fuhr ich im Winter Schlittschuh, wenn das Eis **dick** genug war.
The typing-paper is too **thick**. Haven't you got any thinner paper?
Das Schreibmaschinenpapier ist zu **dick**. Haben Sie nicht dünneres Papier?
The letter was part of a **thick** file that my mother treasured.
Der Brief war Teil einer **dicken** Akte, die meine Mutter hütete.
(2) There was **thick** fog along the south coast all day.
An der Südküste herrschte den ganzen Tag über **dichter** Nebel.
(3) "You must be really **thick**," said one boy to another. "Our teacher has explained it at least three times."
"Du mußt ganz schön **schwer von kapee** sein", sagte ein Junge zum anderen. "Unser Lehrer hat es jetzt schon dreimal erklärt."

Note: **thick** hair = **dichtes** Haar
thick hedge = **dichte** Hecke
thick smoke = **dichter** Rauch
but: **thick** voice = **belegte** Stimme
Compare: That's really a bit **thick** = Das ist ein (ganz) **dicker** Hund.

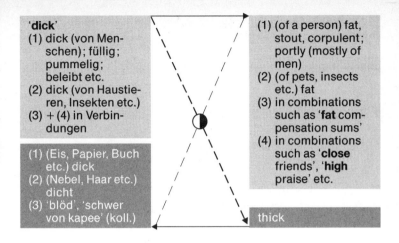

'dick'
(1) dick (von Menschen); füllig; pummelig; beleibt etc.
(2) dick (von Haustieren, Insekten etc.)
(3) + (4) in Verbindungen

(1) (Eis, Papier, Buch etc.) dick
(2) (Nebel, Haar etc.) dicht
(3) 'blöd', 'schwer von kapee' (koll.)

(1) (of a person) fat, stout, corpulent; portly (mostly of men)
(2) (of pets, insects etc.) fat
(3) in combinations such as '**fat** compensation sums'
(4) in combinations such as '**close** friends', '**high** praise' etc.

thick

FALSE FRIENDS IN CONTEXT

Slimming – No Thank You

1. Molly's Reply
You could see the actress had put on weight. She had become ________ (1).
"You know," her husband told her one day, "people must be a bit ________ (2) if they pay to see you looking like that."
"Oh, darling," Molly replied flippantly, "it's fun to be ________ (3) and I don't feel guilty about it."
2. A Different Philosophy of Life
Have you ever heard of the Tongans? If not, don't worry. They live in the South Pacific and are the ________ (4) people in the world. The Tongans have been happy so far.
Now a British team has gone there to teach them the art of slimming – to make them unhappy.

SOLUTION

(1) fat (2) thick (3) fat (4) fattest

ENGEL ≠ angle

angle [ˈæŋgl]

ENGEL

angel [ˈeɪndʒəl]

ENGEL: (1) angel (also fig.)
(2) in combinations such as 'providential **angel**'

(1) "Sei ein **Engel**, fahre nicht zu dicht auf", lautete der Aufkleber auf der Rückseite des Autos vor ihm.
"Be an **angel**, don't drive too close," read the sticker on the back of the car in front of him.
Engel sind übernatürliche Wesen; ich habe bisher noch keine gesehen.
Angels are supernatural beings; I haven't seen one as yet.
"Angela ist kein **Engel**. Man muß ständig ein Auge auf sie haben", sagte ihre Mutter zu der Kindergärtnerin.
"Angela isn't an **angel**. You've got to keep an eye on her all the time," her mother told the kindergarten teacher.
(2) Jeder Autofahrer braucht heutzutage einen Schutz**engel**.
Every car driver needs a guardian **angel** nowadays.
Die russische Stadt Archangelsk heißt auf englisch Erz**engel**.
The Russian city Arkhangelsk is arch**angel** in English.

Note: Rache**engel** = avenging **angel**
Engelschar = host of **angels**
rettender **Engel** = a good **angel**
but: **Engels**geduld haben = have the patience of a saint
Engelshaar = white floss (for Christmas trees)

angle: (1) Winkel (auch math.), Blickwinkel
(2) Aspekt, Gesichtspunkt

(1) The hotel has just a few tables in the **angle** of the crossroads.
Das Hotel hat nur einige Tische in dem **Winkel** an der Straßenkreuzung.
This photograph is taken from a most unusual **angle**.

Dieses Foto ist aus einem ganz ungewöhnlichen **Blickwinkel** aufgenommen.
(2) I'm afraid I haven't looked into the matter from this **angle**.
Leider habe ich die Angelegenheit noch nicht unter diesem **Aspekt** betrachtet.
"We like to think out **angles** the others don't," the manager told me.
"Wir arbeiten gerne **Gesichtspunkte** heraus, auf die die anderen nicht kommen", erzählte mir der Manager.

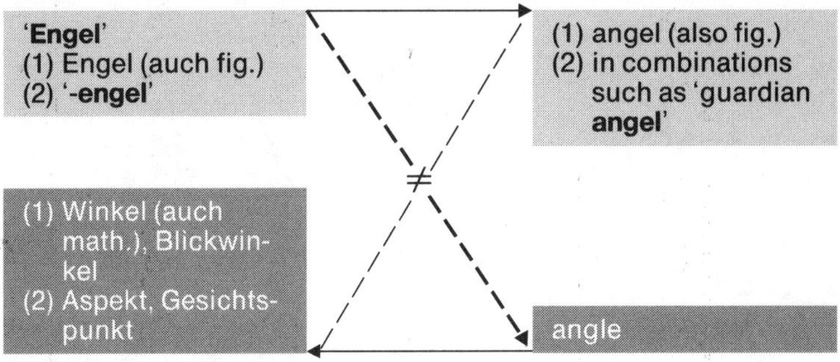

FALSE FRIENDS IN CONTEXT

The Nicest Guy in Town

First Old Lady: I live in constant fear of being mugged. The other day my new handbag with my pension book was snatched out of my hand.
Second Old Lady: Haven't you heard of Billy Tattum? ... Old folk's private guardian ________ (1)? Billy has a karate black belt and is known as a keep-fit fanatic. He's quite a character! Why don't you move to our sheltered housing estate?
First Old Lady: Tell me first from your ________ (2) what he does for you.
Second Old Lady: Every morning Billy knocks on each of the 40 doors on our estate to make sure we are all well. Then he comes back twice a day to have a look round. In the evening he makes his final check to make sure all our doors and windows are shut.
First Old Lady: Seen from that ________ (3) we don't need the New York Guardian ________ (4) round here any more; they're expensive, too.

Second Old Lady: No, Billy's cheaper. He's our unsung ________ (5) and he's been made Citizen of the Year twice for his peace-keeping efforts! Isn't that wonderful? He's the nicest man in town.

SOLUTION

(1) angel (2) angle (3) angle (4) Angels (5) angel

"My wife is an angel. I just adore her..."

FLEISCH ◑ flesh

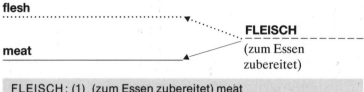

flesh ········ **FLEISCH** (zum Essen zubereitet)

meat ————

FLEISCH: (1) (zum Essen zubereitet) meat
(2) in combinations such as '**meat** dish'

(1) Sie ging auf den Markt, um mageres **Fleisch** zu kaufen; ihr Mann aß am Sonntag gerne **Fleisch**.
She went to the market to buy some lean **meat**. Her husband liked to eat **meat** on Sundays.
(2) "Niemand wußte, daß er Priester war – er sagte, er sei **Fleisch**-importeur", erwiderte Dr. Watson.
"No one knew he was a priest – he said he was a **meat** importer," Dr. Watson replied.

flesh: (1) (rohes, lebendes) Fleisch
(2) Fleisch (fig.)

(1) "I'm built of **flesh** and bone like everyone else," commented the new world heavyweight champion, pointing to his swollen face.
"Ich bin auch nur aus **Fleisch** und Knochen gebaut", kommentierte der neue Schwergewichts-Weltmeister und deutete auf sein geschwollenes Gesicht.
Gold stains proteins left on any surface that has been in contact with **flesh**, as FBI scientists found.
Gold färbt Proteine, die auf Oberflächen zurückbleiben, wenn sie mit **Fleisch** in Kontakt gekommen sind, wie FBI-Wissenschaftler herausfanden.
(2) Looking at the congregation before him, the priest referred to the sins of the **flesh**.
Der Priester bezog sich auf die Sünden des **Fleisches** und schaute auf die Gemeinde vor ihm.
Mary admitted, "I love children, and to have a baby of her own **flesh** and blood is what every woman dreams of."
Mary gab zu: "Ich liebe Kinder, und ein Baby von seinem eigenen **Fleisch** und Blut zu haben, ist, wovon jede Frau träumt."

Note: proud **flesh** = wildes **Fleisch**
butcher = Fleischer

but: in the **flesh** = leibhaftig, in natura
When little children first see a member of the royal family **in the flesh**, they are frequently disappointed and comment on the absence of a crown.
make one's **flesh** creep = Gänsehaut bekommen
The latest stories about the ghost at Glamorgan Castle **made her flesh creep**.
pulp = Frucht**fleisch**

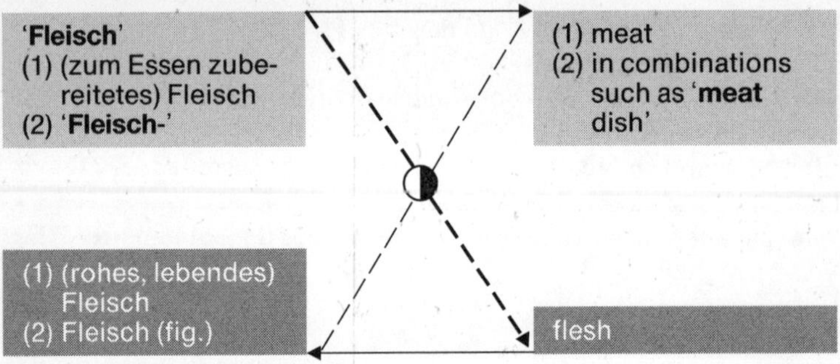

FALSE FRIENDS IN CONTEXT

Britain's Greatest Butchers

I bet you don't know who Britain's greatest butchers are. Neither did I until I read about them – the Vesteys.
Their family fortune is founded on the ________ (1) business and includes the Dewhurst butchers' chain. It is estimated to be worth £1,000 million. The business brain behind all this is the present Lord Vestey. The title was, incidentally, bought by the Vesteys from Lloyd George for £20,000. Today Dewhurst is Britain's biggest ________ (2) selling chain.

SOLUTION

(1) **meat** business (2) **meat** selling chain

Drama on the High Seas

Coastguard: How did you stay alive in the Atlantic without food?
Shipwreck Survivor: I was in a state of shock on the first day, and on the second I almost lost my hand to an enormous dorado fish.
Coastguard: Can you explain exactly what happened to you?
Shipwreck Survivor: I caught a large fish and was hauling it in with the line wrapped around my hand. Suddenly it took off, and I could smell the ________ (3) burning as the line ripped around my hand.
Coastguard: Yes?
Shipwreck Survivor: Then it cut into the ________ (4) of my hand, right down to the bone, before the line caught around a piece of the boat and snapped. It was a bad ________ (5) -wound and I had to stitch it myself. But it didn't work out. So I fixed it with Superglue.
Coastguard: With Superglue?
Shipwreck Survivor: Yes. Then I used fish blood as a sun-blocker until I was picked up by your helicopter near the island of Martinique... after eleven days.

SOLUTION

(3) flesh (4) **flesh** of my hand (5) a bad **flesh**-wound

FLUR ≠ floor

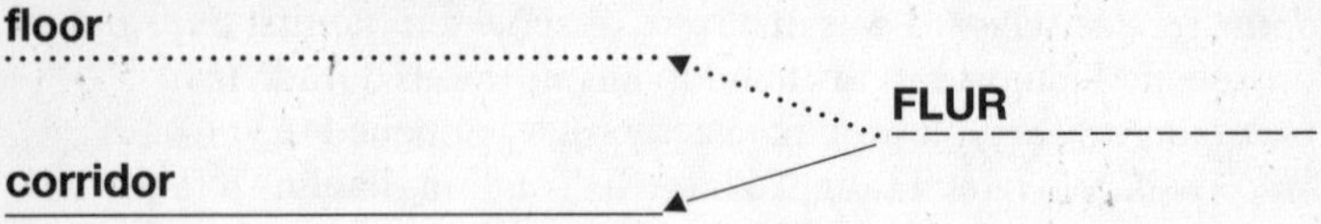

FLUR: (1) corridor
(2) hall(way), landing

Note: **'landing'** kann auch Treppenabsatz, Etagenabsatz oder oberer Treppen**flur** bedeuten.

(1) Ihre Kinder erfüllten die **Flure** mit Lachen.
Her children filled the **corridors** with laughter.
Einige Frauen standen auf einem der **Flure** des Gerichtsgebäudes und diskutierten erregt das Urteil des Mordfalls.
Some women were standing in one of the **corridors** of the court-building, discussing excitedly the verdict in the murder case.
(2) Immer wenn mein Onkel seine Untermieterin auf dem **Flur** (= Treppenabsatz) traf, grüßte er sie stets und eilte die Treppe hinunter.
Whenever my uncle met his lodger on the **landing**, he always greeted her and hurried downstairs.
Schau doch mal im **Flur** nach, ob mein Hut neben dem Spiegel liegt.
Would you go and see if my hat is next to the mirror in the **hall**?

floor: (1) (Fuß-)Boden
(2) Etage, Stock(werk)
(3) Parkett, Tanzfläche

(1) The passenger was lying on the **floor**. He was unconscious.
Der Passagier lag auf dem **Boden**; er war bewußtlos.
(2) Our relatives live on the fifth **floor** of a block of flats.
Unsere Verwandten wohnen im fünften **Stock** eines Hochhauses.
At the London hotel there was a fire on the second **floor**, the same **floor** as last October.
In der zweiten **Etage** des Londoner Hotels war ein Feuer, derselben **Etage** wie im letzten Oktober.
(3) After the state dinner the Thatchers and the Reagans took to the dance **floor** in the White House ballroom.

Nach dem Staatsessen begaben sich die Thatchers und die Reagans auf die **Tanzfläche** des Ballsaals im Weißen Haus.

Note: ground floor (BE), first floor (AE) = Erdgeschoß
first floor (BE), second floor (AE) = erster Stock
second floor (BE), third floor (AE) = zweiter Stock etc.
but: 'mezzanine ['metsəni:n] = Zwischengeschoß

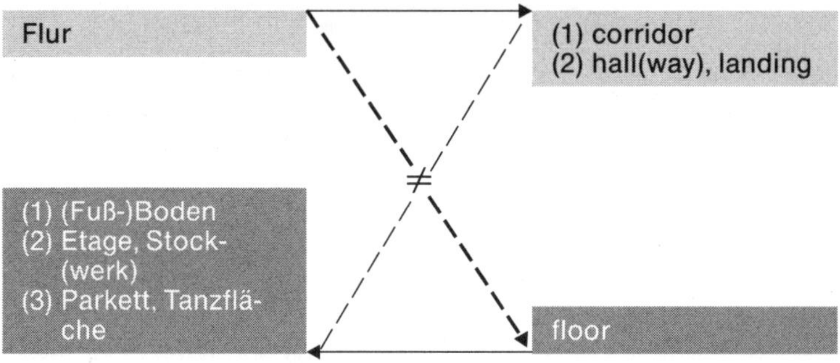

FALSE FRIENDS IN CONTEXT

Busy as a Bee

"Mr. Woodley..." Linda had begun for the third time to talk to her employer, but was cut short.
"How often, Linda, have I told you not to keep anybody waiting in the ________ (1)?" her employer told her. "I'm busy. I'll talk to you later."
Ten minutes later her employer came in again and said, "Now, Linda, tell me what you wanted to say earlier on." She looked at the ________ (2) for a moment as if at a loss how to begin. Then she looked up at Mr. Woodley and said, "There was a man in the ________ (3) who went away with your hat, coat and umbrella."

SOLUTION

(1) corridor/hall (2) floor (3) corridor/hall

FOTOGRAFIE ◑ photography

photography [fəˈtɒgrəfɪ]

die FOTOGRAFIE

photograph [ˈfəʊtəgrɑ:f]

(als Einzelbild)

die FOTOGRAFIE, das FOTO:	(1) (als Einzelbild) photograph
	(2) photo
	(3) ('**Foto-**') in combinations such as '**photographic** magazine'

(1) "Ich habe stets eine **Fotografie** meines verstorbenen Sohns bei mir", erzählte mir die alte Frau im Zug.
"I always have a **photograph** of my dead son with me," the old woman told me on the train.
(2) Als Gorbatschow und Kohl sich die Hand schüttelten, wurden von Pressefotografen aus der ganzen Welt **Fotos** gemacht.
When Gorbachev and Kohl shook hands, **photos** were taken by press photographers from all over the world.
(3) "Die **Foto**ausrüstung werde ich mir im **Foto**handel kaufen", sagte der junge Mann.
"I'll buy my **photographic** equipment from the **photographic** supplier," said the young man.

photography:	(1) Fotografie (als Fach)
	(2) '-**Fotografie**' (in combinations)
	(3) das Fotografieren (als Kunst)

(1) Nowadays **photography** is a course taught at most technical colleges.
Heutzutage ist **Fotografie** ein Kursangebot an den meisten Fachhochschulen.
(2) Colour **photography** is a relatively new development.
Die Farb-**Fotografie** ist eine relativ neue Entwicklung.
(3) **Photography** for advertising purposes is carried out by specialized photographers nowadays.
Das **Fotografieren** zu Werbezwecken wird heute von spezialisierten Fotografen ausgeführt.

"*England from the Air*" is a volume of tip-top **photography**.
"*England aus der Luft*" ist ein Band erstklassigen **Fotografierens**.

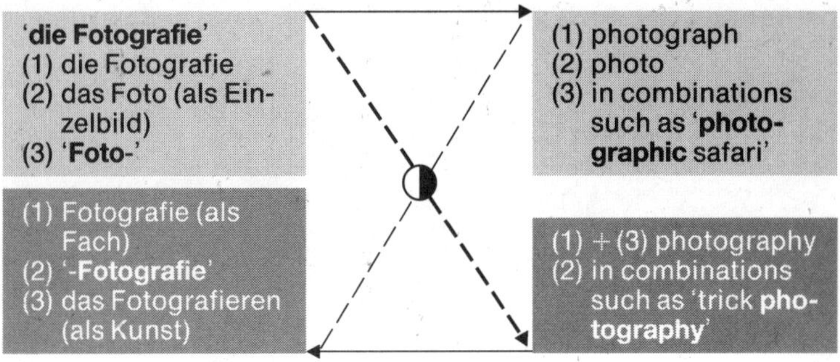

FALSE FRIENDS IN CONTEXT

A Marriage Advertisement

He had remained a bachelor until he was forty. He was a farmer and thought it was time to have someone to look after him. But there was no woman in the village he wanted to marry.
So he hit on the idea of advertising for a wife and promised to send a ________ (1) of himself to every woman who replied to the advertisement.
He got some interesting replies, but there was one letter he particularly liked. It was from a country woman, who mentioned that her father would give her a combine harvester as a dowry.
Without thinking twice, the farmer sent her a telegram, "Interested. But, please, send ________ (2) of combine harvester first. Tom."

SOLUTION

(1) photograph (2) photograph

FOTOGRAF ≠ photograph

photograph [ˈfəʊtəgrɑ:f] .... FOTOGRAF

photographer [fəˈtɒgrəfə] —— (als Beruf)

FOTOGRAF(IN): (1) (als Beruf) photographer
(2) in combinations such as 'press **photographer**'

(1) Nach der Kirche machte der **Fotograf** die Hochzeitsfotos.
After church the **photographer** took the wedding photos.
Später stellte sich heraus, daß der **Fotograf** sein Geschäft aufgegeben hatte. Aus diesem Grunde erhielten sie nie ihre Hochzeitsbilder.
Later it turned out the **photographer** had gone out of business, so they never received their wedding pictures.
(2) Die bekannteste Foto-Zeitschrift der Welt ist 'Der Amateur-**Fotograf**'.
The world's No. 1 photo weekly is 'Amateur **Photographer**'.
Eines der heitersten Bilder von Marilyn Monroe wurde von dem **Fotografen** der feinen Gesellschaft Cecil Beaton gemacht.
One of Marilyn Monroe's most happy pictures was taken by society **photographer** Cecil Beaton.

photograph (or photo): (1) Fotografie (als Einzelbild), Aufnahme, Foto
(2) '**Foto-**' (in combinations)

(1) The three men threatened to send **photographs** to the press unless the money was paid.
Die drei Männer drohten, **Fotografien** an die Presse zu schicken, wenn das Geld nicht bezahlt würde.
"I'm glad a lot of **photographs** were taken at the wedding reception," said the bride. "I'm looking forward to seeing them."
"Ich bin froh, daß auf dem Hochzeitsempfang viele **Aufnahmen** gemacht wurden", sagte die Braut. "Ich freue mich darauf, sie zu sehen."
(2) He suggested holding a **photo** session in an isolated quarry.

Er schlug vor, eine **Foto**-Sitzung in einem abgelegenen Steinbruch durchzuführen.

Note: camera = **Foto**apparat
photofit (picture) = Phantombild
Detectives have issued **photofit pictures** of a woman they believe is a child abductor.

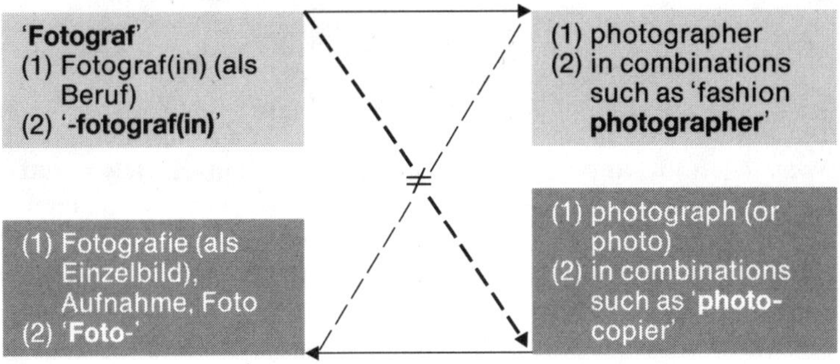

FALSE FRIENDS IN CONTEXT

A Photomontage: Which Side is the Parting?

An elderly lady, whose husband had died some time ago, went to a ________ (1). She showed him a ________ (2) of her former husband and asked whether he could enlarge it. "That's no problem," he answered. The widow looked at the old picture again. "Could you also remove the hat?" she added. "It's a bit tricky to get it off the ________ (3). I'll do my best, but it'll cost you ten pounds more," the ________ (4) told her. "That's all right," she replied casually. "Oh, by the way," he cut her short, "which side did your husband part his hair, on the left or right?" The elderly lady was already on her way out as she replied, "You'll see once you've removed his hat."

SOLUTION

(1) photographer (2) photograph (3) photograph (4) photographer

GOLF ◑ golf

golf [gɒlf]

GOLF

gulf [gʌlf]

(als geogr. Bezeichnung)

GOLF: (1) (als geogr. Bezeichnung) gulf
(2) (Meeresbucht) bay
(3) in combinations such as '**Gulf** War'

Note: (tiefe) Kluft (in den Auffassungen, Beziehungen etc.) = **gulf**
Despite the **gulf** between them, both Kevin and Julie maintained a friendship and respect for each other.

(1) Der **Golf** von Suez ist Teil des Roten Meers, das sich zum **Golf** von Aden öffnet.
The **Gulf** of Suez is part of the Red Sea that opens into the **Gulf** of Aden.
Die Benzinpreise werden wegen der Spannungen am **Golf** wieder steigen.
Petrol prices will rise again because of the tensions in the **Gulf**.
(2) "Über dem **Golf** von Biscaya liegen morgen Wolken, und im **Golf** von Bengalen zieht ein Sturm herauf", lautete die Wettervorhersage.
"There will be clouds over the **Bay** of Biscay tomorrow and there's a storm coming up in the **Bay** of Bengal," was the weather forecast.
(3) Longboat Key ist eine Insel innerhalb einer Inselkette, die sich entlang der dem **Golf** von Mexiko zugewandten Küste Floridas hinzieht.
Longboat Key is an island in a ribbon of islands running down the Mexican **Gulf** coast of Florida.

Note: der Finnische Meer**busen** = the **Gulf** of Finland
der Bottnische Meer**busen** = the **Gulf** of Bothnia
but: Bucht = bay
Near St. Peter Port, the capital of Guernsey, there are quiet, unspoilt **bays** and flat sandy beaches.
Compare: die Danziger **Bucht** = the **Gulf** of Danzig

golf: (1) (als Sportart) Golf
(2) 'Golf-', '-golf' (in combinations)

(1) "Why don't you take up **golf**?" his friend asked him.
"Warum fängst du nicht mit **Golf** an?" fragte ihn sein Freund.
(2) Ian Woosnam hatte ein einziges Ziel für die neue **Golf**saison – den Gewinn eines der vier bedeutenden **Golf**titel der Welt.
Ian Woosnam had a single ambition for the new **golf** season – to win one of the four major **golf** titles in the world.
A letter bomb sent to Wales's oldest **golf** club at Dyfed proved to be a practical joke.
Eine Briefbombe, die an den ältesten **Golf**klub von Wales in Dyfed geschickt wurde, erwies sich als schlechter Scherz.

Note: **golf** course, **golf** links = **Golf**platz, **Golf**anlage
One of the finest and oldest **golf** courses in the world is St. Andrews in Scotland.

but: crazy **golf** (in BE only), mini **golf** (in BE and AE) = Mini-**Golf**
Sidmouth, in Devon, caters for the more mature citizen: bridge, not bingo; putting greens instead of **crazy golf**.

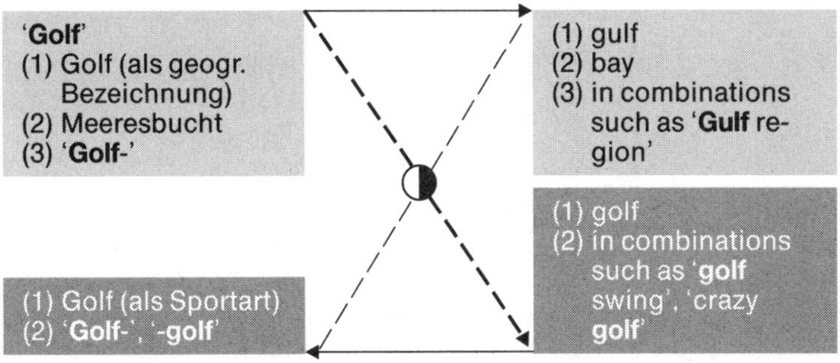

FALSE FRIENDS IN CONTEXT

Star Golfer: 'A Born Cheat'?

Neil: It's a scandal! They've expelled Sylvia from the ________ (1) club.
Mary: Why?
Neil: The papers say she's a born cheat.
Mary: That's simply terrible! This is worse than the ________ (2) War – socially.
Neil: Listen to what it says in the paper, "Nine of the cheating charges were proved wrong, but four others, including moving her ball, were proved..."
Mary: What's Sylvia doing about it?
Neil: First, she's seeking club readmission. And second, she's suing the ________ (3) club, claiming that jealous lady members envy her playing for the County Team.

SOLUTION

(1) **golf** club (2) **Gulf** War (3) **golf** club

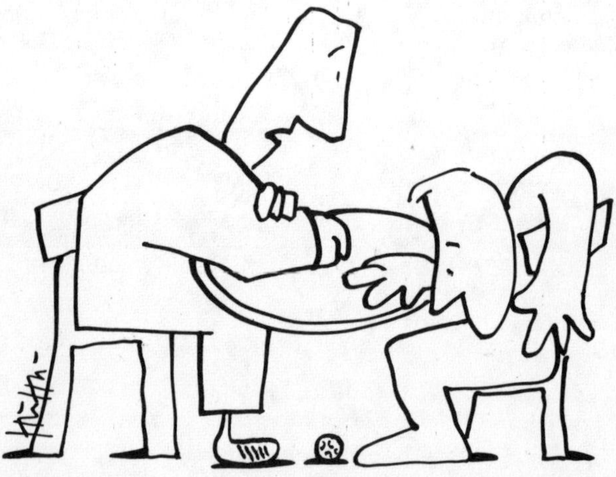

"My girlfriend complains I've changed since I started playing golf"

KANAL ◑ canal

canal [kə'næl]

channel ['tʃænl]

KANAL
(natürlicher Wasserweg)

KANAL: (1) (natürlicher Wasserweg) channel
(2) (tech.: TV, Radio) channel
(3) (diplomatischer Weg etc.) channel(s) (fig.)

(1) Der Nord-**Kanal** trennt Schottland von Nordirland, der St. Georgs-**Kanal** Wales von der Republik Irland.
The North **Channel** separates Scotland from Northern Ireland, St. George's **Channel** Wales from the Republic of Ireland.
Der Ärmel**kanal** ist der meistbefahrene **Kanal** der Welt.
The English **Channel** is the busiest **channel** of the world.
(2) Die Sportnachrichten kommen heute auf **Kanal** 4 (im 4. Programm).
The sports news is on **Channel** Four (on C4) today.
(3) Der Fall wurde über diplomatische **Kanäle** gelöst.
The case was solved through diplomatic **channels**.

Note: der Ärmel**kanal** = the English **Channel** or the **Channel**
der **Kanal**tunnel = the **Channel** Tunnel (between England and France) or the **Chunnel**

canal: (künstlicher) Kanal

Asked to name a land full of **canals**, most of us would think of the Netherlands.
Wenn wir gefragt würden, ein Land mit vielen **Kanälen** zu nennen, würden die meisten an die Niederlande denken.
His car came to a halt just inches from the side of the **canal**.
Sein Auto kam nur Zentimeter vom Rande des **Kanals** zum Halten.
This was the famed Corinth **Canal**, cut through the heart of mainland Greece in 1892 to save a 400-mile detour.
Dies war der berühmte **Kanal** von Korinth, der 1892 durch das griechische Festland getrieben wurde, um sich einen Umweg von 400 Meilen zu ersparen.

Note: the Kiel **Canal** = der Nord-Ostsee-**Kanal**
but: sewer = Abwasser**kanal**
wind tunnel = Wind**kanal**

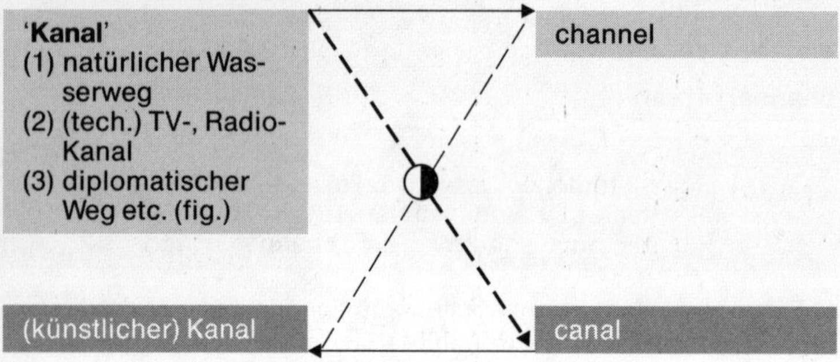

FALSE FRIENDS IN CONTEXT

A Geography Lesson

A geography teacher asked his pupils where the English ________ (1) was. Some of them put up their hands.
"Now, Jack, what about you?" asked his geography teacher, pointing at him.
Jack didn't know the answer. So he replied, "I don't know, sir. We can't get the English ________ (2) on our radio."

SOLUTION

(1) English **Channel** (2) English **channel**

A Letter to the Editor

There have been so many cases of near collisions of aircraft in the past. Why not build off-shore airports in the future? For trans-Atlantic flights an off-shore airport could be built in the Bristol ________ (3) area. This is instead of airports in the Midlands which in some cases have ________ (4) blocking runways at the end. J. F. Deans

SOLUTION

(3) Bristol **Channel** (4) canals

"It can get pretty foggy on the English Channel, you know..."

KROPF ◑ crop

crop

KROPF

goitre [ˈgɔɪtə] (beim Menschen)

KROPF: (1) (beim Menschen als Folge von Jodmangel) goitre (AE goiter)
(2) (**Kropf**bildung) goitre

(1) "Wir müssen Ihren **Kropf** operieren; sonst vergrößert er sich weiter", teilte der Arzt seiner Patientin mit.
"We've got to operate on your **goitre**, otherwise it might grow bigger," the doctor informed his patient.
(2) **Kropf**bildung kann durch regelmäßige Einnahme von jodiertem Speisesalz und Schokolade vermieden werden.
Goitre can be prevented by regularly eating iodised salt and chocolate.

crop: (1) (Verdauungsorgan bei Vögeln, Enten, Gänsen etc.) Kropf
(2) Ernte
(3) Pflanze

(1) "Look at the pigeons. They are sitting quietly on the roof because they've got food in their **crops**," explained the pigeon fancier.
"Schaut die Tauben an. Sie sitzen ruhig auf dem Dach, weil sie ihre Nahrung im **Kropf** haben", erklärte der Taubenzüchter.
(2) "The apple **crop** is good this year. We really can't complain," said one of the farmers in the village pub.
"Die Apfel**ernte** ist dieses Jahr gut. Da können wir uns wirklich nicht beklagen", sagte einer der Bauern in der Dorfkneipe.
(3) There are electric fences to protect valuable **crops** like vegetables from rabbits.
Dort gibt es Elektrozäune, um die wertvollen **Pflanzen** wie Gemüse vor Kaninchen zu schützen.
Runner beans are by far the most popular **crop** on account of the huge harvest.

Stangenbohnen sind bei weitem die beliebteste **Pflanze** wegen der großen Erntemenge.

Note: **crop** = Bürstenschnitt
a good **crop** of students = ein guter Studenten-Jahrgang

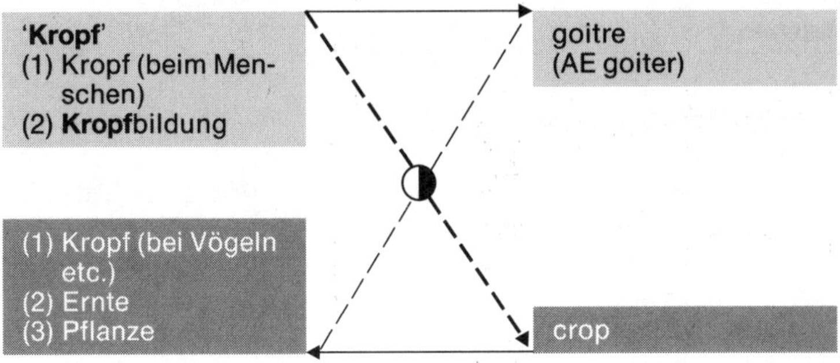

FALSE FRIENDS IN CONTEXT

Living a Strange Life

They had been living all their lives in a remote village high up in the Austrian Alps. Their life was hard as the raw climate of the mountains gave them a ________ (1) only every other year, if at all.
They couldn't remember if anyone from the world outside had ever come up to their village. One afternoon a woman they had never seen before turned up from nowhere.
The children ran after her making fun of her. "You're not to make fun of her. Stop it," an old woman cried. "You can't blame the poor woman for not having a ________ (2)."

SOLUTION

(1) crop (2) goitre

MANN ◑ man

man

MANN
(= Ehemann)

husband

MANN: (Ehemann) husband

"Ich hätte gerne Mr. Brown gesprochen." – "Es tut mir leid, aber mein **Mann** ist im Augenblick nicht da."
"Could I speak to Mr. Brown?" – "I'm sorry, my **husband** isn't at home at the moment."
"Als der Bruch kam, konnte ich nicht länger im Hause meines **Mannes** wohnen bleiben", erklärte die Herzogin.
"When the split came I couldn't stay on at my **husband**'s home any longer," the Duchess explained.

man: (1) Mann
(2) '**Mann**' (in combinations)
(3) Mensch

(1) There's a **man** at the door. John, could you have a look who it is?
An der Tür ist ein **Mann**. John, könntest du einmal nachsehen, wer das ist?
There is no other **man** in my life and I wouldn't have time for one.
Es gibt in meinem Leben keinen anderen **Mann**, und ich hätte auch keine Zeit für einen.
(2) But he is also a **man** of the people.
Aber er ist auch ein **Mann** des Volkes.
He is a **man** in the prime of life and a **man** of action.
Er ist ein **Mann** in den besten Jahren und ein **Mann** der Tat.
(3) **Man** cannot exist without water and oxygen.
Der **Mensch** kann ohne Wasser und Sauerstoff nicht existieren.

Note: (coll.) **Good Lord**, you must be mad! = **Mann**, du bist wohl verrückt!
(coll.) **Gosh**, she's a wonderful woman = **Mann**, ist das eine tolle Frau.

(coll.) **For heaven's sake**, stop it! = **Mann**, hör doch endlich auf!

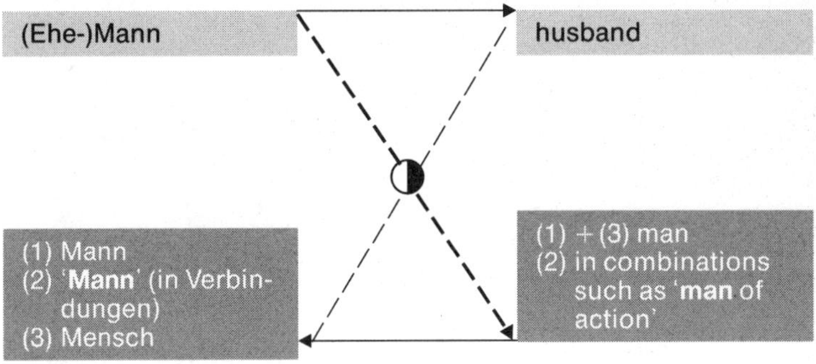

FALSE FRIENDS IN CONTEXT

Wanted: TV Set and Video

Gill: I know the ________ (1) I want. Listen, Becky. The ________(2) I'm going to marry should be able to tell jokes and sing. He should like listening to music, dancing and staying at home in the evening.
Becky (having listened to this and after a little thought): I don't believe what you've told me, Gill. To be frank: you don't want a ________ (3) at all. You want a TV set and video.

SOLUTION

(1) man/husband (2) man (3) man/husband

FALSE FRIENDS TRAPS TEST 2

EASY FALSE FRIENDS

1.a. My father is a professional ________ (**Fotograf ≠ photograph**).
1.b. "Can I have a ________ of you?" he asked her as they said good-bye at the airport (**Fotograf ≠ photograph**).
2.a. The newspaper boy is in the ________ (**Flur ≠ floor**). Henry, could you give him the money?
2.b. Her children filled the ________ with laughter (**Flure ≠ floors**).
3.a. "I'm afraid my ________ is not in (**Mann ◑ man**). You have just missed him," his wife lied on the phone.
3.b. Lord Miles is a ________ famous for never wearing a collar and tie (**Mann ◑ man**).
4.a. As he nodded I noticed his ________ eyebrows (**dick ◑ thick**).
4.b. Carol has become extremely ________ in the last few months (**dick ◑ thick**). She looks like a monster. Do you know why?
5.a. ________ prices have gone up in most European countries in the last few years (**Fleisch ◑ flesh**).
5.b. The latest pop videos have been banned for showing too much ________ (**Fleisch ◑ flesh**).
6. The news of the spy's release reached the British Government through diplomatic ________ (**Kanäle**).
7. "If you eat haddock regularly, you can't develop a ________," the doctor reassured the young woman (**Kropf**).
8. "These ________ of death (Todes**engel**) remind me of those in Auschwitz," commented the Vienna Mayor on the killings of 49 old people.
9. Colour ________ is a fairly recent development (**Fotografie**).
10. Despite the ________ (**Kluft**) between the leaders, President Gorbachev went out of his way to impress the Cubans.

ANSWER SHEET: TRUE FRIENDS TEST 2

EASY FALSE FRIENDS

1.a. My father is a professional **photographer**.
1.b. "Can I have a **photograph** of you?" he asked her as they said good-bye at the airport.
2.a. The newspaper boy is in the **hall**. Henry, could you give him the money?
2.b. Her children filled the **corridors** with laughter.
3.a. "I'm afraid my **husband** is not in. You have just missed him," his wife lied on the phone.
3.b. Lord Miles is a **man** famous for never wearing a collar and tie.
4.a. As he nodded I noticed his **thick** eyebrows.
4.b. Carol has become extremely **fat** in the last few months. She looks like a monster. Do you know why?
5.a. **Meat** prices have gone up in most European countries in the last few years.
5.b. The latest pop videos have been banned for showing too much **flesh**.
6. The news of the spy's release reached the British Government through diplomatic **channels**.
7. "If you eat haddock regularly, you can't develop a **goitre**," the doctor reassured the young woman.
8. "These **angels** of death remind me of those in Auschwitz," commented the Vienna Mayor on the killings of 49 old people.
9. Colour **photography** is a fairly recent development.
10. Despite the **gulf** between the leaders, President Gorbachev went out of his way to impress the Cubans.

MAPPE ≠ map

map

MAPPE

folder etc.

MAPPE: (1) (Akten**mappe**) folder, (Ordner) file
(2) (Aktentasche) briefcase, case; (Schultasche) (school)bag

(1) Wie soll ich bloß den Papierkram in den Griff bekommen? – Am besten, du ordnest ihn in **Mappen**.
I don't know how to cope with all this paper. – The best thing would be for you to arrange it in **folders**.
Kurz vor Dienstschluß bat der Bürovorsteher seine Sekretärin, einige neue **Mappen** (Ordner) zu kaufen.
Shortly before the office closed the chief clerk asked his secretary to buy some new **files**.
(2) Ich habe jetzt überall gesucht. Ich kann meine **Mappe** nicht finden. – Du hast sie wahrscheinlich im Bus liegenlassen.
I've been looking everywhere. I can't find my **briefcase**. – You probably left it on the bus.
"Ich kann nicht mein ganzes Leben mit derselben **Mappe** zur Schule gehen. Schau her, wie alt sie aussieht", stöhnte Maud.
"I can't go to school with the same (**school**)**bag** all my life. Look how tatty it is," moaned Maud.

map: (1) (Land- etc.)Karte
(2) Stadt**plan**
(3) Straßen**karte**

(1) I can't find Southport on the **map**. But as far as I remember it's somewhere near Blackpool.
Ich kann Southport nicht auf der (Land-)**Karte** finden. Aber es muß bei Blackpool sein, soweit ich mich erinnere.
The Britannica Atlas contains **maps** of the world, **maps** of oceans and **maps** of continents.
Der Britannica-Atlas enthält Welt**karten**, **Karten** der Ozeane und **Karten** der Erdteile.

(2) Don't go to London without a street **map**.
Fahre nicht ohne **Stadtplan** nach London.
(3) Before I leave, I'll buy a road **map** of Britain.
Vor meiner Abfahrt kaufe ich noch eine Straßen**karte** von Großbritannien.

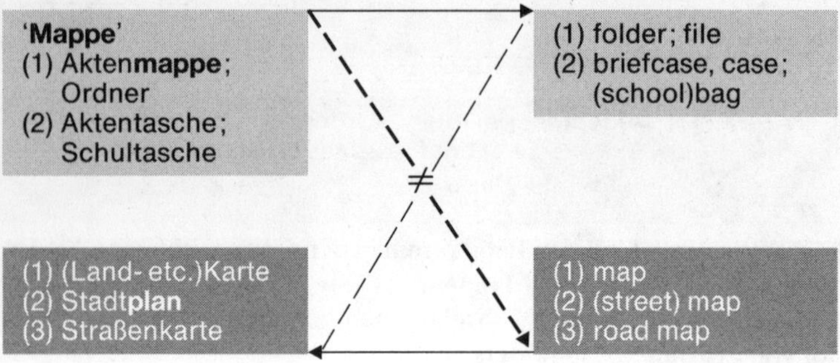

FALSE FRIENDS IN CONTEXT

A Woman on her Own

Detective (at the Southampton main post-office): ...and when did you first discover £ 110,000 had disappeared from the walk-in safe?
Post-Office Official: On Monday morning when the time-lock safe was reopened.
Detective: No traces have been left. Any suspicions?
Post-Office Official: No. But wait a minute. One of our women didn't turn up for work this morning. She's a 44-year-old clerk who always came to the post-office with two ________ (1). One of our men saw her walk out of the main post-office carrying two bulky ________ (2) last Friday.
Detective: Did you find anything in the safe?
Post-Office Official: There were a lot of ________ (3) from overseas places, for instance Rio, Cape Town, Sydney, all in post-office ________ (4). In fact, street ________ (5) from nearly every big city in the world.
Detective: When we checked the woman's home, we found a ________ (6) with ________ (7) of the world in it. Neighbours knew the couple had left for a journey round the world last Friday...

SOLUTION

(1) briefcases, cases (2) briefcases, cases (3) maps (4) post-office **files** (5) street **maps** (6) briefcase, case (7) maps

MEINUNG ≠ meaning

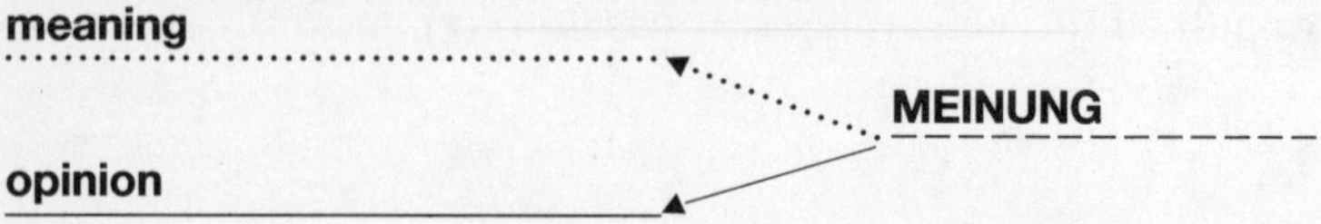

MEINUNG: (1) opinion, view; mind
(2) in combinations such as 'shade of **opinion**'

(1) Ich habe meine eigene **Meinung** zu der Angelegenheit.
I've got my own **opinion** on the matter.
Ich teile Ihre politischen **Meinungen** nicht.
I don't share your political **views**.
Es wird dich vielleicht überraschen, aber ich habe meine **Meinung** darüber geändert.
It may surprise you, but I've changed my **mind** about it.
(2) Wir haben schon unsere **Meinungs**verschiedenheiten, aber im Grunde kommen wir gut miteinander zurecht.
We have our differences of **opinion**, but basically we get on well together.
Es wäre töricht zu glauben, daß Rechtsanwälte und Bankiers jede **Meinungs**schattierung in den Vereinigten Staaten repräsentieren.
It would be foolish to think that lawyers and bankers represent every shade of **opinion** in the United States.

Note: **Meinungs**änderung = change of **opinion**
Meinungsbefragung = (public) **opinion** poll
Meinungsumschwung = swing of **opinion**
but: Da bin ich völlig Ihrer **Meinung** = I entirely agree with you.
Ich teile diese **Meinung** nicht = I don't agree.
Da gehen unsere **Meinungen** auseinander = We obviously differ on this point.

meaning: (1) Bedeutung
(2) Sinn
(3) '**Bedeutung(s)-**', '**Sinn(es)-**' (in combinations)

(1) What is the **meaning** of the new False Friend?
Welche **Bedeutung** hat der neue Falsche Freund?

(2) Life no longer had any **meaning** for her.
Das Leben hatte für sie keinen **Sinn** mehr.
(3) Did you notice the change of **meaning** in that sentence?
Hast du die **Bedeutungs**änderung in jenem Satz gemerkt?
"What is the true **meaning** of Christmas?" the minister asked his listeners.
"Was ist der wahre **Sinn** von Weihnachten?" fragte der Pastor seine Zuhörer.

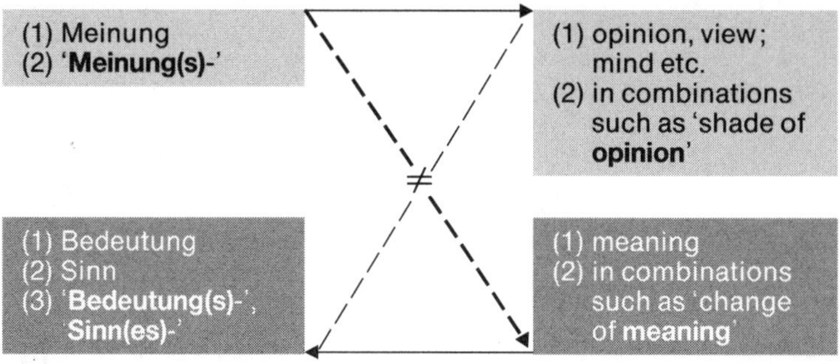

FALSE FRIENDS IN CONTEXT

Goldfinger

Fingerprint Expert: In my ________ (1) genetic fingerprinting is the most important invention in crime history.
FBI Scientist: In the United States FBI scientists have developed a technique which gives a new ________ (2) to the word Goldfinger.
Fingerprint Expert: Tell me more about your new research results.
FBI Scientist: To my ________ (3), gold stains the proteins left on any surface that has been in contact with human flesh. As a result our experts wash the fingerprint in a chemical mixture with tiny particles of gold.
Fingerprint Expert: Is that all you do?
FBI Scientist: By no means. The print is then bathed in a silver solution and an electrical field is passed across it.
Fingerprint Expert: In our ________ (4) this can't work...
FBI Scientist: After a short time an image begins to emerge when the

gold is attracted to the protein in the fingerprint. The new technique works well on computer floppy discs and counterfeit dollars.
Fingerprint Expert: But it can't work on legal dollars because they already have a protein content.
FBI Scientist: That's right. We are in the process of trying it out on many other surfaces.
Fingerprint Expert: I hope it doesn't take too long.

SOLUTION

(1) view, opinion (2) meaning (3) to my mind (4) view, opinion

"We have our differences of opinion, but basically we get on well together, Mum..."

MÖRDER ≠ murder

murder

MÖRDER

murderer/murderess ['mɜ:dərɪs]

MÖRDER(IN): (1) murderer/murderess; killer
(2) in combinations such as 'child **murderer**'
(3) (politischer **Mörder**) assassin [ə'sæsɪn]
(4) (Bruder**mörder**) fratricide (etc.)
(5) (Gift**mörder**) poisoner ['pɔɪznə]

(1) Wragg war kein **Mörder**, sondern eine **Mörderin**. Ihr Name lautete Elizabeth Wragg.
Wragg was not a **murderer**, but a **murderess**. Her name was Elizabeth Wragg.
Der Mann, den er erschossen hatte, lag auf dem Gesicht. Der **Mörder** ging zu ihm hin und drehte den Körper um. Er schaute in das Gesicht seines eigenen Bruders.
The man he had shot lay on his face. The **killer** went up to him and turned the body over. He was looking into his own brother's face.
(2) "Wie kann ein Kinder**mörder** so brutal sein?" fragte mich mein Freund.
"How can a child **murderer** be so brutal?" my friend asked me.
(3) Der **Mörder** von Präsident John F. Kennedy war Lee Harvey Oswald, der zwei Tage später von Jack Ruby erschossen wurde.
The **assassin** of President John F. Kennedy was Lee Harvey Oswald, who was shot dead two days later by Jack Ruby.
(4) Er war zum **Brudermörder** geworden, aber ohne es zu wissen.
He had become a **fratricide**, but without knowing it.
(5) Die **Giftmörderin** hatte ihren Mann mit Rattengift getötet.
The **poisoner** had killed her husband with rat poison.

murder: (1) Mord
(2) '**Mord-**', '**-mord**' (in combinations)
(3) (genocide) Völker**mord**
(4) (assassination) politischer Mord
(5) (fratricide) Bruder**mord** (etc.)
(6) (suicide) Selbst**mord**

(1) This **murder** cannot be cleared up if we don't find the man with the yellow scarf.
Dieser **Mord** kann nicht aufgeklärt werden, wenn wir den Mann mit dem gelben Schal nicht finden.
(2) "She had an attractive body," the **murder** suspect admitted, "but I didn't kill Frances Barnet."
"Sie hatte einen attraktiven Körper", gab der **Mord**verdächtige zu, "aber ich habe Frances Barnet nicht getötet."
(3) Prince Charles accused Brazil of collective **genocide** of the Yanomami Indians.
Prinz Charles beschuldigte Brasilien des kollektiven **Völkermords** an den Yanomami-Indianern.
(4) The **assassination** of Robert Kennedy occurred in the Ambassador Hotel in Los Angeles in 1968 five years after John F. Kennedy's death.
Der **Mord** an Robert Kennedy ereignete sich fünf Jahre nach John F. Kennedys Tod im Jahre 1968 im Ambassador Hotel von Los Angeles.
(5) An English paper commented the next day on the IRA murder, "It was a tragic case of **fratricide**."
"Es war ein tragischer Fall von **Brudermord**", kommentierte eine englische Zeitung am nächsten Tag den IRA-Mord.
(6) **Suicide** was the only way for the artist to reconcile himself with this world.
Selbstmord war für den Künstler der einzige Weg, sich mit dieser Welt zu versöhnen.

Note: character **assassination** = Ruf**mord**
Character **assassination** is the worst kind of slander.
Compare: Bruder**mord** = **fratricide** = Bruder**mörder**
Mutter**mord** = **matricide** = Mutter**mörder**
Vater**mord** = **patricide** = Vater**mörder**
vorsätzlicher **Mord** = **homicide** = vorsätzlicher **Mörder**
Selbst**mord** = **suicide** = Selbst**mörder**
Vater-/Mutter**mord** = **parricide** = Vater-/Mutter**mörder**

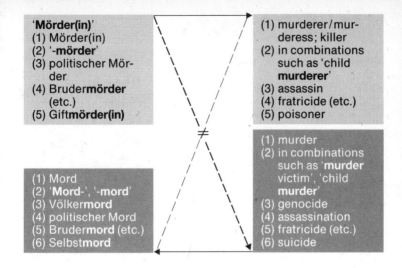

'Mörder(in)'
(1) Mörder(in)
(2) '**-mörder**'
(3) politischer Mörder
(4) Bruder**mörder** (etc.)
(5) Gift**mörder(in)**

(1) murderer/murderess; killer
(2) in combinations such as 'child **murderer**'
(3) assassin
(4) fratricide (etc.)
(5) poisoner

(1) Mord
(2) '**Mord-**', '**-mord**'
(3) Völker**mord**
(4) politischer Mord
(5) Bruder**mord** (etc.)
(6) Selbst**mord**

(1) murder
(2) in combinations such as '**murder** victim', 'child **murder**'
(3) genocide
(4) assassination
(5) fratricide (etc.)
(6) suicide

FALSE FRIENDS IN CONTEXT

Sinatra: 'Put on Hit List'

Reporter (to Chief Editor on the phone): I've just been told of a plot to kill Frank Sinatra. It could make an interesting feature story.
Chief Editor: Perhaps. Give me a few facts.
Reporter: The magazine publisher Larry Flynt is said to have offered Sinatra's potential ________ (1) a million dollars to kill him. I was even shown a photocopy of a million-dollar cheque signed by Flynt.
Chief Editor: But won't it be difficult to prove these facts?
Reporter: At least one thing is certain. Flynt was crippled last night, the victim of a ________ (2) attempt.
Chief Editor: Write up the story and add a few more facts on why Sinatra was put on the hit list by the ________ (3) gang.

SOLUTION

(1) murderer (2) **murder** attempt (3) **murder**gang

NÄCHSTE ◑ next

next

NÄCHSTE

nearest

(= räumlich **nächst**gelegen etc.)

NÄCHSTE(-R, -S): (1) (räumlich nächstgelegen; unmittelbar verwandt) nearest, closest
(2) (in unmittelbarer Nähe) right by; immediate (geogr.)
(3) closest (fig.)

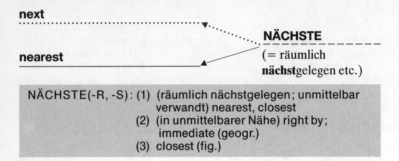

(1) Wo sollen wir übernachten? Das **nächste** Dorf ist drei Meilen entfernt.
Where shall we spend the night? The **nearest** village is three miles away (= das per Luftlinie **nächste**, also räumlich **nächst**gelegene Dorf).
Zu meinem 55. Geburtstag lade ich nur die **nächsten** Verwandten ein.
I'll only invite my **closest** relatives on my fifty-fifth birthday.
(2) Das neue Hotel wurde in **nächster** Nähe der Themse gebaut.
The new hotel was built **right by** the Thames.
Die Römer hatten ihr Lager südlich **nächst** der Mauer aufgeschlagen.
The Romans had set up their camp in the **immediate** south of the wall.
(3) Seine letzte Aussage dürfte der Wahrheit am **nächsten** kommen.
His last statement is probably **closest** to the truth.

next: (in der Reihen- oder Abfolge) nächste(-r, -s), nächstfolgend (auch zeitlich)

Where shall we spend the night? The **next** village is three miles away (= das entlang der Landstraße in der Reihenfolge **nächste** Dorf).
Wo sollen wir übernachten? Das **nächste** (= **nächst**folgende) Dorf ist drei Meilen entfernt.
The PNC2 system is the **next** generation of computers for Britain's police.
Das PNC2-System ist die **nächste** Computer-Generation für die britische Polizei.
My birthday is not until May **next** year.
Ich habe erst im Mai **nächsten** Jahres Geburtstag.

"Then we climbed the **next** highest hill," said the witness.
"Dann stiegen wir den **nächst**höchsten Hügel hinauf", sagte der Zeuge.

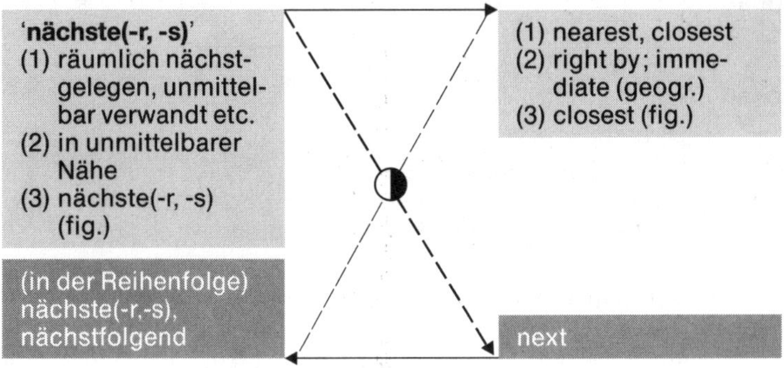

FALSE FRIENDS IN CONTEXT

Directing People

She had thought a cruise would be more romantic. As the ship was pitching and rolling more than usual, the little lady felt something funny going on in her stomach. So she left her cabin.
"I'm sorry," she said to the sailor standing ________ (1) to her on deck. "I'm feeling seasick. How far is it to the ________ (2) stretch of land?
"Six miles," was the sailor's quick answer.
"In which direction?" the little lady asked.
"Straight down, of course," came the reply.
"And where's the ________ (3) lavatory?" she asked, turning pale.
"Turn round. Behind you."

SOLUTION

(1) **next** to (2) nearest (3) nearest

PERLE ◑ pearl

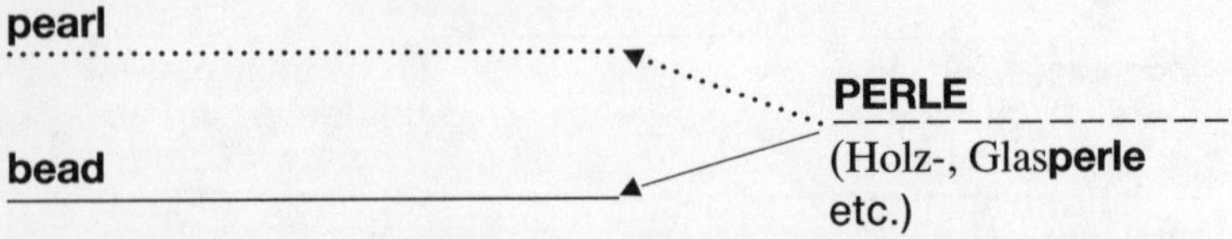

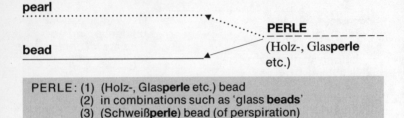

PERLE: (1) (Holz-, Glas**perle** etc.) bead
(2) in combinations such as 'glass **beads**'
(3) (Schweiß**perle**) bead (of perspiration)

(1) Im nächsten Sommer werden die Modeschöpfer Bikinis herausbringen, die mit Muscheln, Münzen und **Perlen** besetzt sind.
Next summer fashion designers will launch bikinis decorated with shells, coins and **beads**.
In einem kleinen Laden entdeckte Joanna eine Holz-**Perlen**kette. Ohne viel zu überlegen, kaufte sie noch eine Glas-**Perlen**kette für ihre Mutter.
In a small shop Joanna found a string of wooden **beads**. Without thinking twice she also bought a necklace of glass **beads** for her mother.
(2) Es war heiß im Laden, und die Stirn des Ladenbesitzers war mit Schweiß**perlen** übersät.
It was hot in the shop, and the shopkeeper's forehead was covered with **beads** of perspiration.

pearl: (1) (natürliche, echte) Perle
(2) '**Perl(en)-**', '**-perle**' (in combinations)
(3) Perle (fig.)

(1) "My husband has given me a necklace of real Oriental **pearls** – besides a number of other gifts," Samantha confided to a friend.
"Mein Mann hat mir eine Halskette mit echten orientalischen **Perlen** geschenkt – neben einigen anderen Geschenken", vertraute Samantha einer Freundin an.
(2) Down at the harbour a **pearl** diver offered me a necklace of real **pearls**.
Unten am Hafen bot mir ein **Perlen**taucher eine echte **Perlen**kette an.
Fortunately I didn't have enough money with me. Later a fellow passenger told me I had been offered cheap artificial **pearls**.

Glücklicherweise hatte ich nicht genügend Geld bei mir. Später erzählte mir ein Mitreisender, daß ich billige Kunst**perlen** angeboten bekommen hätte.
(3) When he laughed the young man showed his teeth, which looked like **pearls**.
Wenn er lachte, zeigte der junge Mann seine Zähne, die wie **Perlen** aussahen.

Note: mother of **pearl** = **Perl**mutt
but: dew drops = Tau**perlen**
sparkling wine = **Perl**wein

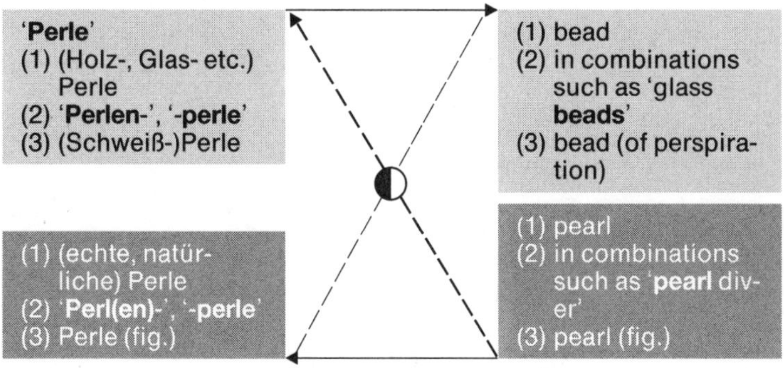

FALSE FRIENDS IN CONTEXT

A Car Wash with a Difference

Car Owner: What's so special about New Hot Wax?
Attendant (at petrol station): Well, it both cleans your car better and contains more waxes than any other wash-and-wax product.
Car Owner: I seem to have heard that before.
Attendant: The new product contains enough wax to last a full four weeks. You can see for yourself. After four weeks there are still ________ (1) drops.
Car Owner (still sceptical): What about protection in the winter months?
Attendant: When you've washed your car with New Hot Wax, you've waxed it at the same time. With a white car like yours New Hot Wax

gives a brilliant lasting shine in which even your teeth will look like _______ (2).

SOLUTION

(1) **bead** drops (2) pearls

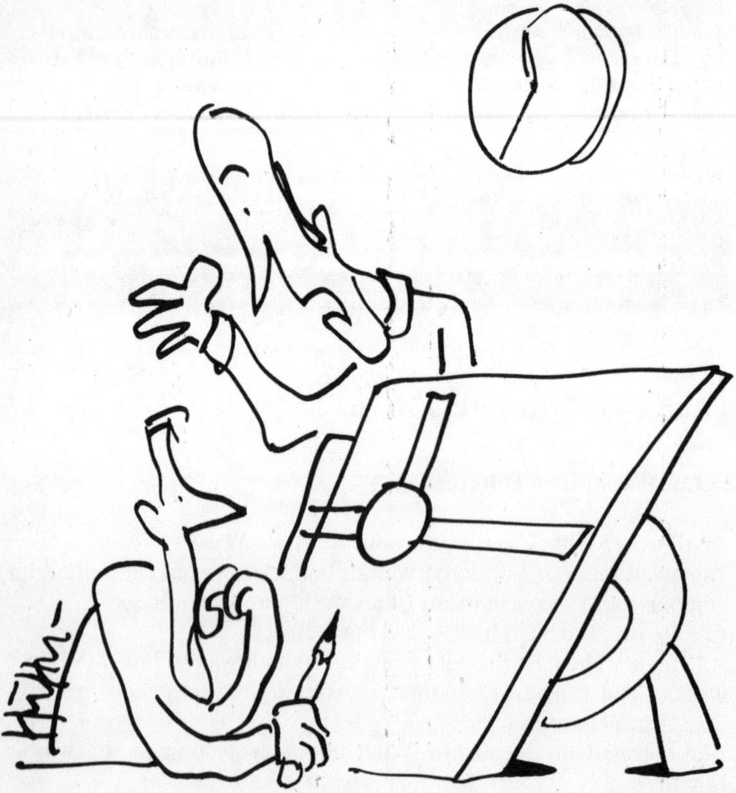

"I would rather see beads of perspiration on your forehead than invisible inspiration on your board!"

RENTE ≠ rent

rent

RENTE

pension ['penʃn]

(Alters**rente** etc.)

RENTE: (1) (Alters**rente**) pension (**see** Pension ≠ pension)
(2) (Leib**rente**) annuity (from an insurance company)

(1) Wieviel **Rente** bekommen Sie?
How much do you get as a **pension**?
Ich erhalte nur 149 Pfund Alters**rente** pro Monat. Es ist ein Skandal!
I only get £ 149 a month old-age **pension**. It's a scandal!
Entschuldigung, aber ist Altersruhegeld dasselbe wie Alters**rente**? – Natürlich, das war ja der Trick, mit dem sie uns reingelegt haben.
I'm sorry, but is retirement **pension** the same as old-age **pension**? – Of course, but that was the trick they used to catch us out.
(2) Glücklicherweise bekomme ich noch eine kleine Leib**rente** von der Versicherung meines Mannes; sonst könnte ich nicht mit dem Geld auskommen.
Fortunately, I also get a small **annuity** from my husband's insurance, otherwise I couldn't make ends meet.

Note: Witwen**rente** = widow's **pension**
Invaliditäts**rente** = disability **pension**
Kriegswitwen**rente** = war-widow's **pension**
but: Altersruhegeld = retirement **pension**

rent: (1) Miete, Mietzins
(2) '**Miet**-' (in combinations)
(3) Pacht(geld)

(1) Is your **rent** as high as ours? We can hardly afford to live in this house.
Ist Ihre **Miete** auch so hoch wie unsere? Wir können uns kaum dieses Haus leisten.
The **rent** is £ 750 every month. That's an exorbitant **rent**.
Der **Mietzins** beträgt £ 750 pro Monat. Das ist eine unverschämt hohe **Miete**.

(2) Our neighbour's **rent** arrears were enormous, so he moved out.
Die **Miet**rückstände unseres Nachbarn waren enorm, daher zog er aus.
(3) The **rent** for the land and the wood went up last year; it is £6,500 a year now.
Die **Pacht** für das Land und den Wald stieg letztes Jahr; sie beträgt jetzt 6.500 Pfund im Jahr.

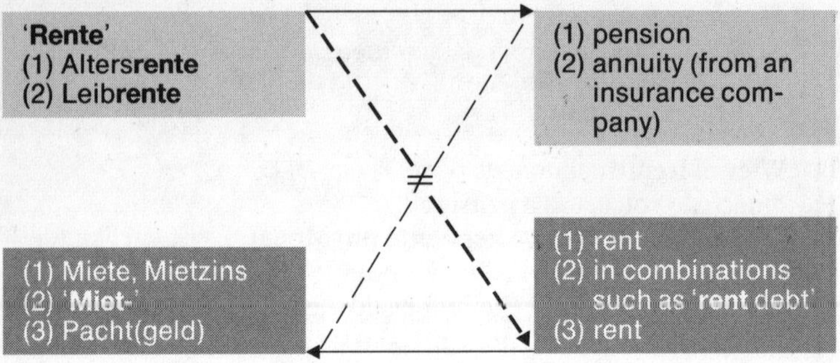

FALSE FRIENDS IN CONTEXT

Playing for Time

Landlord: Why are you always behind with your ________ (1)? I won't tolerate it any longer. I'll throw you out if you don't pay now!
Scotsman: But as I've already told you, I can't give you the ________ (2) today. Please, give me a little more time.
Landlord: Right, then, I'll give you four more days. But, then...
Scotsman: O.K. then... And my four days are Good Friday, August Bank Holiday, the Fifth of November and Christmas Day...

* * *

You old fool, I've got to save up for my old-age ________ (3), the Scotsman thought at the back of his mind.

SOLUTION

(1) rent (2) rent (3) pension

SAUCE ◑ sauce

sauce

SAUCE
(= Braten**sauce**)

gravy

SAUCE: (Braten**sauce**) gravy

“Ich möchte keine **Sauce** zu den Koteletts, sonst schmecken sie anders”, sagte der alte Herr.
“I don’t like **gravy** with the chops, otherwise they taste different,” said the old gentleman.
Bis ich dann mal aufgestanden bin, ist es Zeit, die **Sauce** für den Sonntagsbraten anzurichten.
By the time I’ve got up, it’s time to make the **gravy** for the Sunday roast.
“Ich habe gerade meinen Schlips mit Mineralwasser bekleckert, und es hat die (**Braten**-)**Saucen**flecke völlig entfernt”, sagte er scherzhaft und schaute seine Frau an.
“I just spilt some mineral water down my tie and it’s completely removed the **gravy** stains,” he said jokingly, looking at his wife.

Note: Spesen-, Vergünstigungs- = **gravy** (in combinations, mainly in AE)
Many left-wing trade unionists were eager enough to go on **gravy** trips to East Germany in the past.
Only after a world record attempt will Elliott hit the **gravy** trail for two months.

sauce (alle anderen **Saucen**arten):
(1) süße Saucen (sweet sauces in combinations such as ‘chocolate **sauce**’, ‘custard **sauce**’)
(2) pikante Saucen (savoury sauces in combinations such as ‘cheese **sauce**’, ‘mushroom **sauce**’, ‘onion **sauce**’)

(1) “Food should be elementary and healthy. So there’s no need for all those heavy **sauces**,” continued the head chef of the Dorchester Hotel.

“Das Essen sollte einfach und gesund sein. Daher braucht man nicht unbedingt die vielen schweren **Saucen**”, fuhr der Chefkoch des Dorchester Hotels fort.
“What’s for pudding today?” – “Chocolate blancmange with custard **sauce**.”
“Was gibt’s heute zum Nachtisch?” – “Schokoladen-Pudding mit Vanille-**Sauce**.”
(2) A lot of chefs say that Cheddar cheese, whether mild or tasty, makes a perfect cheese **sauce**.
Viele Köche behaupten, daß sich aus Cheddarkäse, ob mild oder pikant, eine ideale Käse-**Sauce** herstellen läßt.

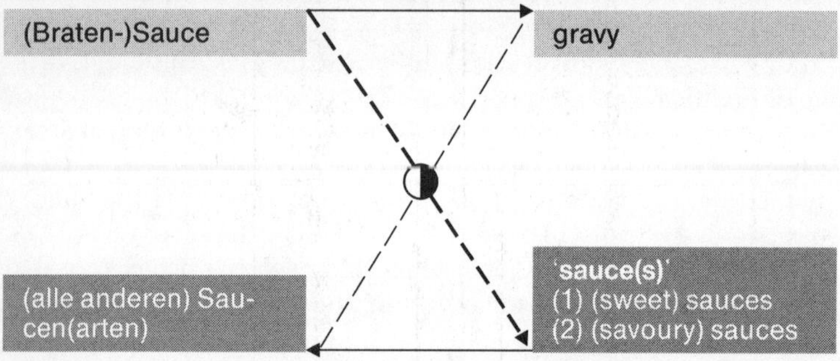

FALSE FRIENDS IN CONTEXT

Living a Good Life

Doctor (advising a housewife on dieting): While you’re on a diet, avoid having ________ (1) with your desserts and any kind of ________ (2) on your meat. Do you remember what it says in the cookery books? Make the ________ (3) by melting three ounces of butter in a pan...
Housewife: And pour the ________ (4) into a buttered fireproof dish... I know what you mean.
Doctor: So take care to avoid hidden fats...

* * *

Housewife (at home): Be careful when you eat your roastbeef, and don’t spill ________ (5) down you, John.

Husband: I just spilt some mineral water down my tie and it's completely removed the ________ (6) stains.

SOLUTION

(1) sauce (2) gravy (3) sauce (4) sauce (5) gravy (6) **gravy** stains

"Some more tomato sauce, Sir?"

SCHMAL ≠ small

small

SCHMAL
(= eng; gering etc.)

narrow etc.

SCHMAL: (1) (eng) narrow
(2) (hager) thin
(3) (gering) slight
(4) (feingliedrig) slender

(1) Ein **schmaler** Pfad führte den Hügel hinauf.
A **narrow** path led up the hill.
(2) "Der ist aber **schmal** im Gesicht geworden, seit ich ihn das letzte Mal gesehen habe", dachte Allen, als er den Postboten beim Weggehen beobachtete.
"He's grown **thin** in the face since I last saw him," Allen thought as he watched the postman going away.
(3) "Unsere Firma macht im Augenblick nur einen **schmalen** Gewinn. Daher suche ich mir am besten eine neue Stelle", kam Jackie der Gedanke.
"Our firm is only making a **slight** profit at the moment. So I'd better look for a new job," it occurred to Jackie.
(4) Ihre **schmalen** Hände zitterten, als sie Franks Gesicht berührten.
Her **slender** hands trembled as they touched Frank's face.

small: (1) klein, gering
(2) niedrig
(3) bescheiden

(1) We are only a **small** club.
Wir sind nur ein **kleiner** Verein.
In addition, there is a **small** membership fee.
Außerdem wird ein **geringer** Mitgliedsbeitrag erhoben.
(2) The **small** crowds in football stadiums show that people are only interested in good football.
Die **niedrigen** Zuschauerzahlen in den Fußballstadien zeigen, daß die Leute nur an gutem Fußball interessiert sind.

(3) My first husband only left me a **small** inheritance. So I've only a **small** income.
Mein erster Mann hinterließ mir nur ein **bescheidenes** Vermögen. Daher verfüge ich nur über ein **bescheidenes** Einkommen.

Note: Fiona won a **small fortune** in the pools =
Fiona gewann im Lotto **viel Geld**.
Steve inherited a **small fortune** from his aunt. =
Steve erbte von seiner Tante ein **kleines Vermögen**.

but: the **small** print = das **Klein**gedruckte
(die Verkaufsbedingungen)

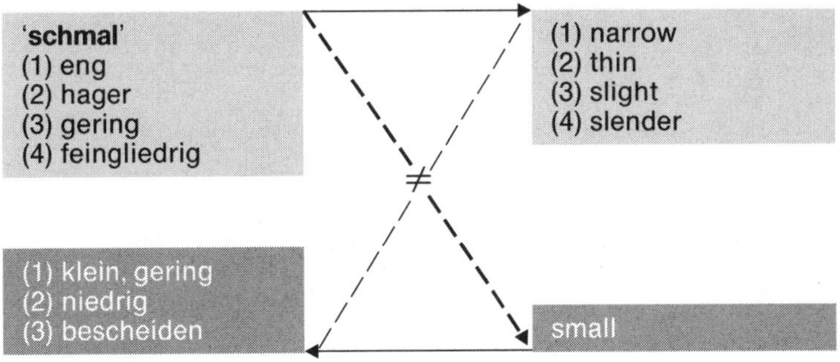

FALSE FRIENDS IN CONTEXT

The Very Limit

Tourist (making a complaint): It was a ________ (1) bump, but it hurt my knee while on holiday in Majorca, and the medical costs came to £24. This was quite a sum for my ________ (2) holiday budget.
Legal Adviser: This isn't covered by the National Health Service as it happened abroad.
Tourist, looking ________ (3) in the face: That's just the point. I had insurance for all medical eventualities. But my claim has been rejected because it is under £25.
Legal Adviser: Have you got the insurance form with you? There must be a catch somewhere.
Tourist, with her ________ (4) hands trembling: Here you are, sir.
Legal Adviser (after looking through the clauses): It's here in the ________ (5) print. I'm afraid you're £1 down on your luck. Be more careful next time before signing a travel insurance policy.

SOLUTION

(1) small (2) small (3) thin (4) slender (5) small

"My husband only left me a small inheritance – I managed to build it up during my second and third marriage."

SCHNECKE ≠ snake

snake

SCHNECKE

snail

SCHNECKE: (1) snail (with shell), slug (without shell)
(2) snail (fig.)

(1) **Schnecken** mit einem Gehäuse auf dem Rücken können Sonne besser ertragen als **Schnecken** ohne Gehäuse.
Snails, which have a shell on their backs, can bear the sun better than **slugs**, which don't.
Der nordamerikanische Everglade-Milan befolgt eine höchst eingeschränkte Diät, indem er nur **Schnecken** verzehrt.
The North American Everglade kite has a most restricted diet, eating only **snails**.
(2) Der Riesenlaster vor uns bewegte sich nur im **Schnecken**tempo.
The giant lorry in front of us only moved at a **snail**'s pace.

Note: In der biologischen Fachsprache lauten die Bezeichnungen
Gehäuse**schnecken** = **snails**
Nackt**schnecken** = **slugs**

snake: (1) Schlange
(2) '**Schlangen-**', '**-schlange**' (in combinations)

(1) Yvonne stellte sich tot, um sich davor zu schützen, von der **Schlange** angegriffen zu werden – einer 10 Fuß langen Python.
Yvonne played dead to save herself from being attacked by a **snake** – a ten-foot python.
(2) "Do you know the **snake** charmers of Burma and the **snake** dancers of the Hopi Indians?" he asked. "Would you like to come and see them?" he said, inviting her.
"Kennst du die **Schlangen**beschwörer von Burma und die **Schlangen**tänzer der Hopi-Indianer?" fragte er. "Möchtest du sie sehen?" lud er sie ein.
Most people are afraid of **snake**bites.

Die meisten Menschen fürchten **Schlangen**bisse.
It is little known, however, that poisonous **snakes** only bite in self-defence.
Es ist jedoch wenig bekannt, daß Gift**schlangen** nur zur Selbstverteidigung den Biß ausführen.

Note: serpent = **Schlange** (in der Mythologie, Literatur, Bibel etc.)
The golden **serpent** is a figure in legends, folktales and in literature.
Near Pontypridd, Wales, a nasty **serpent** drags victims into a local pool, so legend has it.
but: grass **snake** = Ringel**natter**
smooth **snake** = Schling-, Glatt**natter**
While still a schoolboy at Canford, in Dorset, Hilary Hook supplied the London Zoo with several specimen of the rare smooth **snake**.

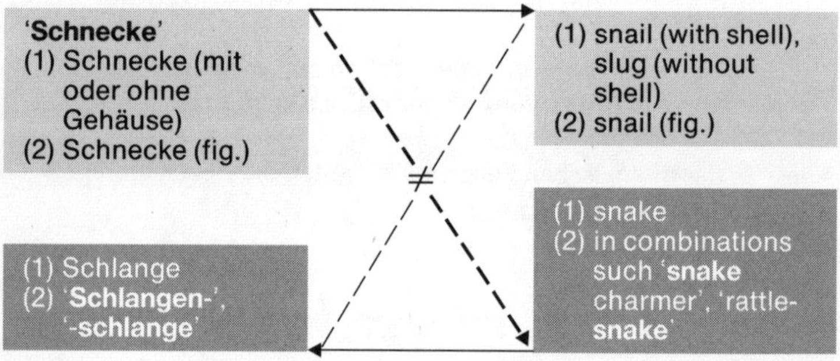

FALSE FRIENDS IN CONTEXT

Sharing your Fear

Have you ever thought of sharing your fear with other people? If not, the following statistics give you an insight into what people are afraid of.
If, like many other people, you are terrified of ________ (1) don't worry – 390 out of 1,000 people share your fear.

In every 1,000 people, here is the number afraid of:

heights 307
storms 211
flying 198
dentists 198
crying 182
travelling alone 74

and ________ (2) (with shell) ... 0 – everyone thought they were harmless.

SOLUTION

(1) snakes (2) snails (with shell)

Did you know...?

Did you know that ________ (3) provide valuable fertiliser to enable the desert to bloom?
Did you know that a rattle________ (4) needs a meal only once every five weeks?

SOLUTION

(3) snails (4) rattle**snake**

SCHWIMMEN ◑ swim

swim

SCHWIMMEN
(= im oder auf dem Wasser treiben)

float

SCHWIMMEN (passiv): (im oder auf dem Wasser treiben)
(1) float
(2) drift

(1) Weiter unten am Fluß fanden die Kinder eine Flasche, die im Wasser **schwamm**; sie enthielt eine Botschaft in einer Sprache, die sie nicht verstanden.
Further down the river the children found a bottle **floating** in the water. It contained a message in a language they didn't understand.
Nach dem Tanker-Unglück **schwammen** Tausende toter Fische und Vögel auf dem Ölteppich.
After the tanker disaster thousands of dead fish and birds were left **floating** in the oil slick.
(2) Nach dem starken Regen **schwamm** viel Holz den Fluß hinunter.
After the heavy rain a lot of wood was **drifting** downstream.

Note: Treibeis = **floating** ice
but: Milchauto = milk**float**
Why do Skodas have a fifth gear? To overtake milk**floats**. (This is a car joke!)
schwimmendes Hospital = **floating** hospital
The Royal Yacht Britannia is going to be used as a **floating** hospital.
schwimmendes Restaurant = **floating** restaurant
The world's biggest **floating** restaurant is on Hongkong Island.
schwimmender Sarg = **floating** tomb [tuːm]
The burnt-out ferry 'Scandinavian Star' with a death toll of 160 was called a **floating** tomb.

swim: schwimmen (aktiv)

In the afternoon we **swam** to the little island in the middle of the lake. We looked into the hut, and then **swam** back in ten minutes because we felt cold.
Nachmittags **schwammen** wir zur kleinen Insel in der Mitte des Sees. Wir schauten in die Hütte und **schwammen** dann in zehn Minuten zurück, weil uns kalt wurde.
It used to be a joy in the summer months to **swim** in the lake.
In den Sommermonaten machte es gewöhnlich Freude, in dem See zu **schwimmen**.

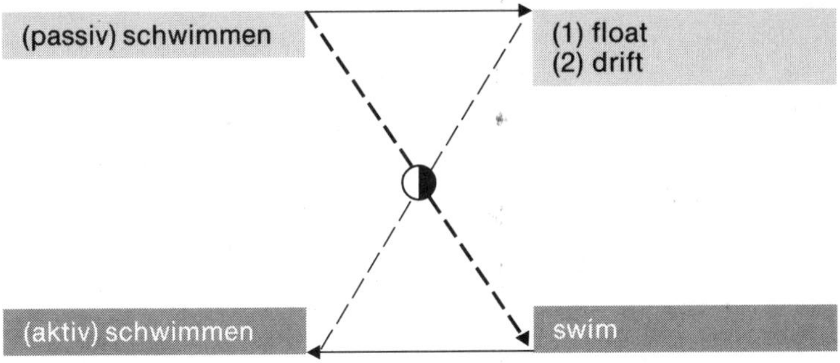

FALSE FRIENDS IN CONTEXT

An Adventure in the Jungle . . .

An expedition was trying to cross a river in the Amazon jungle. As there was no bridge and no boat, one of the explorers suggested they should ________ (1) across the river at midday.
Explorer to a native, ________ (2) next to him: We are lucky there are no piranhas about.
Native (looking unconcerned): I think the crocodiles keep them off. They only snap at things ________ (3) by when it's hot at midday.

SOLUTION

(1) swim (2) swimming (3) floating

. . . and a Rescue at Sea

Two men sunbathing on the beach with their wives near Skegness were alerted when they heard two boys shouting for help and waving their arms frantically.
They jumped into the water at once and ________ (4) about 80 yards to rescue the two teenagers whose dinghy was ________ (5) out to sea. Once ashore the boys ran off without a word of thanks.

SOLUTION

(4) swam (5) was floating, was drifting

"Honestly, I expected the floating restaurant to be somewhat different, darling..."

FALSE FRIENDS TRAPS TEST 3

EASY FALSE FRIENDS

1.a. As the secretary had some time left in the afternoon, she arranged the documents in a ________ (**Mappe ≠ map**).
1.b. Antique ________ of London and ________ of English counties always find a buyer (**Mappen ≠ maps**).
2.a. "What is the ________ of all this?" demanded my father when he entered the room (**Meinung ≠ meaning**).
2.b. This idea is as old as the hills. But it is not a popular ________ (**Meinung ≠ meaning**).
3.a. The Amazon Indians watched as the white woman was trying to ________ across the crocodile-infested river (**schwimmen ◑ swim**).
3.b. Thousands of dead fish ________ on the Derwent River which had been contaminated (**schwimmen ◑ swim**).
4.a. "I only get a small war-widow's ________," the old woman complained. "Why don't war widows get more ________ (**Rente ≠ rent**)?"
4.b. In the early days of her career, Marilyn Monroe posed nude for photographer Tom Kelly because she needed the money to pay her ________ (**Rente ≠ rent**).
5.a. I'm only going to invite my ________ relatives to our wedding (**nächsten ≠ next**).
5.b. "When are we going to meet ________?" Chrissy asked her lover (**nächstes ≠ next**).
6. The steak was tender and juicy, but it was served without any ________ (**Sauce**).
7. The ________ (**Mörder**) had escaped in the darkness, but the police managed to catch him next morning.
8. "What a nice string of wooden ________ (**Perlen**)," Linda said to her mother. "Will you buy me one?"
9. I could see my grandfather's face had grown ________ (**schmal**). He had become very ill.
10. "Look at the ________ (**Schnecke**) crawling slowly along. I like its shell," the child said to her mother.

ANSWER SHEET: TRUE FRIENDS TEST 3

EASY FALSE FRIENDS

1.a. As the secretary had some time left in the afternoon, she arranged the documents in a **folder**.
1.b. Antique **maps** of London and **maps** of English counties always find a buyer.
2.a. "What is the **meaning** of all this?" demanded my father when he entered the room.
2.b. This idea is as old as the hills. But it is not a popular **view**.
3.a. The Amazon Indians watched as the white woman was trying to **swim** across the crocodile-infested river.
3.b. Thousands of dead fish **floated** on the Derwent River which had been contaminated.
4.a. "I only get a small war-widow's **pension**," the old woman complained. "Why don't war widows get more **pension**?"
4.b. In the early days of her career, Marilyn Monroe posed nude for photographer Tom Kelly because she needed the money to pay her **rent**.
5.a. I'm only going to invite my **nearest/closest** relatives to our wedding.
5.b. "When are we going to meet **next**?" Chrissy asked her lover.
6. The steak was tender and juicy, but it was served without any **gravy**.
7. The **murderer** had escaped in the darkness, but the police managed to catch him next morning.
8. "What a nice string of wooden **beads**," Linda said to her mother. "Will you buy me one?"
9. I could see my grandfather's face had grown **thin**. He had become very ill.
10. "Look at the **snail** crawling slowly along. I like its shell," the child said to her mother.

SEE ◑ sea

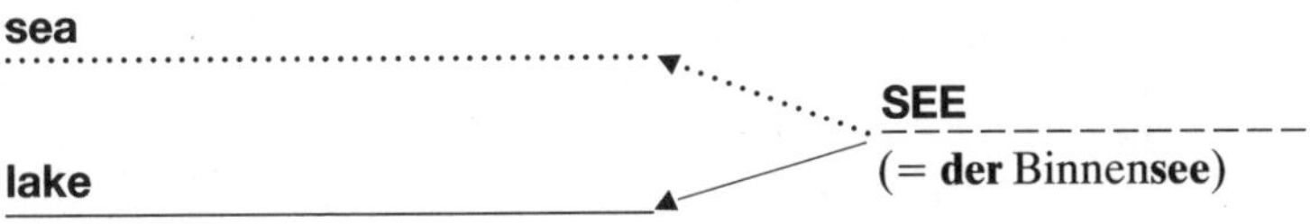

(der) SEE: (1) (Binnen**see**) lake
(2) in combinations such as '**lake**side', 'park **lake**'

(1) Es war dunkel geworden. Der **See** war nach dem Regen ruhig.
It had become dark. The **lake** was calm after the rain.
Milton Keynes, Großbritanniens Neue Stadt, hat künstliche **Seen** mit einer 'Küste', die länger ist als die der Insel Jersey.
Milton Keynes, Britain's New Town, has artificial **lakes** with a 'coastline' longer than the island of Jersey.
(2) Der Boden**see** ist der größte Binnen**see** in Deutschland.
Lake Constance is the biggest inland **lake** in Germany.
Die Studenten saßen an einem Land**see** und unterhielten sich mit zwei Schönheiten von der Gesundheitsfarm.
The undergraduates were sitting by a country **lake** talking to two health farm beauties.

Note: (Binnen-)**See** = loch [lɔx] (Scot.)
Riccarton near Edinburgh is an old estate around a small **loch**.

sea: (1) (die) See, (das) Meer
(2) '**See-**', '**-see**'; '**Meer(es)-**', '**-meer**' (in combinations) (**see** Golf ≠ golf)

(1) It was broad daylight. **The sea** was as smooth as glass.
Es war schon heller Tag. **Die See** war so glatt wie ein Spiegel.
(2) Even far out on the North **Sea**, when land was no longer in sight, **sea**gulls accompanied our ocean liner.
Sogar weit draußen auf der Nord**see**, als das Land nicht mehr in Sicht war, begleiteten **See**möwen unseren Ozeandampfer.
The tiny island was just above **sea** level.
Die winzige Insel lag gerade über dem **Meeres**spiegel.

Note: **sea** front = Strandpromenade
sea wall = Damm, (Meeres-)Deich

The gale force winds brought floods and breached **sea** walls at the **sea** front.

but: Baltic **Sea** = Ost**see**
Barents **Sea** = Barents**see**
Black **Sea** = Schwarzes **Meer**
Irish **Sea** = Irische **See**
Red **Sea** = Rotes **Meer**
White **Sea** = Weißes **Meer**

Compare: **sea** of colours = Farben**meer**
sea of flowers = Blumen**meer**
sea of spectators = Zuschauer**meer**

but: seal = **See**hund
sole = **See**zunge
starfish = **See**stern

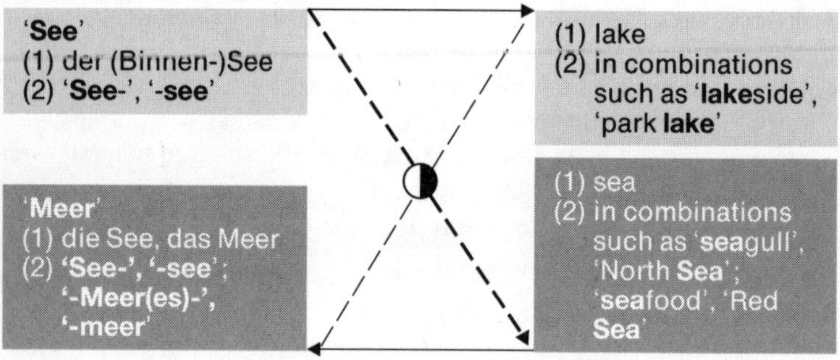

FALSE FRIENDS IN CONTEXT

Lucky to be Alive

After their tour of Britain the top ten band "Living In A Box" went for a holiday to the luxury resort of Los Ardos on the Mexican coast. One day when the ________ (1) was calm two of them hired a boat, hoping to do some fishing. However they got into difficulties...
(Their boat was hit by a wave and capsized. An hour later after struggling ashore the two told the other band members what had happened):
Band Leader: When we went out the ________ (2) was smooth. Out of nowhere a big wave grew to about 25 feet high, lifted the boat up like a nutshell, flipped us over and eventually crashed us on the shore. Look at the cuts and bruises we've got.

Youngest Band Member (still suffering from shock): I'm not going out to ________ (3) again. From now on I'm going swimming in a ________ (4) or in the hotel swimming-pool.
Another Band Member: You're lucky to be alive!

SOLUTION

(1) sea (2) sea (3) sea (4) lake

"You can't really swim in the sea, but you could develop a film in there, honey!"

SEITE ◑ side

side .... **SEITE**

page etc. ——— (Buch**seite** etc.)

SEITE: (1) (Buch-, Zeitungs**seite** etc.) page
(2) aspect
(3) party; point (fig.)

(1) Schau dir die erste **Seite** an; ich glaube, das dritte Wort ist falsch.
Look at the first **page**; I think the third word is wrong.
(2) Diese **Seite** des Problems ist noch nicht betrachtet worden.
This **aspect** of the problem hasn't been considered as yet.
(3) Ich habe von ihrem Tod nur von dritter **Seite** erfahren.
I heard of her death only from a third **party**.
"Wie jeder Mensch hat auch Frank seine starken und schwachen **Seiten**; seine starken **Seiten** überwiegen aber", beeilte sich Helen hinzuzufügen.
"Like everyone Frank has his strong and weak **points**; his strong **points** predominate however," Helen hastened to add.

Note: **Seiten**hieb = sarcastic remark; gibe (AE jibe)
Seitenspiegel = wing mirror (of a car)
Seitensprung = (have) an affair; extramarital escapade
Seitenstreifen = verge; hard shoulder (on a motorway)

side: (1) (Straßen- etc.) Seite
(2) (Berg-)Flanke
(3) Mannschaft (Sport)
(4) '**Neben-**' etc. (in combinations)

(1) "Don't cycle on the wrong **side** of the road, Fred," his mother shouted.
"Fahr' bloß nicht auf der falschen Straßen**seite**, Fred", rief seine Mutter.
The police pushed several demonstrators to one **side**.
Die Polizei stieß mehrere Demonstranten zur **Seite**.
The club president took me to one **side** before the meeting began.

Der Vereinspräsident nahm mich vor Beginn der Sitzung auf die **Seite**.
(2) "Let's climb the northern **side** of the Matterhorn; this **side** of the mountain is too dangerous for me," insisted the older climber.
"Laßt uns die Nord**flanke** des Matterhorns besteigen. Diese Berg**flanke** ist mir zu gefährlich", beharrte der ältere Bergsteiger.
(3) Queens Park Rangers fielded a strong **side**, but the game ended in a draw.
Queens Park Rangers schickte eine starke **Mannschaft** aufs Feld, aber das Spiel endete unentschieden.
(4) While the film star left the theatre through a **side** entrance, autograph hunters waited for her at the main entrance.
Während die Filmschauspielerin das Theater durch den **Neben**eingang verließ, warteten die Autogrammjäger am Haupteingang auf sie.

Note: take **sides** (with) = Partei ergreifen (für) etc.
"We are not **taking sides**, we are on the side of the game," stated the MTC (= **M**en's **T**ennis **C**ouncil) spokesman.
Compare: **side** dishes = Beilagen (zu einer Mahlzeit)
side saddle = Damensitz (zu Pferde), Damensattel
side salad = Salat (als Beilage)
but: bed**side** lamp = Nachttischlampe
bed**side** table = Nachttisch

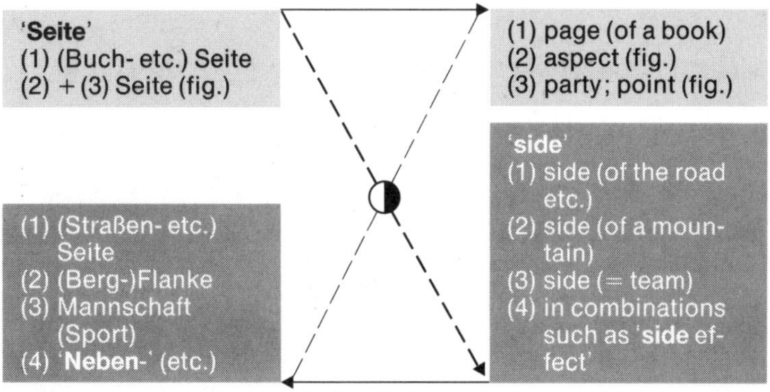
'Seite'
(1) (Buch- etc.) Seite
(2) + (3) Seite (fig.)
(1) page (of a book)
(2) aspect (fig.)
(3) party; point (fig.)
(1) (Straßen- etc.) Seite
(2) (Berg-)Flanke
(3) Mannschaft (Sport)
(4) 'Neben-' (etc.)
'side'
(1) side (of the road etc.)
(2) side (of a mountain)
(3) side (= team)
(4) in combinations such as 'side effect'

FALSE FRIENDS IN CONTEXT

Kisses Aren't Forever

Medical Correspondent: Is there really a danger in kissing? Or is there another ________ (1) to this intimate form of encounter?
Dr. Methuen (at the Medical and Diagnostic Centre in London): Kissing is an accepted way of showing affection. The other ________ (2) of the coin is that each kiss could take three minutes of your life because of the strain on your heart.
Medical Correspondent: Isn't there a difference between a private kiss between lovers and a public kiss on stage or TV?
Dr. Methuen: It will depend how often, how long and how passionate the embrace is if recorded by a cardiac monitor.
Medical Correspondent: Still. A private kiss may also be recorded in the ________ (3) of a diary. I don't think a screen kiss, an advertising kiss or a scientific kiss is recorded in the same way.
Dr. Methuen: The scientific ________ (4) reveals a passionate embrace can be very dangerous because the pulse rate soars to nearly 200 beats per minute, 130 above normal.
Medical Correspondent: But kissing will go on between lovers. The good ________ (5) is love is sealed by a kiss. The bad ________ (6) is lovers are determined to kiss again.

SOLUTION

(1) aspect (2) side (3) pages (4) aspect (5) point (6) point

SENDER ≠ sender

sender .... **SENDER**

(radio) transmitter etc. ← (= Radio-Sender etc.)

SENDER: (1) (broadcasting) station, (TV) station (auch: Sendestation)
(2) (radio, TV) transmitter (als Gerät)

(1) "Ich werde BBC Radio 2 nicht in einen Popmusik-**Sender** umwandeln", kündigte die neue Intendantin an. "Es wird einige Änderungen beim **Sender** geben, aber keine Kehrtwendungen."
"I won't be turning BBC Radio 2 into a pop **station**," announced the new controller. "There'll be some changes for the **station**, but no U-turns."
Nahezu alle britischen Radio**sender** beginnen ihre Sendungen schon um 6 Uhr morgens.
Nearly all British radio **stations** start broadcasting as early as 6 o'clock in the morning.
(2) Können wir nicht einen neuen **Sender** für den Lake District kaufen? Der alte **Sender** stammt aus den ersten Nachkriegsjahren.
Can't we buy a new (**radio**) **transmitter** for the Lake District? The old **transmitter** dates from the early post-war years.

sender: (1) Einsender
(2) Absender

(1) The first prize goes to the **sender** of the first correct solution opened.
Der erste Preis geht an den **Einsender** mit der ersten richtigen eingegangenen Lösung.
(2) "There was no **sender**'s address on your envelope, so we had to open the letter as the address was wrong," the postman informed Mr. Harding.
"Der **Absender** auf Ihrem Umschlag fehlte; daher mußten wir den Brief öffnen, da die Anschrift nicht stimmte", informierte der Postbote Herrn Harding.

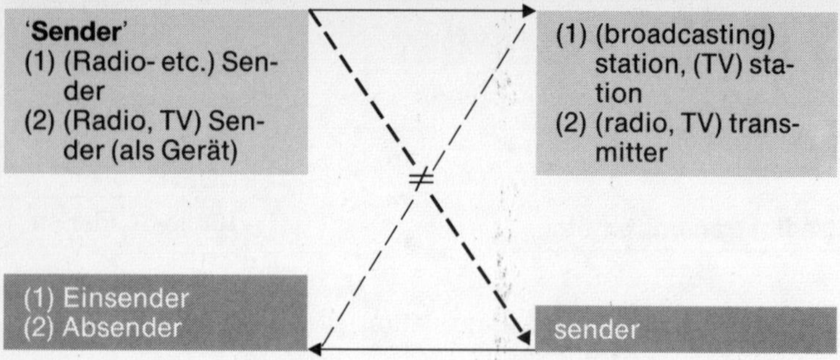

FALSE FRIENDS IN CONTEXT

Lady Chatterley at Bedtime

(Recording of a controversial phone-in on BBC Radio Four)
First Caller: I'm a regular Radio Four listener. Its 'Book at Bedtime' is unique: no other ________ (1) has a similar programme. For me a reading of D. H. Lawrence's novel 'Lady Chatterley's Lover' is just another in a long series.
Second Caller: ... What I don't understand is why this radio ________ (2) chooses to relate the sexual relationship between Lady Chatterley and her gamekeeper Mellors, but then presents a decimated text with a ban on all four-letter words etc.
Third Caller: I believe the author of 'Lady Chatterley's Lover' wanted to break down sexual and linguistic taboos. Radio Four is taking a backward step with its shortened version. They'd be better off using an old ________ (3) if they want to reach little old ladies with nothing to do at bedtime. Its method is rather like playing golf without a ball.
Fourth Caller: A 'Book at Bedtime' is listened to by a wide cross-section of people. They have a right to hear the unexpurgated version of 'Lady Chatterley's Lover'. I suggest having a radio competition for each of the 15 minute episodes of the 15 parts to find out the bits missing from Lawrence's expurgated Radio Four version. The ________ (4) of the first three correct entries should get a *de luxe* edition of 'Lady Chatterley's Lover' – unexpurgated.

SOLUTION

(1) (radio) **station** (2) radio **station** (3) transmitter (4) senders

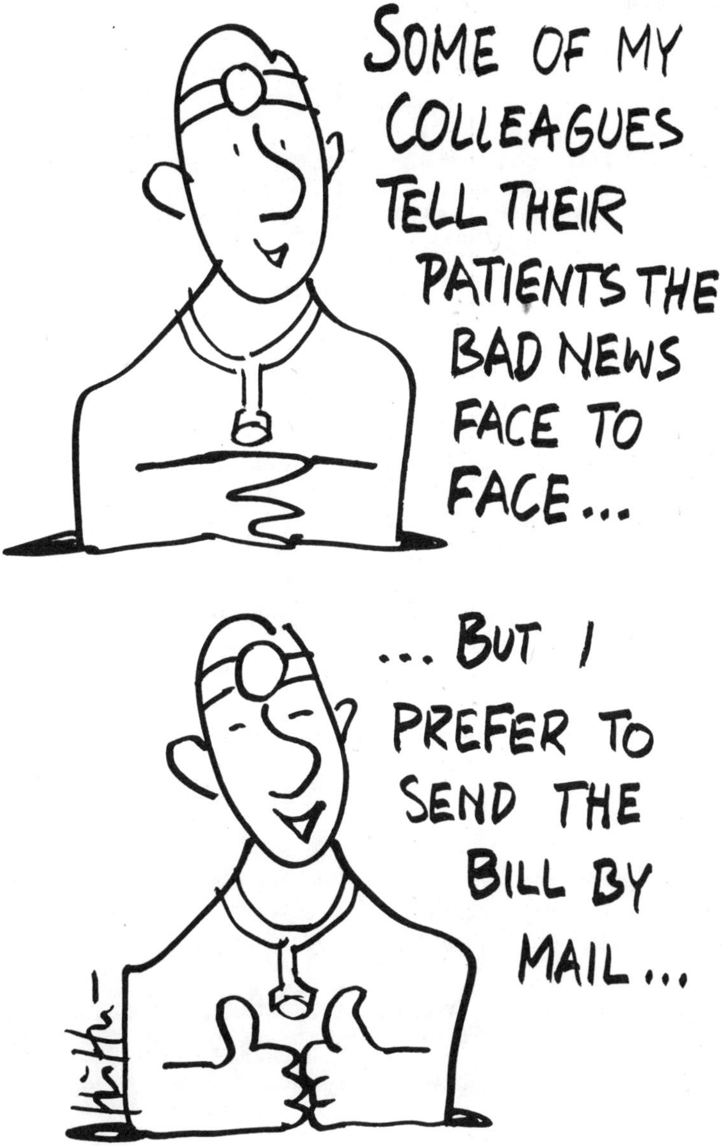

SPAREN ≠ spare

spare [speə]

SPAREN

save

SPAREN: (1) (sparen für) save (up), (sparen an) economize (on)
(2) (sich etwas ab**sparen**) stint o.s. (for)
(3) (sich etwas vom Munde ab**sparen**) scrimp and save (for)

(1) "Wir müssen zwar Geld, aber auch Energie **sparen**. Die Ölreserven sind knapp geworden", kündigte der neue Energieminister an.
"It is true we've got to **save** money, but energy as well. Our oil reserves have become much reduced," announced the new Energy Secretary.
"Liebling", versuchte seine Frau ihn zu warnen, "wenn wir den Bungalow im Lake District kaufen, werden wir jahrelang **an** vielen Dingen **sparen** müssen."
"Darling," his wife tried to warn him," if we buy the bungalow in the Lake District, we'll have to **economize on** many things for years."
(2) "Hör mal, ich kann **mir** auch nicht noch den nächsten Urlaub **absparen**", muckte seine Frau auf.
"Look here, I can't **stint myself for** our next holiday as well," his wife protested.
(3) Viele Studenten müssen sich auch heute noch die Bücher **vom Munde absparen**.
Many students still have to **scrimp and save for** their books even today.

Note: **Spar**kasse = savings bank
but: **Spar**büchse = money box
Sparschwein = piggy bank

spare: (1) (Verb) übrig haben, erübrigen
(2) (Verb) befreien (von), verschonen
(3) (Adj.) zusätzlich; übrig

(1) Surely everyone can **spare** a few pence to help the flood victims.
Jeder **hat** sicherlich ein paar Pfennige **übrig**, um den Opfern der Flutkatastrophe zu helfen.
"Mr. Jones, can you **spare** me a moment, please?" asked the gardener.
"Herr Jones, können Sie einen Augenblick Zeit für mich **erübrigen**?" fragte der Gärtner.
(2) The early retirement of the Archbishop of Canterbury may **spare** Britain a tricky problem.
Die vorzeitige Pensionierung des Erzbischofs von Canterbury kann Großbritannien **von** einem heiklen Problem **befreien**.
(3) Unfortunately my girlfriend didn't have a **spare** tyre.
Unglücklicherweise hatte meine Freundin keinen **zusätzlichen** Reifen.
"Have you got any **spare** money?" the beggar asked me.
"Haben Sie etwas Geld **übrig**?" fragte mich der Bettler.

'sparen'
(1) sparen (für), sparen (an)
(2) sich etwas ab**sparen**
(3) sich etwas vom Munde ab**sparen**

(1) save (up), economize (on)
(2) stint o.s. (for)
(3) scrimp and save (for)

≠

(1) (Verb) übrig haben, erübrigen
(2) (Verb) befreien (von), verschonen
(3) (Adj.) übrig, zusätzlich

(1) + (2) (verb) spare
(3) (adj.) spare

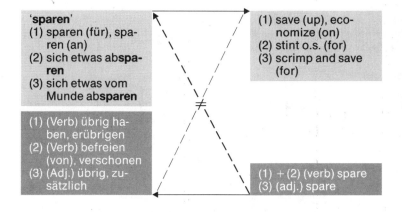

FALSE FRIENDS IN CONTEXT

An Icecream for a Turkey

Father: Sorry, children, I can't buy you an icecream this time. I bought you one an hour ago. You know I can't ________ (1) any more today; we're going on holiday soon.
Kate: Oh, why do we have to ________ (2) all the time?

Mother: We won't be able to go to Turkey if you go on like this. Be a good girl, Kate, will you?
Kate: I don't want to ________ (3) for a turkey, Daddy, I want another icecream.

SOLUTION

(1) spare (2) save (3) save (up)

STRASSE ◑ street

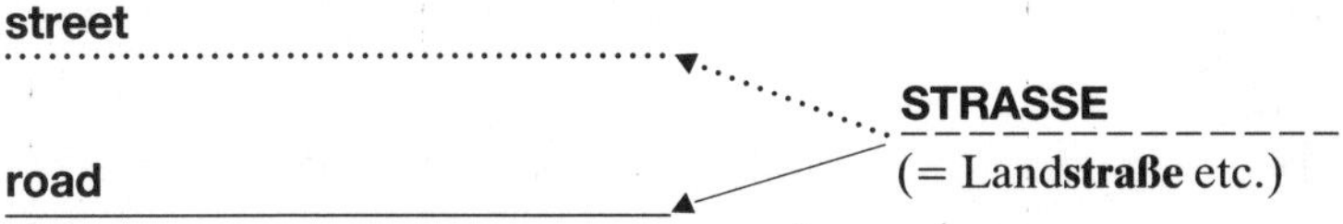

> STRASSE: (1) (Land**straße**; **Straße** in den neueren Vorstädten) road
> (2) in combinations such as '**road** atlas', 'trunk **road**'
> (3) (Meeres**straße**) strait(s)

Note: In most cases '**road**' is used nowadays (except in **street** names), although the accepted meaning of '**street**' is **road** in a town with houses or buildings along it and usually a pavement on each side.

Compare: At the moment they are repairing the **road** in the High **Street**.

but: Even in the heart of London '**road**' is used in many **street** names such as Edgeware **Road**, Marylebone **Road**, Borough **Road**, Vauxhall Bridge **Road** etc. It is interesting to note that King's **Road** and Buckingham Palace **Road** lead to Buckingham Palace.

(1) Alle **Straßen** nach York sind heute vormittag durch Eis und Schnee blockiert. Daher bleiben wir heute am besten zu Hause.
All **roads** to York are blocked by ice and snow this morning. So we'd better stay at home today.
(2) "Haben Sie auch einen **Straßen**atlas von England?" – "Leider nein. Aber vielleicht bekommen Sie einen an der Tankstelle dort drüben."
"Have you also got a **road** atlas of England?" – "I'm afraid we haven't got one. But you'll get one at the garage over there."
"Benutzen Sie am Freitagnachmittag nie Fern**straßen**", riet er mir.
"Never use trunk **roads** on a Friday afternoon," he advised me.

Note: Land**straße** = country **road**
Straßenschwelle (in Fußgängerzonen etc.) = **road** hump (in pedestrian precincts etc.)

Zubringer**straße** = feeder **road**
Zufahrts**straße** = slip**road**
but: Umgehungs**straße** = bypass

(3) Die Fahrt durch die **Straße** von Dover war heute morgen sehr stürmisch.
The passage through the **Straits** of Dover was very stormy this morning.

Note: die **Straße** von Florida = the **Straits** of Florida
die **Straße** von Hormus = the **Strait** of Hormuz
die **Straße** von Sizilien = the **Strait**(s) of Sicily
Surprisingly, the Sicilian **straits** are not deeper than 1,500 feet.

street: (1) (**Straße** im Zentrum von Städten oder älteren Vorstädten) street
(2) '**Straßen-**', '**-straße**' (in combinations)

(1) Jessica had never been in a town with so many narrow **streets**.
Jessica war noch nie in einer Stadt mit so vielen engen Straßen.
(2) A stranger stood under the **street** lamp looking at the houses.
Ein Fremder stand unter der **Straßen**laterne und schaute die Häuser an.
Then he slowly walked up the High **Street** to the town hall.
Dann ging er langsam die Haupt**straße** zum Rathaus hinauf.

Note: High **Street** (mainly BE) = Haupt**straße**
Main **Street** (mainly AE)
village High **Street** = Haupt**straße** eines Dorfes
village **street** = Dorf**straße**
street party = **Straßen**fest
but: high-**street** stores = in der Haupt**straße** gelegene Kaufhäuser
Compare the **main stress** in each of the following (London) **street** names (followed by its postal district number):
'Earl **Street** EC2 Earl '**Road** SE1
'Hall **Street** EC1 Hall '**Road** NW8
'Chester **Street** SW1 Chester '**Road** NW1
'Monmouth **Street** WC2 Monmouth '**Road** W2
'Abingdon **Street** SW1 Abingdon '**Road** W8
'Albany **Street** NW1 Albany '**Road** SE5

When the word '**street**' forms part of the name, the main stress is always on the first syllable of the first word.
However, when '**road**' is used, the main stress always falls on '**road**'.

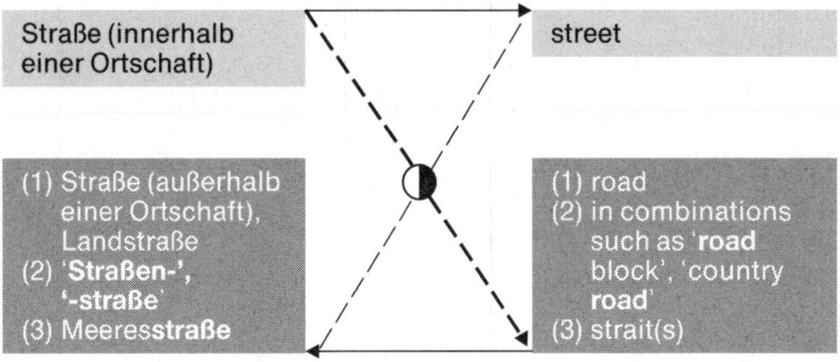

FALSE FRIENDS IN CONTEXT

There's Madness in Fast Driving

A lonely figure had been waiting nearly all day on the coast ________ (1) when an MG pulled up and offered him a lift.
It was still a long way to Swansea and it would be getting dark in half an hour. The driver put his foot down as they drove along a narrow ________ (2) near the cliffs. Soon the MG was going at 100 miles an hour. The hitch-hiker leaned over to the driver, "You're a good driver, but could you slow down when you take the corners?"
The driver smiled as he accelerated again and remarked, "If you're frightened by the way I'm driving, shut your eyes while we're going along the cliffs. Don't worry, I'm doing the same!"

SOLUTION

(1) coast **road** (2) road

Yellow for Pedestrians

A woman was taking her driving test.
Examiner: And what are the double yellow lines in the middle of the ________ (3) for?
Woman: Pedestrians!

SOLUTION

(3) street

"Believe me, I was just looking for the sliproad to the M 4 when I slipped..."

STROM ◑ stream

stream

STROM

(= großer Fluß etc.)

river etc.

STROM: (1) (großer Fluß, **Strom**) (a great or large) river
(2) (elektrischer **Strom**) (electric) current
(3) (Meeres-, Luft**strom**) (ocean, air) current

(1) Der Mississippi ist mit 3779 km einer der längsten **Ströme** der Welt.
The Mississippi, with its 3,779 km, is one of the longest **rivers** in the world.
(2) In den meisten Ländern arbeitet der elektrische **Strom** mit 220 Volt.
In most countries the electric **current** is 220 volts.
(3) Der kalte Humboldt**strom** ist auch als Peru**strom** bekannt.
The cold Humboldt **Current** is also known as the Peru **Current**.
Ein feuchter, warmer Luft**strom** strich durch die Stadt.
A humid air **current** moved lightly through the town.

Note: **Strom**rechnung = electricity bill
Stromversorgung = electricity supply
Stromzähler = electric meter
but: **Strom**sperre = power cut

stream: (1) kleiner Fluß, Bach
(2) Flut (fig.)
(3) Strom (fig.)

(1) 'Little **streams** make great rivers,' is an English proverb.
'Kleine **Bäche** bilden große Ströme', lautet ein englisches Sprichwort.
If you follow the little **stream** for half a mile, it flows into the village pond.
Wenn du dem kleinen **Bach** eine halbe Meile folgst, fließt er in den Dorfteich.

Note: '**burn**' is the Scottish term for '**Bach**'.
These **burns**, the Laret and the Sproutson, have always been famous for their salmon.

(2) The comic's blue jokes have already brought a **stream** of complaints from TV viewers.
Die schlüpfrigen Witze des Komikers haben bereits eine **Flut** von Beschwerden von den Fernsehzuschauern ausgelöst.
(3) A seemingly endless **stream** of people filed past the statesman's coffin as a farewell gesture.
Ein nicht endenwollender **Strom** von Menschen defilierte am Sarg des Staatsmanns als Abschiedsgeste vorüber.

Note: blood**stream** (med.) = Blut**strom**
Compare: **stream(s)** of blood = **Ströme** von Blut
The revolution of the Kurds was drowned in **streams** of blood.
stream of consciousness = Bewußtseins**strom**
stream of lava = Lava**strom**
Gulf **Stream** = Golf**strom**
Orbiting space satellites have been used to map the path of the Gulf **Stream**.
but: the flow of time = der **Strom** der Zeit

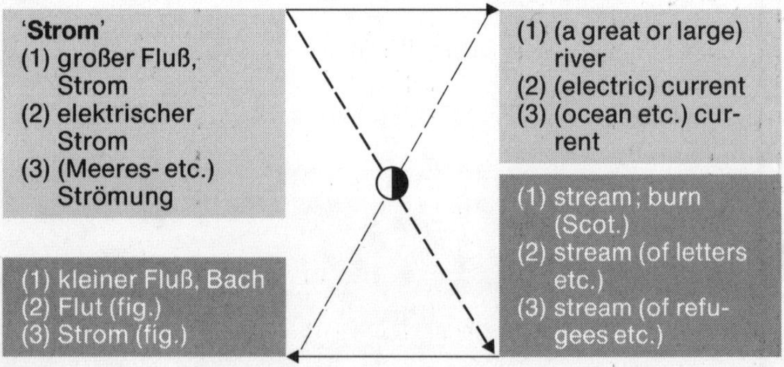

FALSE FRIENDS IN CONTEXT

It's the Title that Counts

It was a very hot summer when Queen Elizabeth and Prince Philip were on the royal visit to Australia. On one occasion Prince Philip asked his hosts whether the long ________ (1) of people could be presented to them outside on the terrace. It was a little cooler there, and the ________ (2) offered a whiff of fresh air.

Among the people presented to them was a young couple announced as 'Mr. and Dr. Finchley'. The Duke looked at them with a questioning frown. Mr. Finchley hastened to explain that his wife was a doctor of medicine and added, "She's much more important than I am."

Prince Philip replied with a knowing smile, "I think we have that trouble in my family, too."

SOLUTION

(1) stream (2) river

Taking the Plunge

Recently I was walking down a village High Street that had a ________ (3) running alongside. Suddenly a mother duck jumped into the ________ (4) looking back at her eleven young to join her. One by one they took the plunge – and swam immediately to her.

SOLUTION

(3) stream (4) stream

Tablett ≠ tablet

tablet [ˈtæblɪt]

TABLETT
(Servierbrett)

tray [treɪ]

TABLETT: (1) (Servierbrett) tray
(2) (Silber**tablett**, Silberschale) (silver) salver

(1) Mutter brachte mir Frühstück auf einem **Tablett** ans Bett. Da ich krank war, wollte sie mich aufmuntern.
Mother brought me breakfast in bed on a **tray**. As I was ill, she wanted to cheer me up.
(2) Lord Soames' Diener brachte das Telegramm auf einem **Silbertablett** in das Frühstückszimmer und verließ es dann sofort.
Lord Soames' butler brought the telegram into the breakfast room on a **silver salver** and then left at once.

Note: Ablagekasten (eines Fotokopiergeräts) = **tray** (of a photocopier)
Place the original neatly on the **tray** and slide the original forward until it stops.

tablet: (1) Tablette
(2) '**Tabletten-**', '**-tablette**' (in combinations)
(3) (Ton-, Marmor- etc.) Tafel; (Gedenk-)Platte

(1) "You can't get these **tablets** without a prescription. So it's no good going to the chemist's," said my mother two days later.
"Du kannst diese **Tabletten** nicht ohne Rezept bekommen. Es hat also keinen Zweck, zur Apotheke zu gehen", sagte meine Mutter zwei Tage später.
(2) On our voyage we had also a bottle of vitamin **tablets**, which became vital later.
Auf unserer Seereise hatten wir auch eine Flasche Vitamin**tabletten** dabei, die später lebenswichtig wurden.
(3) It took the archaeologists a long time to decipher the inscriptions on the clay **tablets** they had discovered in the cave.

Die Archäologen brauchten lange Zeit, um die Inschriften auf den Ton**tafeln** zu entziffern, die sie in der Höhle gefunden hatten.
Chris looked at the memorial **tablet** outside the church, but couldn't read the name on it.
Chris schaute sich außerhalb der Kirche die Gedenk**platte** an, aber er konnte den Namen darauf nicht lesen.

Note: sleeping **pills** (also sleeping **tablets**) = Schlaf**tabletten**

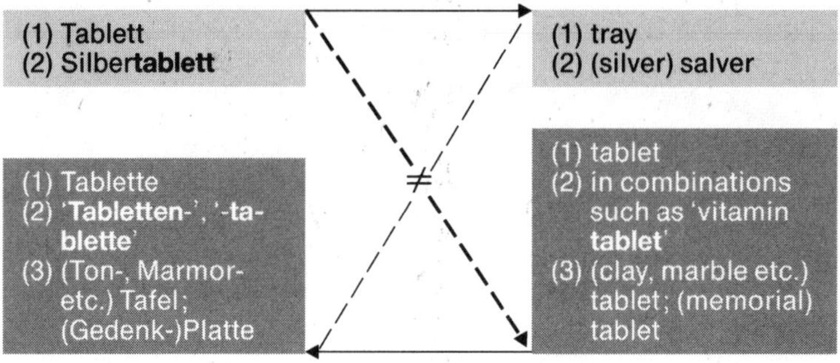

FALSE FRIENDS IN CONTEXT

Good-Bye to All That

Lord Lobster (at his breakfast table): Times were different before the war. Then butlers ironed the creases out of 'The Times' before bringing it into the breakfast room on a silver ________ (1).
Lady Lobster: Yes, I know, things have gone from bad to worse. Nowadays you're lucky to get a butler at all. How did you sleep last night?
Lord Lobster: I had to take two painkilling ________ (2) before I finally fell asleep at five.
Lady Lobster: You don't look well. You must have some form of food poisoning. I'll call the doctor to see you. You must take some more ________ (3) and get some fresh air. I'll fetch the ________ (4) and tell the maid to clear the breakfast table.

SOLUTION

(1) salver (2) tablets (3) tablets (4) tray

WENN ◑ when

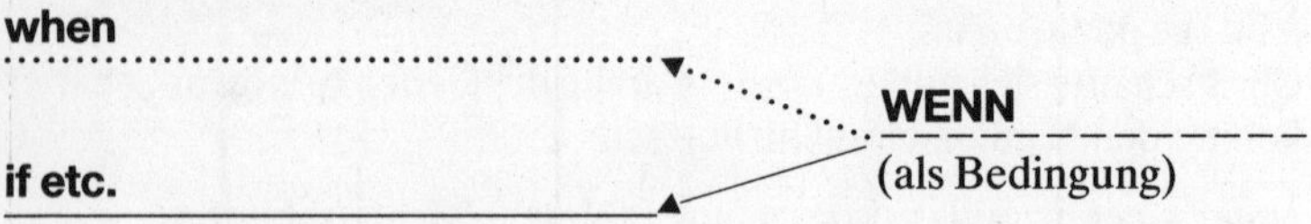

> WENN: (1) (als Bedingung) if
> (2) (zeitliche Bedingung) when
> (3) (verneinte Bedingung: **wenn** nicht) unless

(1) **Wenn** du darauf bestehst, öffne ich eine Flasche Wein.
If you insist, I'll open a bottle of wine.
(2) **Wenn** der Winter kommt, fahren wir nach Kalifornien.
When the winter comes, we're going to California.
(3) Ich komme im Frühjahr nachgereist, **wenn nichts** Außergewöhnliches dazwischenkommt. Ich komme aber nicht, **wenn** ihr **nicht** vorher anruft.
I'll follow you in the spring, **unless** something extraordinary should happen. But I won't go **unless** you give me a ring first.

Note: ob = if (or: whether)
The Prime Minister paused to ask his Press Secretary **if** he had heard the reporter's question.

> when: (1) wann (in Fragen)
> (2) als (mit Zeitbezug oder mit Angabe des Zeitpunkts)

(1) **When** are you coming tomorrow? – About six.
Wann kommst du morgen? – Etwa um 6 Uhr.
Since **when** have you been waiting? he asked abruptly.
Seit **wann** wartest du schon? fragte er schroff.
(2) **When** the police arrived, the bank robbers had disappeared with the loot – £ 650,000.
Als die Polizei ankam, waren die Bankräuber bereits mit der Beute verschwunden – 650.000 Pfund.

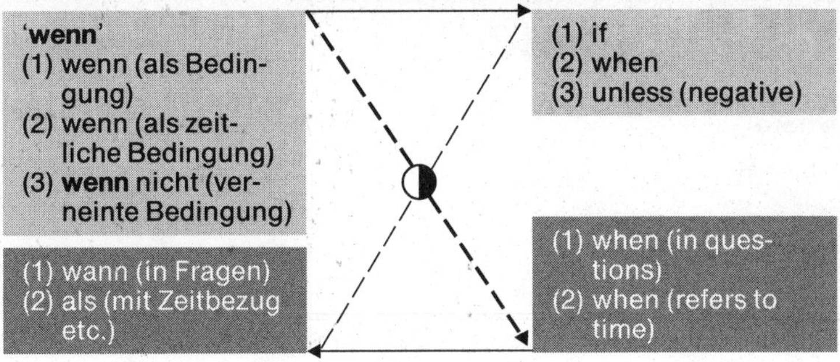

FALSE FRIENDS IN CONTEXT

Torn Two Ways by Love

Jenny's nagging mother tries to warn her daughter:

– " ________ (1) your skirt is too short, men will be eyeing you up."

– " ________ (2) you had a man's children and he then left you for another woman, how do you think you would feel?"

– " ________ (3) you get married, you'll have a wedding in Lincoln Cathedral."

– " ________ (4) you have a child, you'll have to look after it."

– "You'll be in trouble, ________ (5 = wenn nicht) you see your fiancé tomorrow."

But Jenny's reaction is not what her mother expects and comes in the form of ten flippant two-letter words:

" ________ (6) it is to be, it is up to me!"

SOLUTION

(1) if (2) if (3) when (4) when (5) unless (6) if

WER ≠ where

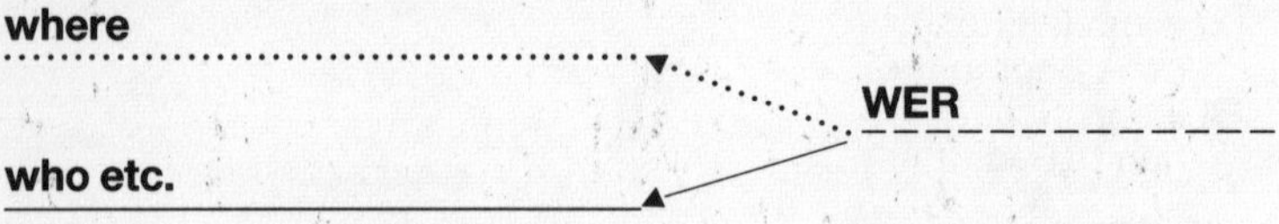

WER: (1) who, whoever
(2) which of (in 'restricted choice' questions)

(1) **Wer** hat den ganzen Papierkram auf meinen Schreibtisch gelegt? Schau dir die Unordnung an. **Wer** hat das gemacht?
Who put all these papers on my desk? Look at the mess. **Who** did it?
Wer kann uns nur morgens um drei Uhr angerufen haben?
Whoever can have rung us up at three o'clock in the morning?
(2) **Wer** von euch möchte morgen zu dem Konzert gehen?
Which of you wants to go to the concert tomorrow?
Die endgültige Auswahl, **wer** von ihnen einen Platz im Raumfahrt-Projekt Juno erhält, wird nicht vor April getroffen.
The final choice of **which of** them will win a place on the space project Juno will not be made before April.

where: (1) wo
(2) woher, wohin etc.

(1) **Where** is my purse? It was in my handbag a minute ago.
Wo ist meine Geldbörse geblieben? Sie war noch vor einer Minute in meiner Handtasche.
(2) **Where** do you want to go? – I'm going **where** I have been wanting to go all evening, to the bathroom.
Wohin willst du gehen? – Ich gehe jetzt hin, **wohin** ich schon den ganzen Abend gehen wollte, zum Badezimmer.
Where are you **from**?
Woher sind Sie?
Where do you come **from**?
Woher kommen Sie?

Note: There were moments **when** I would have liked to cry.
Es gab Augenblicke, **wo** ich am liebsten geweint hätte.

How do you know we're going on holiday tomorrow? =
Woher weißt du, daß wir morgen in Urlaub fahren?

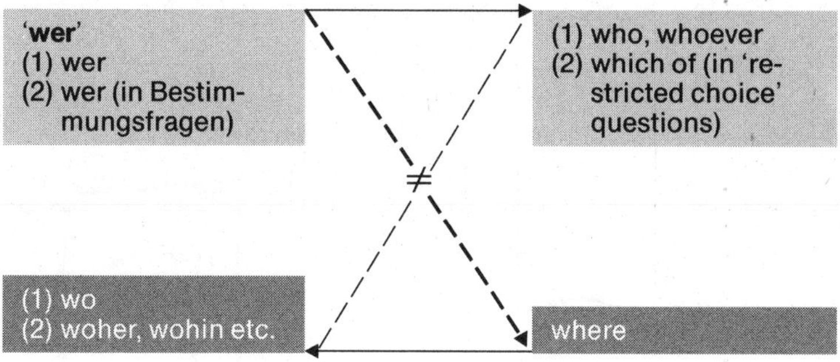

FALSE FRIENDS IN CONTEXT

Britain's Model Town

Kevin: Do you know the town ________ (1) dreams come true?
Lynn: Venice or Florence perhaps but ________ (2) knows.
Kevin: No, darling, it's Milton Keynes in Buckinghamshire.
Lynn: Really? I wonder ________ (3) would have guessed that. But tell me why!
Kevin: First of all, it's a perfectly new town ________ (4) you can walk to work. I like to look out of the window at work and to breathe clean air. You simply live longer that way.
Lynn: What about shopping and, more importantly, jobs?
Kevin: There's a huge shopping complex in the town centre ________ (5) you can walk into 140 stores including your favourites Marks and Spencer and John Lewis all under one roof. Milton Keynes is a dream come true for job-hunters. It's worth moving there after the summer.
Lynn: Are you joking?
Kevin: No Lynn.
Lynn: But you'll miss watching Tottenham Hotspurs at White Hart Lane and I'll miss my friends here.
Kevin: Soccer is not everything in life. We'll meet new friends.
Lynn: You're right. It's the chance for a new life.

Kevin: Milton Keynes is Britain's most prosperous town. It's a model town ________ (6) dreams come true.
Lynn: I've started dreaming already!

SOLUTION

(1) where (2) who (3) who (4) where (5) where (6) where

You want to know where the Nazis came from? – From outer space, if you believe the history books…"

WO ≠ who

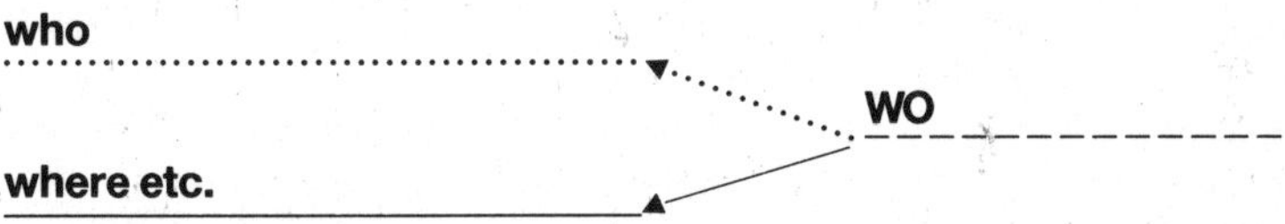

WO: (1) where
(2) which … in, which … from; **or**: in which, from which etc.
(3) when (refers to time)

(1) "**Wo** bist du jetzt?" fragte Carols Mann sie am Telefon. "Ich habe dich überall gesucht."
"**Where** are you now?" Carol's husband asked her on the phone. "I've been looking for you everywhere."
Das ist der Laden, **wo** ich das Lexikon kaufte.
That's the shop **where** I bought the dictionary.
(2) Hier ist das Buch, **wo** ich das Coleridge-Zitat fand.
Here is the book **in which** I found the Coleridge quotation.
Die entsetzten Angler sprangen um ihr Leben, als ein Auto auf den Deich stürzte, von **wo** aus sie gefischt hatten.
Horrified anglers leapt for their lives as a car crashed into the sea wall **from which** they had been fishing.
(3) Der Schuß auf den Präsidenten fiel zu einem Zeitpunkt, **wo** alle Menschen zu den Fallschirmspringern am Himmel hochschauten.
The shot was fired at the president at a moment **when** everybody was looking up at the parachutists in the sky.

Note: **Woher** weißt du das? = How do you know that?

who: (1) wer (als Fragewort)
(2) wem, wen (in Fragen)
(3) der, die etc. (in Relativsätzen)

(1) "**Who**'s got a new ball," shouted the tennis player.
"**Wer** hat einen neuen Ball", schrie der Tennisspieler.
(2) **Who** are you talking about? **Who** do you want to give this present to?
Über **wen** sprechen Sie gerade? **Wem** möchten Sie das Geschenk geben?

(3) It's always better in life to seek out somebody **who** can help you.
Es ist immer besser im Leben, sich jemanden auszusuchen, **der** einem helfen kann.
The play 'Chains of Love' is about a group of women **who** throw a party to explore their emotions.
Das Stück 'Ketten der Liebe' handelt von einer Gruppe von Frauen, **die** eine Party gibt, um mehr über ihre Gefühle zu erfahren.

Note: which = wer (in 'restricted choice' questions)
Which of you is the elder?

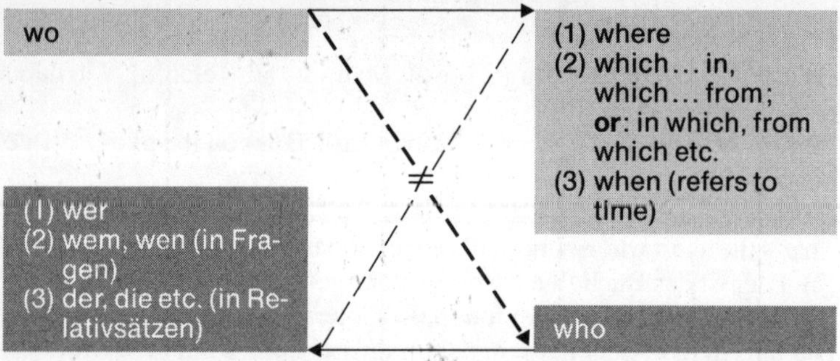

FALSE FRIENDS IN CONTEXT

Top Brains: Problem Gifts

Mother: Did you read about 12-year-old Ian Oates ________ (1) has been named as one of Britain's top brains?
Father: No, I didn't.
Mother: I was talking to our neighbour this afternoon. Linda scored 179 in the intelligence test ________ (2) she was only nine.
Father: And ________ (3) is Linda?
Mother: She's our neighbour's daughter. You know her, don't you?
Father: Of course I do. But isn't it wrong to treat such gifted children as geniuses?
Mother: They are ordinary children ________ (4) behave exactly as other children except that they possess a particular talent.
Father: In fact, the label 'genius' suggests that they'll succeed ________ (5) others fail.

Mother: They are, in effect, more likely to suffer problems than less gifted children.

SOLUTION

(1) who (2) when (3) who (4) who (5) where

"Who did it?"

FALSE FRIENDS TRAPS TEST 4

EASY FALSE FRIENDS

1.a. A steep rise in ________ accidents has brought a new ________ safety offensive from the police (**Straße ◑ street**).
1.b. "A man called me a whore in the ________ the other day," the young woman complained (**Straße ◑ street**).
2.a. You'll wonder why on earth Tom waited so long to sail the ________ (**Seen ◑ seas**).
2.b. Time and again his sister had invited them all to visit her in Canada where she has a house beside a ________ (**See ◑ sea**).
3.a. "I don't think I can ________ on so many things over the next twenty years," she warned her husband (**sparen ≠ spare**).
3.b. Everybody can ________ a pound to help the poor people in Romania (**sparen ≠ spare**).
4.a. Birmingham will get a new private ________ next year (**Sender ≠ sender**).
4.b. There is a first prize of £ 50 and two runners-up prizes of £ 10 for the ________ of the first three correct solutions (**Sender ≠ sender**).
5.a. The Amazon is still one of the most dangerous ________ in the world (**Ströme ◑ streams**).
5.b. There were salmon in the little ________, but he was not allowed to catch them (**Strom ◑ stream**).
6. ________ (**wenn**) you can't come, give me a ring tomorrow.
7. ________ (**wer**) of you cannot come to the dance on Saturday?
8. Her butler brought the letter in on a silver ________ (**Tablett**).
9. "You've got the wrong ________ (**Seite**) in the wrong paper," his wife said looking at him.
10. The mountain guide felt lost in the snowstorm and he didn't know ________ (**wo**) he was.

ANSWER SHEET: TRUE FRIENDS TEST 4

EASY FALSE FRIENDS

1.a. A steep rise in **road** accidents has brought a new **road** safety offensive from the police.
1.b. "A man called me a whore in the **street** the other day," the young woman complained.
2.a. You'll wonder why on earth Tom waited so long to sail the **seas**.
2.b. Time and again his sister had invited them all to visit her in Canada where she has a house beside a **lake**.
3.a. "I don't think I can **economize on** so many things over the next twenty years," she warned her husband.
3.b. Everybody can **spare** a pound to help the poor people in Romania.
4.a. Birmingham will get a new private **station** next year.
4.b. There is a first prize of £ 50 and two runners-up prizes of £ 10 for the **senders** of the first three correct solutions.
5.a. The Amazon is still one of the most dangerous **rivers** in the world.
5.b. There were salmon in the little **stream**, but he was not allowed to catch them.
6. **If** you can't come, give me a ring tomorrow.
7. **Which of** you cannot come to the dance on Saturday?
8. Her butler brought the letter in on a silver **salver**.
9. "You've got the wrong **page** in the wrong paper," his wife said looking at him.
10. The mountain guide felt lost in the snowstorm and he didn't know **where** he was.

TEIL II

NOT SO EASY FALSE FRIENDS

ACHSE ◑ axis

axis [ˈæksɪs]

ACHSE

axle [ˈæksl]

(Rad**achse** etc.)

ACHSE: (1) (Rad**achse** etc.) axle (tech.); (**see** Achsel ≠ axle)
(2) in combinations such as '**axle** load', 'rear **axle**'

(1) An diesem Lastwagen stimmt etwas mit der **Achse** nicht.
There's something wrong with the **axle** of that lorry.
(2) Im neuen Jaguar XJS Cabriolet sitzt der Fahrer nur knapp vor der Hinter**achse**.
In the new Jaguar XJS Convertible the driver sits just in front of the rear **axle**.

axis: (1) (geogr., math., polit. etc.) Achse
(2) '**Achs(en)-**', '**-achse**' (in combinations)

Note: The plural of '**axis**' is '**axes**' [ˈæksi:z]

(1) Strictly speaking, the **axis** of the earth does not form a straight line.
Genau genommen bildet die **Achse** der Erde keine gerade Linie.
(2) In World War II the **Axis** Powers Germany, Italy and Japan opposed the Allied Powers.
Im Zweiten Weltkrieg standen die **Achsen**mächte Deutschland, Italien und Japan den Alliierten Mächten gegenüber.
In the Van Gogh painting the yellow flowers are arranged about a diagonal **axis**.
In dem Van Gogh-Gemälde sind die gelben Blumen um eine Diagonal**achse** angeordnet.

Note: **axis** of rotation = Rotations**achse**
axis of symmetry = Symmetrie**achse**
but: He's always on the move = er ist immer auf **Achse**
turn right round = sich um die eigene **Achse** drehen

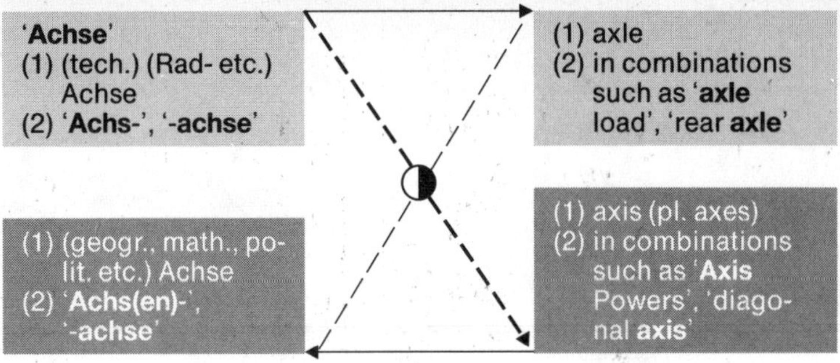

FALSE FRIENDS IN CONTEXT

Now You're Talking our Language

British Politician: Mrs. Thatcher's vision of Europe differs from that of the leaders of other EEC countries. But since the Madrid summit the Iron Lady has isolated Britain from the Paris–Bonn–Brussels ________ (1).
German Politician: I fully agree there. Politically, the ________ (2) countries are 'pro-European', while Britain is 'anti-European' – at least that is the general feeling.
British Politician: It is, however, not what most British people want. In effect, the ________ (3) is good at making the British feel guilty. The British are for a Single Market but oppose a European central bank and a joint currency.
German Politician: Within a future EEC this is a price worth paying for national independence.
British Politician: What a future EEC needs most of all is a single, common European language. Let's take an example. If new cars with a faulty ________ (4) have to be recalled, there'll be confusion and delay, because the recall has to be translated into every EEC language. But faulty ________ (5) do not wait, they break if not changed in time.
German Politician: I can see what you mean.
British Politician: The language of the ________ (6) countries should be English.

SOLUTION

(1) axis (2) axis (3) axis (4) axle (5) axles (6) axis

"A secret meeting of the axis powers, I guess…"

ACHSEL ≠ axle

axle

ACHSEL
(beim Menschen)

under the arm etc.

ACHSEL: (1) (Achsel beim Menschen) under the arm
(2) (**Achsel**höhle) armpit
(3) in combinations such as '**shoulder**-straps'

(1) Die Ballett-Tänzerin puderte sich vor ihrem Auftritt unter den rasierten **Achseln**.
The ballet dancer powdered **under her** shaved **arm** before going on stage.
Weißt du, meine neue Bluse sitzt unter den **Achseln** nicht richtig; sie stammt aus dem Sommerschlußverkauf.
You see, my new blouse doesn't fit well **under the arm**; it's from the summer sales.
(2) "Das einzige, was ich nicht an den U-Bahn-Fahrten während der Hauptverkehrszeiten ausstehen kann", sagte John in scherzhaftem Ton, "ist der **Achsel**geruch, der einen beim Einsteigen fast umhaut."
"The one thing I don't like about travelling on the tube during the rush hour," said John in a jocular tone, "is the smell of the sweaty **armpits** that nearly knocks you out when you get on."
Plötzlich gab das Eis nach, und er stürzte bis zu den **Achseln** in den kalten See.
Suddenly the ice gave way and he plunged into the cold lake up to his **armpits**.
(3) "Darf ich", sagte der Pfarrer und streifte ihr die **Achsel**träger herunter.
"May I," said the vicar and slipped off her **shoulder**-straps.

Note: mit den **Achseln** zucken = shrug (one's shoulders)
mit einem **Achsel**zucken = (with a) shrug (of the shoulders)
Achselklappen (mil.) = **shoulder**-straps

axle: (1) (tech.) Achse
(2) '**Achs-**', '**-achse**' (in combinations) (**see** Achse ≠ axis)

(1) "Never weld a broken **axle**," the mechanic warned me. "Your car has to have a new one."
"Schweiße nie eine gebrochene **Achse**", warnte mich der Monteur. "Ihr Auto muß eine neue haben."
(2) "Did you do the **axle** test? If not, the **axle** suspension of your car doesn't work. You should do something about it," my friend told me.
"Hast du den **Achs**test gemacht? Wenn nicht, die **Achs**federung deines Autos funktioniert nicht mehr. Da mußt du etwas unternehmen", sagte mir mein Freund.

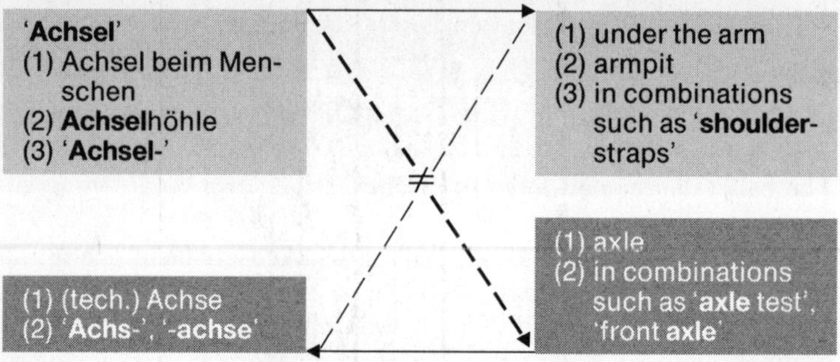
'**Achsel**'
(1) Achsel beim Menschen
(2) **Achsel**höhle
(3) '**Achsel-**'
(1) under the arm
(2) armpit
(3) in combinations such as '**shoulder-**straps'
≠
(1) (tech.) Achse
(2) '**Achs-**', '**-achse**'
(1) axle
(2) in combinations such as '**axle** test', 'front **axle**'

FALSE FRIENDS IN CONTEXT

Snake Fanciers

First Customs Officer (to colleague): The Sealink ferry has been delayed for more than three hours because a king snake was loose on board.
Second Customs Officer: Quite a few people went to the world-famous Snake Day at Utrecht in Holland.
First Customs Officer: Passengers will be trying everything to get snakes into the country.

* * *

First Customs Officer: And what's in the bag hidden in your ______ (1)?
First Passenger: Two small pets.
First Customs Officer, looking briefly in the bag after removing it from the passenger's _______ (2)-strap: They're not pets. It's a milk snake

and a corn snake. I'm afraid they have to be held at the animal quarantine centre at Heathrow for a time.

* * *

Second Customs Officer (after checking another passenger): What's under your ________ (3)?
Second Passenger: Oh, it's my personal guardian.
Second Customs Officer: May I have a look? What you've taped to your body is a deadly Ottoman viper. It has to go to the quarantine centre in any case.

* * *

Third Customs Officer: You gave 'snake charmer' as your profession. Have you anything to declare?...

SOLUTION

(1) in your **armpit** (2) **shoulder**-strap (3) under your arm

AKT ◑ act

act

AKT

nude

(in der Malerei etc.)

AKT : (1) (painting from the) nude etc.
(2) in combinations such as '**nude** model'

(1) Einen **Akt** zu zeichnen verlangt die ganze Aufmerksamkeit des Künstlers.
Drawing a **nude** demands the artist's full attention.
Francesca Annis war die erste Schauspielerin, die die Irrenszene als Lady Macbeth ganz als **Akt** spielte.
Francesca Annis was the first actress to play the mad scene as Lady Macbeth completely in the **nude**.
(2) Eines der gelungensten von Anders Zorns **Akt**-Gemälden 'Les Baigneuses' wurde bei Christie für 1,76 Millionen Pfund verkauft.
One of the most successful of Anders Zorn's **nude** paintings 'Les Baigneuses', sold for £ 1.76 at Christie's.
Ihr Mann ist wütend wegen der **Akt**fotos von seiner Frau im 'Playboy', als sie 17 war.
Her husband is furious because of **nude** photographs of his wife in 'Playboy' when she was 17.

act: (1) Akt, Tat, Handlung **see** Akt(e) ≠ act(s)
(2) Akt (im Drama)
(3) Gesetz
(4) Nummer (im Zirkus etc.)

(1) It was an **act** of humanity to help the Vietnamese refugees.
Es war ein **Akt** der Menschlichkeit, den vietnamesischen Flüchtlingen zu helfen.
The childmurder was an irresponsible **act**.
Der Kindesmord war eine unverantwortliche **Tat**.
Turning off the alarm system was a wrongful **act**.
Die Abschaltung des Alarmsystems war eine widerrechtliche **Handlung**.
(2) It seemed a very long second **act**. But the next hour went in a flash.

Es schien ein sehr langer zweiter **Akt**. Aber die nächste Stunde verging wie im Nu.
(3) The 1986 Animal **Act** controls experimental tests on animals.
Das Tier**gesetz** von 1986 regelt experimentelle Tests mit Tieren.
(4) By coincidence, he was organizing circus **acts** in France last week.
Per Zufall organisierte er in der letzten Woche Zirkus**nummern** in Frankreich.

Note: an **act** of defiance = eine Trotz**handlung**
In a childish **act** of defiance my son didn't brush his teeth.
get one's **act** together (coll.) = die Dinge in Ordnung bringen; systematisch planen/arbeiten
At last everybody has decided to get their **act** together and things are beginning to happen.

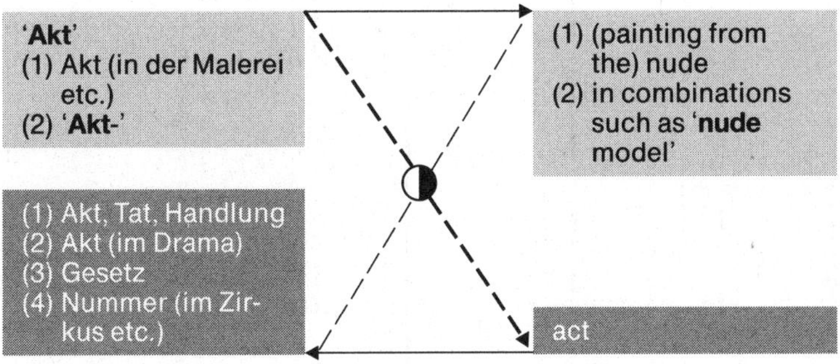

FALSE FRIENDS IN CONTEXT

Rubbing it in

Part One
Chief Hospital Executive: Tell me all the details you have and who's responsible.
Matron: About twenty patients were unable to get any help because Auxiliary Nurse Hobson turned off their alarm buzzers during night shifts.
Chief Hospital Executive: So their lifeline was cut. This is an irresponsible ________ (1) and I will report it to the hospital management at once.

Part Two (a month later)
Member of Industrial Tribunal (addressing Auxiliary Nurse Hobson): ... What have you got to say?
Auxiliary Nurse Hobson: Switching off the emergency alarm system was an ________ (2) of generosity, not inhumanity. The patients wanted to sleep and not be disturbed by the buzzers.
Member of Industrial Tribunal: You were sacked for several ________ (3) of misconduct: first of all for ill-treating patients by saying, 'Don't ring again!' and destroying the picture of a ________ (4) model calling it trash. Second for negligence of duties to stroke patients. Third for switching off the alarm buzzers.

* * *

Part Three (after the hearing)
Head of Industrial Tribunal (summing up): ... All these ________ (5) were totally inhumane. By sabotaging NHS (= **N**ational **H**ealth **S**ervice) equipment and turning off the nurse call alarm system, you violated the Health and Safety at Work ________ (6).

SOLUTION

(1) act (2) **act** of generosity (3) **acts** of misconduct (4) **nude** model
(5) acts (6) Health and Safety at Work **Act**

AKTE(N) ≠ act(s)

act(s)

AKTE(N)

file(s) etc.

> AKTE(N): (1) file(s), record(s)
> (2) in combinations such as '**filing** cabinet', 'client **files**'

(1) Die jetzige **Akte** im Mordfall Robson ist unvollständig.
The present **file** on the Robson murder case is incomplete.
Die Prozeß**akten** wurden vernichtet, als Hochwasser in das Kellergeschoß eindrang.
The **records** of the trial were ruined when floodwater got into the basement.
(2) Der **Akten**schrank ist leer. Alle Personal**akten** sind verschwunden.
The **filing** cabinet is empty. All the personal **files** have disappeared.

Note: **Akten**tasche = briefcase
aktenkundig machen = place on record
This fact **was placed on record** immediately.
Aktenzeichen = reference
but: Nagelfeile = nail-**file**

> act(s): (1) Tat(en), Handlung(en) (**see** Akt ◑ act)
> (2) Gesetz(e)
> (3) Apostelgeschichte (Bibel)

(1) These **acts** of violence by these youths can no longer be ignored.
Diese Gewalt**taten** von diesen Jugendlichen können nicht länger hingenommen werden.
Such an **act** can only aggravate the problems.
Solch eine **Handlung** kann nur die Probleme verschlimmern.
(2) The 1944 Education **Act** paved the way for Great Britain's present educational system.
Das Erziehungs- und Bildungs**gesetz** von 1944 ebnete den Weg für das heutige Erziehungswesen in Großbritannien.

(3) The **Acts** of the Apostles is the fifth book of the New Testament. Die **Apostelgeschichte** ist das fünfte Buch im Neuen Testament.

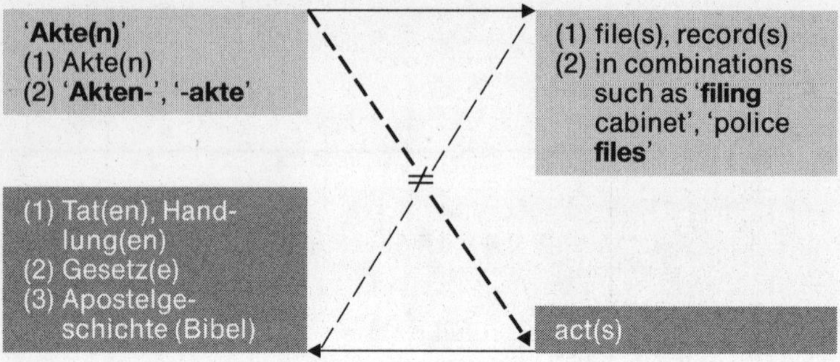

FALSE FRIENDS IN CONTEXT

Doctors' Secret Humour

First Doctor: There are rumours we keep secret medical ________ (1) on our patients.
Second Doctor: It depends on what you mean by 'secret'. I know of a medic who wrote in a patient's ________ (2): 'He thinks more of his cat than his wife.'
Third Doctor (amid general laughter): I remember one item from a confidential medical ________ (3): 'I've met the patient, I've met his wife, his children and his pet rabbit. And the rabbit is the most intelligent of them all.'
First Doctor (after the laughter has died down): I know of a colleague who wrote out a prescription for Valium. He added: 'Take as you please, as anything I say will make no difference.' It was meant, of course, to give the chemist a giggle – but it ended up written on the patient's pill bottle label.
Second Doctor: But joking apart, the CFI (= **C**ampaign for the **F**reedom of **I**nformation) argues that these funny remarks stay on a patient's ________ (4) for life.
Third Doctor: We've got to be more careful. The group is demanding a new ________ (5) granting access to all medical ________ (6).
First Doctor: Do you know what my secretary says in such cases? 'I haven't lost it – I filed it! It's the ________ (7) I've lost!'

SOLUTION

(1) records (2) patient's **file** (3) medical **file** (4) records, file (5) a new **act** (6) files, records (7) file

ALARMIEREN ◑ alarm

alarm [ə'lɑ:m]

ALARMIEREN

alert [ə'lɜ:t]

ALARMIEREN: (1) alert
(2) call

(1) Sie versuchte verzweifelt, ihren Mann wiederzubeleben, ehe sie eine Freundin **alarmierte**, die einen Krankenwagen herbeirief.
She desperately tried to revive her husband before **alerting** a friend, who called an ambulance.
Die alte Frau wurde durch schnelles Handeln ihres zehnjährigen Neffen Terry gerettet, der einen Lebensretter **alarmierte**.
The old woman was saved by the quick thinking of her ten-year-old nephew Terry, who **alerted** a lifeguard.
(2) Als die Einbrecher das Küchenfenster zertrümmerten, **alarmierte** meine Frau die Polizei.
When the burglars smashed the kitchen window, my wife **called** the police.

Note: in **Alarm**zustand versetzen = put on the alert
When the Russians approached, the troops were **put on the alert**.

alarm: (1) (jdn.) warnen
(2) sich fürchten; (jdn.) beunruhigen
(3) be alarmed (at): sich fürchten (vor); beunruhigt sein (über)

(1) The Greens thought of **alarming** the public through the mass media.
Die Grünen dachten daran, die Öffentlichkeit über die Massenmedien zu **warnen**.
(2) The inhabitants of Osaka were **alarmed** when they heard details of the earthquake in Kobe.
Die Einwohner von Osaka **fürchteten sich**, als sie Einzelheiten von dem Erdbeben in Kobe hörten.

This bad news didn't **alarm** the European tourists staying at Osaka in the least.
Diese schlechte Nachricht **beunruhigte** die europäischen Touristen, die sich in Osaka aufhielten, nicht im geringsten.
(3) With the World Cup Finals only five weeks away, the English Football Association **were alarmed at** the provocative message.
Knapp fünf Wochen vor der Endrunde der Weltmeisterschaft **war** der englische Fußballverband **über** die provokative Botschaft **beunruhigt**.

Note: be alarming = beunruhigend sein
Even more **alarming is** that many union leaders hold a mistaken belief.

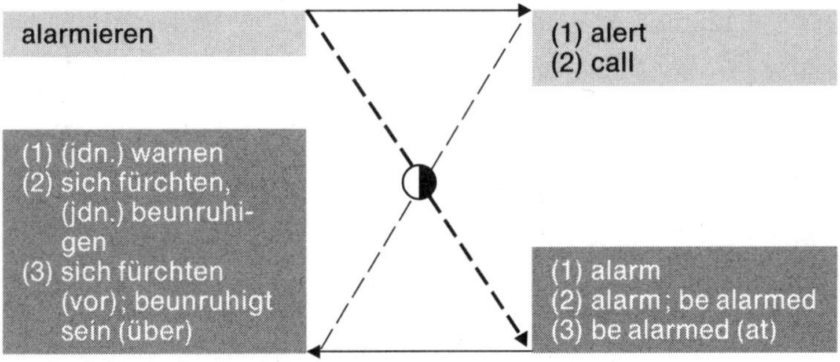

FALSE FRIENDS IN CONTEXT

Mother to the Front

Mother (in her shop in Farnham, trying to ring her son ten miles away in Guildford): Bill, ________ (1) the...
Bill knew at once what was going on. He heard his brave mother being attacked by a thug... on the other end of the phone.

* * *

Bill, dialling 999 to ________ (2) the Farnham police: Bill Hunter speaking from Guildford. Go to my mother's corner shop at 5, Oldfield Road in Farnham. I've just had a phone call. A thug's beating her up.

Police Officer: Right, we'll send a police-car round straight away.

* * *

In a taxi on the way to Farnham:
Bill: Quick! I'm ________ (3) about my mother.
Taxi Driver: Why?
Bill: Someone's been attacking her in her corner shop. I could hear it on the phone.

* * *

Mother: You needn't have been so ________ (4), Bill. I slammed the till hurting his fingers. Then I grabbed my cane and beat the thug off. The villain made off through the back door when this man came in.

SOLUTION

(1) alert (2) alert (3) alarmed (4) alarmed

The Helpful and the Unconcerned

A young man was standing beside an overturned sports car.
Motorist, stopping and getting out of his Ford asking somewhat ________ (5): Anybody hurt in the accident? I'll ________ (6) the police and ring for an ambulance.
Young Man (calmly): There's no reason to be ________ (7). There hasn't been an accident. I've just finished repairing my exhaust pipe.

SOLUTION

(5) alarmed (6) call, alert (7) alarmed

ALLEE ≠ alley

alley ['ælɪ]

ALLEE

avenue ['ævənju:]

ALLEE: (often a tree-lined) avenue

Note: The use of '**avenue**' in street names is quite common in BE and AE. Leadenhall **Avenue**, Maida **Avenue** and Peabody **Avenue** are streets in London. The annual Steuben Parade is held on New York's Fifth **Avenue**.

Es war beeindruckend zu beobachten, wie der Rolls-Royce die breite **Allee** zum Schloß des Multi-Millionärs hochfuhr.
It was impressive to watch the Rolls-Royce going up the broad **avenue** to the multi-millionaire's castle.
Wenn man den Wohnblock baut, wird der Blick die **Allee** hinauf nach Süden zerstört.
If they are going to build the block of flats, the view up the **avenue** to the south will be ruined.

Note: Weg, Methode = alley (fig.)
The best **avenue** to a powerful golf swing is building a solid foundation in your feet.

alley: (1) Gasse
(2) kleine Gasse, Gäßchen
(3) '**-gäßchen**', '**-gasse**' (in combinations)

(1) One of the findings of the Home Office report was that most rapes are committed in dark **alleys** by total strangers.
Eines der Ergebnisse des Berichts des Innenministeriums war, daß die meisten Vergewaltigungen von völlig Fremden in dunklen **Gassen** begangen werden.
(2) In Brighton, the **alleys** known as the Lanes, were full of antique shops.
In Brighton waren die **kleinen Gassen**, die als die 'Lanes' bekannt sind, voller Antiquitätenläden.

(3) Shortly after midnight our neighbour heard two shots in the back **alley** near the harbour.
Kurz nach Mitternacht hörte unser Nachbar zwei Schüsse in dem Hinter**gäßchen** beim Hafen.

Note: **alley**way = Seitengäßchen, Durchgang
The police will keep watch on the narrow streets and **alleyways** which wind their way up to the castle.
but: bowling **alley**, skittle **alley** = Kegelbahn

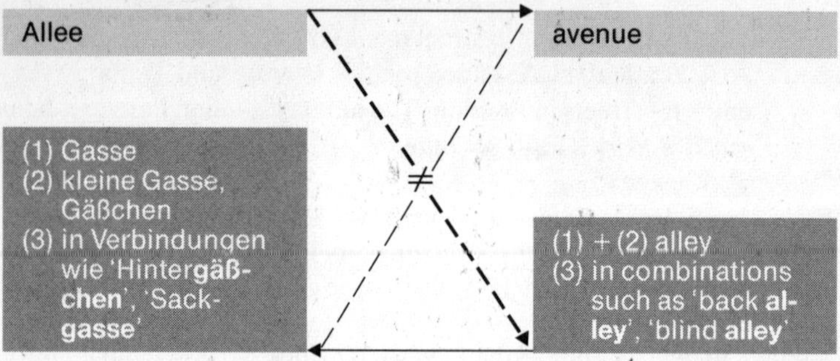

FALSE FRIENDS IN CONTEXT

Difficult Situations

Quizmaster: What is a street with trees lining both sides?
Jennifer (the candidate): I think it's called an ________ (1).
Quizmaster: That's right. Two points for you. And what is it when boys crowd in on both sides?
Jennifer (after some thought): A tight corner.

* * *

A 34-year-old woman was raped after being dragged into a narrow ________ (2) in Handsworth, Birmingham, on Wednesday night. Police investigations are under way.

SOLUTION

(1) avenue (2) alley

ANTENNE ◑ antenna

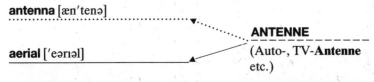

antenna [æn'tenə]

ANTENNE
(Auto-, TV-**Antenne** etc.)

aerial ['eərɪəl]

ANTENNE: (Auto-, TV-, Radio-**Antenne**) aerial (BE), antenna (mainly AE)

Note: The plural of **antenna** in this sense is **antennas** (in AE).

Der neue Mazda hat sogar eine Scheinwerfer-Waschanlage, eine Mittelarmlehne und – was am wichtigsten ist – eine Motor-**Antenne**.
The new Mazda even has headlamp washers, a centre armrest and, most important, an electric **aerial**.
Die zehn roten Milane wurden mit winzigen Radiosendern und **Antennen** versehen, um ihren Aufenthaltsort feststellen zu können.
The ten red kites were fitted with tiny radio transmitters and **aerials**, so they could be tracked.

Note: Luftsalto, Luftschraube (in der Ski-Akrobatik) = **aerial** (sport).
She is an excellent skier, but it is in the breathtaking **aerial** routines (Luftakrobatik-Programm) that Jilly excels. (**Aerials** are the official term for somersaults accomplished after the skier has raced down a mountain at a speed of 60 mph before being catapulted into space.)

antenna: (1) Fühler (bei Insekten etc.)
(2) Fingerspitzengefühl, Gespür (fig.)

Note: The plural of **antenna** in this case is **antennae** [æn'teni:] (in BE and AE).

(1) There were two lobsters with their **antennae** in full array.
Es gab zwei Hummer mit ihren **Fühlern** in voller Aufstellung.
(2) Sensitive **antennae** are called for among small business advisers because of bankruptcies.
Wegen der Konkurse müssen Berater von Kleinunternehmen schon über **Fingerspitzengefühl** verfügen.

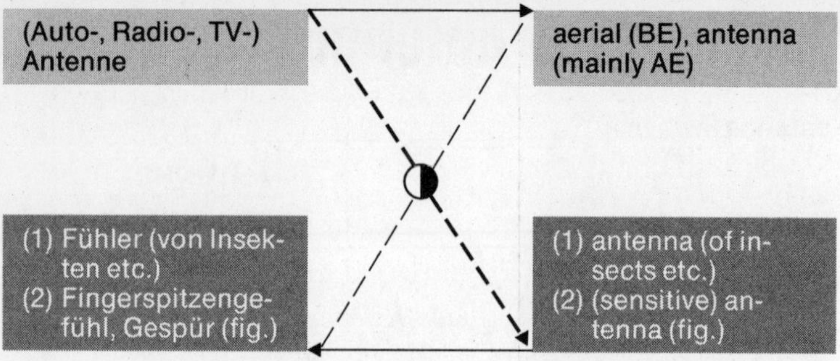

FALSE FRIENDS IN CONTEXT

That'll Teach them a Lesson

Football Manager: All players have to turn up in time for the return flight to Sunderland.
Assistant (impressing it on the players): Everyone has to be at the terminal half an hour before take-off.

* * *

Football Manager (at take-off time): I wonder where four of our players are.
Assistant: I'd better ring the police.

* * *

Assistant (ten minutes later): Howard, Gates, Soly and Webb are in police cells.
Football Manager: What for?
Assistant: The police found six cars with ________ (1) ripped off, and two cars had dented panels. So they arrested them.
Football Manager: Surely, that's not enough evidence.
Assistant: When the police arrived on the scene, Gates was hurling an ________ (2) across the road.
Football Manager: I'm going to see the Superintendent of Exeter police about it. Perhaps I can put in a good word for them. But before the next home match against Tottenham I'll make each of them collect two snails.

Assistant: What for?
Football Manager: So they can hand them over to the groundsman with their ________ (3) outstretched. That'll teach them a lesson.

SOLUTION

(1) aerials (2) aerial (3) antennae

A Question and a Straight Answer

What do you call a Skoda with an ________ (4)? – A dodgem (= Autoskooter auf der Kirmes).

SOLUTION

(4) aerial

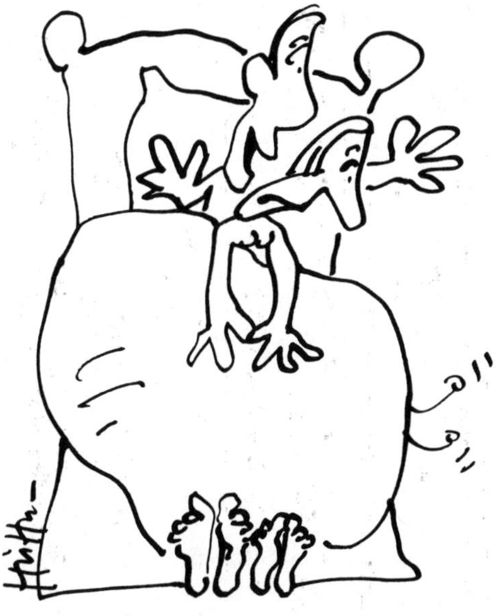

"We've got to be careful! My wife has really got an antenna for my affairs!!"

ART ≠ art

art

ART

kind etc.

ART : (1) kind, type, sort
(2) (**Art** und Weise) way
(3) (Wesen) nature
(4) (Verhalten) behaviour

(1) "Diese **Art** von Notlüge kenne ich schon", pfiff ihn der Fahrkartenkontrolleur an.
"I've heard that **kind** of white lie before," snapped the ticket inspector.
Meine Schwester mochte diese **Art** von Büchern nicht; daher kaufte sie auch keines.
My sister didn't like this **type** of book, so she didn't buy any.
Auf der Tier-Ausstellung konnten wir Hunde aller **Art** sehen.
At the pet show we saw all **sorts** of dogs.
(2) Der neue Trainer war mit der **Art** und Weise, wie der Klub geleitet wurde, unzufrieden.
The new coach wasn't satisfied with the **way** the club was being run.
Robert Maxwell, der Besitzer der neuen Zeitung 'The European', war mit der **Art** und Weise des Absatzes sehr zufrieden.
Robert Maxwell, proprietor of the new paper 'The European', was very pleased with the **way** sales were going.
(3) Es war nicht ihre **Art**, so etwas Schreckliches zu tun.
It wasn't in her **nature** to do such a terrible thing.
(4) Ich kann seine **Art** nicht ausstehen.
I can't stand his **behaviour**.

Note: Das ist nicht seine **Art** = That's not his **way** of doing things.
Aber hör' mal, das ist doch keine **Art**! =
Look here, that's no **way** to talk!
but: Tier**art** = species
That **species** died out more than fifty years ago.

art: (1) Kunst
(2) '**Kunst-**' (in combinations)

(1) "I do not excel at **art**, although I am left-handed," the new student maintained.
"Ich bin in **Kunst** nicht überragend, obwohl ich Linkshänder bin", behauptete der neue Student.
(2) The Czech master spy passed himself off as a Dutch **art** dealer.
Der tschechische Meisterspion gab sich als holländischer **Kunst**händler aus.
"Enjoyment of **art** has little to do with **art** theory," said Liliane Lijin, the first woman in Britain to approach the Tate Gallery for a women's **art** exhibition.
"**Kunst**genuß hat wenig mit **Kunst**-Theorie zu tun", sagte Liliane Lijin, die erste Frau in Großbritannien, die bei der Tate Galerie wegen einer Frauen-**Kunst**ausstellung vorsprach.

Note: **art** gallery = **Kunst**galerie
art historian = **Kunst**historiker
art lover = **Kunst**freund
but: **artificial** silk = **Kunst**seide
Compare: figure skater = Eis**kunst**läufer
imitation leather = **Kunst**leder
pause for effect = **Kunst**pause
trick cyclist = **Kunst**fahrer

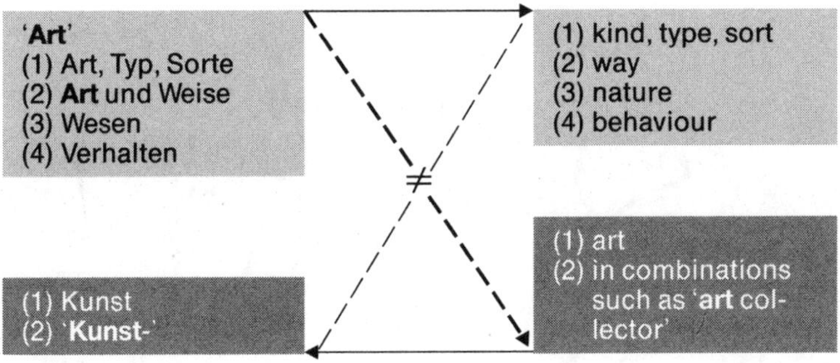

FALSE FRIENDS IN CONTEXT

The Spy with no Name

Mr. Amis: I've met all ________ (1) of people in my life, but I've never come across that ________ (2) of man before.
Mrs. Case: You mean that fellow in the flat downstairs?
Mr. Amis: Yes. He passed himself off as an ________ (3) dealer. Three weeks ago he lured a nude model to his love-nest and beat her up. When I went to complain he bawled, "That's no ________ (4) to talk to me!" and banged the door in my face.
Mrs. Case: Well, he took painting lessons at the Camden ________ (5) Centre twice a week.
Mr. Amis: Now, they've found out Van Haarlem was just a cover name. The judge said he's a Czech master spy with no name.

SOLUTION

(1) sorts (2) type, kind (3) **art** dealer (4) way (5) Camden **Arts** Centre

"Terribly sorry, Sir! That's not modern art. It's a mirror..."

AUSGESPROCHEN ≠ outspoken

outspoken ['aʊt'spəʊkən]

AUSGESPROCHEN

decided etc.

AUSGESPROCHEN: (1) adj.: decided, marked, pronounced
(2) adv.: decidedly, extremely, markedly

Note: '**marked**' is mostly used in a negative sense.

(1) Mein Onkel hat eine **ausgesprochene** Vorliebe für englische Briefmarken aus dem letzten Jahrhundert.
My uncle has a **decided** preference for English stamps of the last century.
Es bestand **ausgesprochene** Abgeneigtheit, die Angelegenheit zu diskutieren.
There was a **marked** unwillingness to discuss the matter.
Der neue Rektor der Universität hat einen **ausgesprochen** schottischen Akzent.
The new Vice-Chancellor of the university has a **pronounced** Scottish accent.
(2) Die Stimmung der Labour-Abgeordneten war **ausgesprochen** gedrückt.
The mood of the Labour M. P.s was **decidedly** gloomy.
Ausgesprochen schlechtes Wetter unterbrach alle weiteren Segel-Wettbewerbe.
Extremely bad weather stopped all further sailing competitions.
Experten in Großbritannien betrachteten den neuen Haushalt mit **ausgesprochen** gemischten Gefühlen.
Experts in Britain viewed the new budget with **markedly** mixed feelings.

outspoken: (1) offen, freimütig
(2) unverblümt, ungeschminkt

(1) B. Andreatta was an **outspoken** critic of the Italian banks.
B. Andreatta übte **offene** Kritik an den italienischen Banken.
Many Russians are very **outspoken** nowadays about their country.

Viele Russen äußern sich heutzutage sehr **freimütig** über ihr Land.
(2) The **outspoken** criticism of the reporter surprised everyone.
Die **unverblümte** Kritik des Reporters überraschte alle.
One of the M. P.s echoed some of the Trade Secretary's more **outspoken** views.
Einer der Abgeordneten gab einige recht **ungeschminkte** Ansichten des Handelsministers wieder.

Note: (to) be (**very**) **outspoken** = kein Blatt vor den Mund nehmen, **offen** seine Meinung sagen
He's not popular with his colleagues because he's **very outspoken**.
but: After the meeting we had a **frank** discussion =
Nach der Sitzung führten wir eine **offene** Aussprache.
She has an **open** and honest manner =
Sie hat eine **offene**, ehrliche Art.

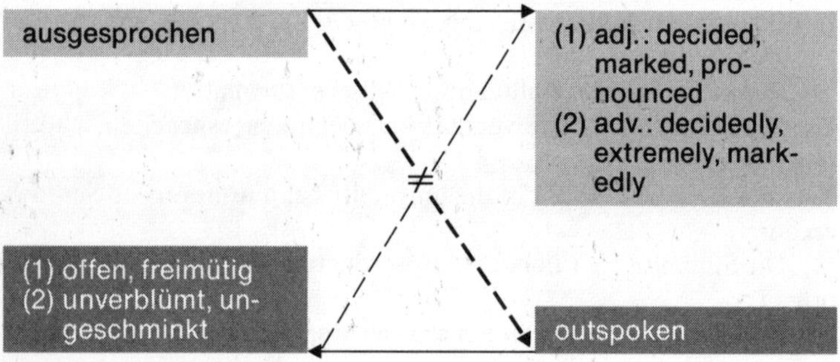

FALSE FRIENDS IN CONTEXT

A Modern Village War

Guardian Correspondent: Many people in Britain's industrial areas still live in ________ (1) unhealthy housing conditions.
Architect: I fully agree. That's where Prince Charles's "New Vision of Britain" starts from. His plan is for four new villages, where people both live and work.
Guardian Correspondent: That's where the problem began. People in

the Dorchester area and even tenants of his own Duchy of Cornwall are against his scheme.
Architect: Prince Charles has been one of the most ________ (2) critics of architects in recent years. On the other hand, he also called the London Docklands a ________ (3) success for property developers.
Guardian Correspondent: I agree. Many angry families have recently protested in a series of public meetings against the new "live where you work" villages. The people of the Poundbury development don't want to be the Prince's guinea pigs.

SOLUTION

(1) **decidedly** unhealthy (2) outspoken (3) a **pronounced** success

BLANK ≠ blank

blank

BLANK

bright, shining etc.

BLANK: (1) adj.: bright, shining, shiny
(2) verb: ('**blank** sein'), be broke (coll.); be penniless
(3) verb: (**blank** putzen) polish sth.

(1) Seine **blanken** Augen erfreuten seine Mutter.
His mother was delighted at his **bright** eyes.
Alice konnte in der **blanken** Oberfläche des Spiegels jede Einzelheit des Raums erkennen.
Alice could see every detail of the room reflected in the **shining** mirror.
Ihre **blanken** schwarzen Schuhe paßten zu ihrem Kleid.
Her **shiny** black shoes went with her dress.
(2) Um acht betraten die beiden die Kneipe. Als die Kneipe schloß, waren die jungen Herren **blank**. Aber sie machten sich nichts daraus.
At eight the two entered the pub. When the pub closed, the young gentlemen were **broke**. But they didn't care.
Zum zweiten Mal in diesem Monat war er **blank**. Was sollte er nun machen?
He was **penniless** for the second time this month. What should he do?
(3) Hast du deine Schuhe **blank** geputzt?
Have you **polished** your shoes?

Note: **blankes** Eis = **smooth** ice
blanker Hohn = **utter** nonsense
blanker Unsinn = **pure** contempt
but: Seine Nerven lagen **blank** = He was **in a terrible state** of nerves

blank: (1) leer; unausgefüllt (auch fig.)
(2) ausdruckslos, verständnislos
(3) verblüfft

(1) The exam candidate looked at the **blank** page before him. He couldn't think of anything to write.

Der Examenskandidat schaute auf das **leere** Blatt vor sich. Er konnte nichts zu Papier bringen.
When the interviewer asked me what books I liked to read, my mind suddenly went **blank**.
Als der Leiter des Einstellungsgesprächs mich fragte, welche Bücher ich gerne lesen würde, war mein Kopf plötzlich wie **leer**.
Many people thought the **blank** wall was 'a work of art' by John Lennon and began analysing it. But the picture had simply been removed.
Viele Menschen dachten, die **unausgefüllte** Wand sei 'ein Kunstwerk' von John Lennon, und begannen es zu analysieren. Aber das Bild war einfach entfernt worden.
(2) There was a **blank** look on the defendant's face as the judge sentenced him to fifteen years in prison.
Das Gesicht des Angeklagten nahm einen **verständnislosen** Ausdruck an, als der Richter ihn zu 15 Jahren Gefängnis verurteilte.
(3) When her husband told her he was going to leave her, Eileen looked **blank** for a moment.
Als ihr Mann ihr sagte, daß er sie verlassen würde, schaute Eileen einen Augenblick **verblüfft** drein.

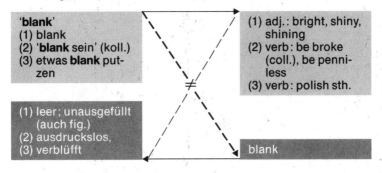

'**blank**'
(1) blank
(2) '**blank** sein' (koll.)
(3) etwas **blank** putzen

(1) adj.: bright, shiny, shining
(2) verb: be broke (coll.), be penniless
(3) verb: polish sth.

≠

(1) leer; unausgefüllt (auch fig.)
(2) ausdruckslos,
(3) verblüfft

blank

FALSE FRIENDS IN CONTEXT

A Cheque to Bank on

Linda: Our bank account is in the red.
Malcolm, looking ________ (1) for a moment: What? Really? But there was more than £ 800 in it on Monday, and now it's only Wednesday.

Linda: Maybe but now we are ________ (2).
Malcolm: Don't look so worried, darling. Let's check our latest bank statement. Look what it says down here: Someone handed in a cheque for £ 845! What did you buy, Linda?
Linda: Nothing. I didn't sign a cheque for £ 845. But let me think ... A moment later with ________ (3) eyes: Wait a minute! The owner of the van asked me to give him a signed, but otherwise ________ (4) cheque when we moved house last week.
Malcolm: You didn't sign a ________ (5) cheque, did you?
Linda: Why not? What's wrong with that, darling?

SOLUTION

(1) blank (2) penniless (3) bright (4) blank (5) blank

DOM ≠ dome

dome [dɔʊm]

DOM

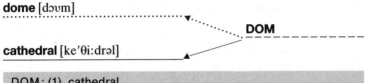

cathedral [ke′θi:drəl]

DOM: (1) cathedral
(2) in combinations such as '**cathedral** town'

(1) Besuchen Sie in jedem Fall den **Dom** von Salisbury. Die schönsten mittelalterlichen Glasmalereien in England sind jedoch im **Dom** von Canterbury.
You must visit Salisbury **Cathedral**. The finest mediaeval stained glass windows in England are, however, in Canterbury **Cathedral**.
(2) Was er besonders an der **Dom**stadt mochte, war die alte **Dom**schule.
What he particularly liked about the **cathedral** town was its old **cathedral** school.
Es ist geplant, 7 Millionen Pfund für die **Dom**reparaturen aufzubringen.
The plan is to raise £ 7 million for **cathedral** repairs.

dome: (1) Kuppel, Gewölbe
(2) Kuppelgebäude
(3) Glatze
(4) (überdachtes) Stadion (mainly in AE)

(1) The pilgrims stopped when they first caught sight of the **dome** of St. Peter's in Rome.
Die Pilger hielten inne, als sie zum ersten Mal die **Kuppel** des St. Petersdoms in Rom erblickten.
What would happen in the event of an explosion inside the **dome** of the reactor container at Sizewell B?
Was würde im Explosionsfall innerhalb des **Gewölbes** des Reaktorbehälters von Sizewell B passieren?
(2) The SunAqua Park, the recently opened giant plastic **dome**, was heated to a delicious 84 F.
Der SunAqua Park, das kürzlich eröffnete riesige Plastik-**Kuppelgebäude**, war auf wohltuende 28,8 °C erwärmt.

(3) You could see the manager had aged. His hair was greying at the sides, and on his head a **dome** had even appeared.
Man konnte sehen, daß der Manager gealtert war; sein Haar wurde an den Seiten zusehends grau, und sogar eine **Glatze** hatte sich auf dem Kopf entwickelt.
(4) Chicago may build a $ 300 million **dome** just to keep the 'Bears'.
Chicago wird wahrscheinlich ein **überdachtes Stadion** bauen, nur um die 'Bears' (= die Mannschaft der 'Chicago Bears') zu halten.

Note: '**dome**' is also used in names of roofed stadiums in the United States, Canada and Australia.
New Orleans claims its Super**dome**, Houston its Astro**dome**, Minnesota its Humphrey Metro**dome**, Seattle its King**dome**, Toronto its Sky**dome** and Perth its Burswood Super**dome** which lose millions of dollars a year but bring billions in business.
but: an onion **dome** = ein Zwiebelturm
a **domed** forehead = eine gewölbte Stirn

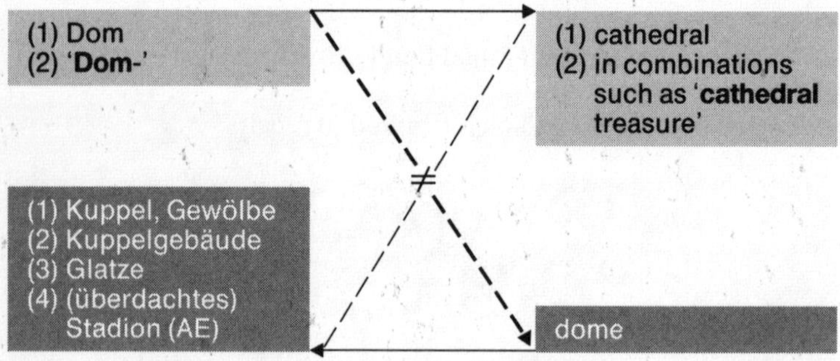

FALSE FRIENDS IN CONTEXT

The Image of his Father

Little Terry walked across the street and past the old ________ (1). But today he didn't give the building a second look.
He was going to have his hair cut and was on his way to the hairdresser near the market square. When he had settled down in the chair, the

hairdresser asked him, "Now, young man, how would you like to have your hair cut?"
Without much thought, little Terry replied, "Like my father's, with a ________ (2) on top."

SOLUTION

(1) cathedral (2) dome

The Peace of Chianti-shire

Paul: We've spent two days in Florence now with its squares, the Michelangelo masterpieces and the magnificient ________ (3) of the thirteenth century ________ (4), the Duomo.
Victoria: Where shall we go now?
Paul: I know. Let's head back into the lush green of Tuscany, it's what British tourists call Chianti-shire.
Victoria: But didn't we want to go to the ________ (5) city of Siena?
Paul: It's a little south of here. We could go there first.
Victoria: Let's do that then. Siena has banned traffic completely. So we can walk in silent streets enjoying the bells in the main square near the ________ (6). It's going to be magical, Paul!
Paul: And then we'll enjoy the peace of Chianti-shire!

SOLUTION

(3) domes (4) cathedral (5) **cathedral** city (6) cathedral

FALSE FRIENDS TRAPS TEST 5

NOT SO EASY FALSE FRIENDS

1.a. Horrified tourists saw a man jump to his death from the Whispering Gallery in the ________ of St. Paul's on September 7th, 1989 (**Dom ≠ dome**).
1.b. Hundreds of people who could find no room in the packed ________ stood outside during the service (**Dom ≠ dome**).
2.a. "We'll no longer accept such ________ of hooliganism," the headmaster told his pupils (**Akten ≠ acts**).
2.b. "Could you bring me the ________ on the Warburton case," said the solicitor to his secretary (**Akten ≠ acts**). "I've got to look something up for the report I'm writing."
3.a. A group of tourists walked along a grandiose ________ lined with trees on both sides (**Allee ≠ alley**).
3.b. She did not talk to him in the usual way; she was snarling like a Calcutta ________ cat (**Allee ≠ alley**).
4.a. The young man used this ________ of argument because he wanted to get a job (**Art ≠ art**).
4.b. She put her ________ before marriage and motherhood (**Art ≠ art**). That's why she won the Turner Prize for ________ (**Art ≠ art**).
5.a. James Pickles is regarded by many in Britain as an ________ judge (**ausgesprochen ≠ outspoken**).
5.b. Fortunately his financial situation looked ________ encouraging (**ausgesprochen ≠ outspoken**).
6. Interpol has been ________ (**alarmiert**) in case the man has gone abroad.
7. My new Volvo drives me mad. Now the ________ (**Achse**) is broken.
8. It was easy for Picasso to find ________ (**Akt-**) models on the Côte d'Azur.
9. Unobtrusively, James Bond carried his gun under his ________ (**Achsel**).
10. Margie did not understand why Frank did not love her any more. So she just gave him a ________ (**ausdruckslos, verständnislos**) look.

ANSWER SHEET: TRUE FRIENDS TEST 5

NOT SO EASY FALSE FRIENDS

1.a. Horrified tourists saw a man jump to his death from the Whispering Gallery in the **dome** of St. Paul's on September 7th, 1989.
1.b. Hundreds of people who could find no room in the packed **cathedral** stood outside during the service.
2.a. "We'll no longer accept such **acts** of hooliganism," the headmaster told his pupils.
2.b. "Could you bring me the **files** on the Warburton case," said the solicitor to his secretary. "I've got to look something up for the report I'm writing."
3.a. A group of tourists walked along a grandiose **avenue** lined with trees on both sides.
3.b. She did not talk to him in the usual way; she was snarling like a Calcutta **alley** cat.
4.a. The young man used this **kind** of argument because he wanted to get a job.
4.b. She put her **art** before marriage and motherhood. That's why she won the Turner Prize for **art**.
5.a. James Pickles is regarded by many in Britain as an **outspoken** judge.
5.b. Fortunately his financial situation looked **decidedly** encouraging.
6. Interpol has been **alerted** in case the man has gone abroad.
7. My new Volvo drives me mad. Now the **axle** is broken.
8. It was easy for Picasso to find **nude** models on the Côte d'Azur.
9. Unobtrusively, James Bond carried a gun under his **arm**pit.
10. Margie did not understand why Frank did not love her any more. So she just gave him a **blank** look.

FABRIK ≠ fabric

fabric [ˈfæbrɪk]

FABRIK

factory

FABRIK:	(1) (allg.) factory
	(2) in combinations such as '**factory** site', 'bicycle **factory**'
	(3) (Produktionsstätte, -anlage) plant
	(4) (Werk, [Stahl-]Hütte etc.) works
	(5) (rohstoffverarbeitende Fabrik) mill

(1) Die Arbeitsbedingungen in der **Fabrik** sind schlecht; deshalb werde ich kündigen.
Working conditions in the **factory** are bad, so I'll give in my notice.
(2) Das alte **Fabrik**gelände ist in ein modernes Einkaufszentrum verwandelt worden.
The old **factory** site has been converted into a modern shopping centre.
(3) Die Luft in der Umgebung von Chemie**fabriken** (Chemie-**Anlagen**) stinkt meist.
The air near chemical **plants** usually stinks.
(4) Die Produktion bei den Fiat-Auto**werken** mußte um 50% gedrosselt werden.
Production at the Fiat Motor **Works** had to be cut by 50 per cent.
(5) Die Papier**fabrik** wird heute nicht mehr genutzt.
The paper **mill** is no longer used today.

Note: Industrie**anlage** = industrial **plant**
Textil**fabrik** = textile **mill**
Seiden**fabrik** = silk **mill**
but: Gaswerk = gas **works**
Wasserwerk = water **works**
Stahlwerk = steel **works**

fabric: (1) Gewebe, Stoff
(2) (Gesellschafts-) Gefüge
(3) Bausubstanz

(1) In the film 'The Man in the White Suit' Alec Guinness plays the part of a chemist who invents a **fabric** that will never wear out.
In dem Film 'Der Mann im weißen Anzug' spielt Alec Guinness die Rolle eines Chemikers, der ein **Gewebe** erfindet, das nie verschleißt.
These **fabrics** were bought in the Far East.
Diese **Stoffe** sind im Fernen Osten gekauft worden.
(2) The First World War radically altered the **fabric** of English society.
Der Erste Weltkrieg veränderte das **Gefüge** der englischen Gesellschaft völlig.
(3) The present owner has tried hard, but he hasn't been able to maintain the **fabric** of the house.
Der jetzige Besitzer hat alles versucht, aber konnte die **Bausubstanz** des Hauses nicht erhalten.

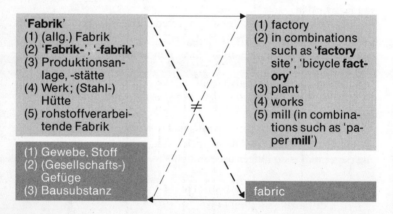

'Fabrik'
(1) (allg.) Fabrik
(2) **'Fabrik-'**, **'-fabrik'**
(3) Produktionsanlage, -stätte
(4) Werk; (Stahl-) Hütte
(5) rohstoffverarbeitende Fabrik

(1) factory
(2) in combinations such as '**factory** site', 'bicycle **factory**'
(3) plant
(4) works
(5) mill (in combinations such as 'paper **mill**')

≠

(1) Gewebe, Stoff
(2) (Gesellschafts-) Gefüge
(3) Bausubstanz

fabric

FALSE FRIENDS IN CONTEXT

Managing the Household Budget

Mrs. Hardcastle: Our bedroom curtains are old and tattered. We need new ones. This time I want tailored curtains with cushion covers and bedspreads to match.

Mr. Hardcastle: Hm. That'll cost us a pretty penny. A bit of a burden on the household budget.
Mrs. Hardcastle: I've found out where I can get tailored curtains at ________ (1) prices. Last Friday I sent for a brochure from Coningsby with ________ (2) samples in 36 shades. What's more, they even advised me on measuring, hanging and caring for ________ (3). The brochure came today.
Mr. Hardcastle: The price lists look good. No High Street prices and quality ________ (4). Go ahead with it, darling.

SOLUTION

(1) **factory** prices (2) **fabric** samples (3) fabrics (4) quality **fabrics**

FAMILIÄR ≠ familiar

familiar [fə'mɪljə]

FAMILIÄR
(die Familie betreffend; ungezwungen etc.)

personal etc.

FAMILIÄR: (1) personal
(2) in combinations such as '**family** peace'
(3) relaxed, informal
(4) intimate

(1) "Leider kann ich an der Herbst-Konferenz aus **familiären** Gründen nicht teilnehmen", entschuldigte sich unser Bekannter aus Bristol.
"Unfortunately I can't come to the autumn conference for **personal** reasons," our friend from Bristol apologized.
(2) "Die häufigen anonymen Anrufe haben den **familiären** Frieden gestört", sagte Herr Coburn der Polizei.
"The frequent anonymous calls have disturbed our **family** peace," Mr. Coburn told the police.
(3) Sie mochte die **familiäre** Atmosphäre auf ihrer neuen Arbeitsstelle.
She liked the **relaxed** atmosphere in her new office.
Die Gespräche zwischen den beiden Gewerkschaftsführern nahmen einen fast **familiären** Charakter an.
The talks between the two trade union leaders took an almost **informal** turn.
(4) Obwohl wir uns seit mehr als zwanzig Jahren nicht gesehen hatten, schlug mein früherer Schulfreund sofort einen **familiären** Ton an.
Although we had not met for more than twenty years, my former schoolfriend dropped into an **intimate** tone.

familiar: (1) (wohl-)bekannt, (wohl-)vertraut
(2) vertraut, freundschaftlich
(3) (plump-)vertraulich
(4) geflügelt (such as '**familiar** quotation')

(1) Ken and Trevor were almost as **familiar** as old friends.
Ken und Trevor waren miteinander fast so **bekannt** wie alte Freunde.
The spires of Ely Cathedral were a **familiar** sight to regular church-goers.
Die Türme des Doms von Ely waren für die regelmäßigen Kirchenbesucher ein **vertrauter** Anblick.
(2) Her daughter was on **familiar** terms with the actor.
Ihre Tochter hatte zu dem Schauspieler **freundschaftliche** Beziehungen.
(3) But she found him too **familiar** after a short time.
Aber sie fand ihn schon nach kurzer Zeit zu **vertraulich**.
(4) "Look up the saying in one of the dictionaries. It is probably a **familiar** quotation," the librarian suggested.
"Schlagen Sie doch die Redensart in einem der Lexika nach. Wahrscheinlich ist es ein **geflügeltes** Wort", schlug die Bibliothekarin vor.

Note: all-too-**familiar** = allzu vertraut, allzu bekannt
For him, the House of Commons was filled with **all-too-familiar** faces.

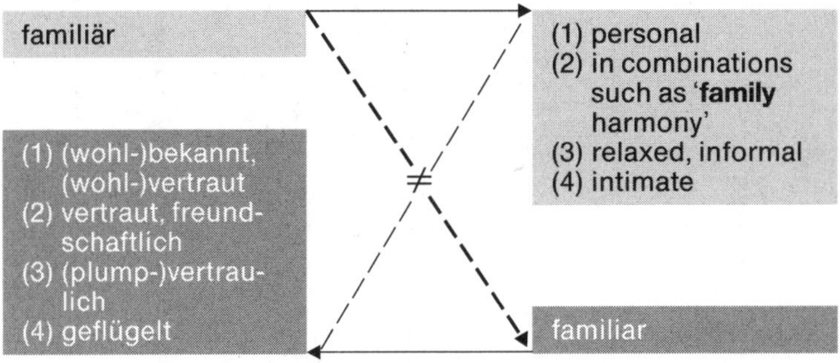

FALSE FRIENDS IN CONTEXT

A Festive Note

Are you ________ (1) with musical underpants? If not, listen to this: A solicitor formally addressed Stafford Magistrates' Court – only to be accompanied by ________ (2) Christmas carols.
While applying for a motoring case to be adjourned, he leant against

the desk; thus triggering off Jingle Bells and other ________ (3) songs. The other solicitors and courtroom staff collapsed into laughter. Blushing, he continued his appeal while a ________ (4) mood spread around the courtroom. He carried on talking – and the tune carried on playing. An almost ________ (5) atmosphere had developed in the courtroom when Rudolph the Red-nosed Reindeer came to an end. Later the solicitor apologized, "Once started, the music doesn't stop. The musical underpants were a present and I had to accept them for ________ (6) reasons."

SOLUTION

(1) familiar (2) **familiar** Christmas carols (3) **familiar** songs (4) **relax-ed** mood (5) **intimate** atmosphere (6) **personal** reasons

"My friends say, I'm a workoholic, but honestly: I am more familiar with alcohol than with work..."

FLIRT ≠ flirt

flirt → **FLIRT** (als Vorgang)

flirtation → **FLIRT** (als Vorgang)

FLIRT: (als Vorgang) flirtation

Charme und der Sinn für Spaß und **Flirt** haben Diana zum beliebtesten Mitglied der Königlichen Familie gemacht.
Charm and a sense of fun and **flirtation** have turned Diana into the most popular member of the Royal Family.
Jane erinnert sich, daß alles mit einem Telefon**flirt** anfing.
Jane recalls that it all started with a **flirtation** on the phone.

Note: Jane ist sein neuester **Flirt** = Jane is his latest flame (or girlfriend)

flirt: (1) (noun) (Frau) die Kokette; Schäkerin; Flittchen
(2) (noun) (Mann) Courschneider/Courmacher; Schäker
(3) (verb) flirten (mit), kokettieren (mit)
(4) liebäugeln (mit)

(1) Princess Stephanie of Monaco has been called a royal '**flirt**'.
Prinzessin Stephanie von Monaco ist als königliche '**Kokette**' bezeichnet worden.
A former boyfriend dismissed her as a 'terrible' **flirt**.
Ein früherer Freund tat sie als 'billiges' **Flittchen** ab.
Mind you, she's not one of those **flirts**.
Bedenke, daß sie nicht eine von diesen **Schäkerinnen** ist.
(2) Lionel had the reputation of being a calculating **flirt**.
Lionel stand im Ruf, ein berechnender **Courschneider** zu sein.
(3) As every young lady she likes to be **flirted with**. In fact, she **flirts with** everybody.
Wie jede junge Frau hat sie es gerne, wenn man mit ihr **flirtet**. Tatsächlich **flirtet** sie **mit** jedermann.
(4) At the end of last summer I **flirted with** the idea of going to Madrid, even though I hadn't the money.
Ende letzten Sommers **liebäugelte** ich **mit** dem Gedanken, nach Madrid zu fahren, obwohl ich nicht das Geld dafür hatte.

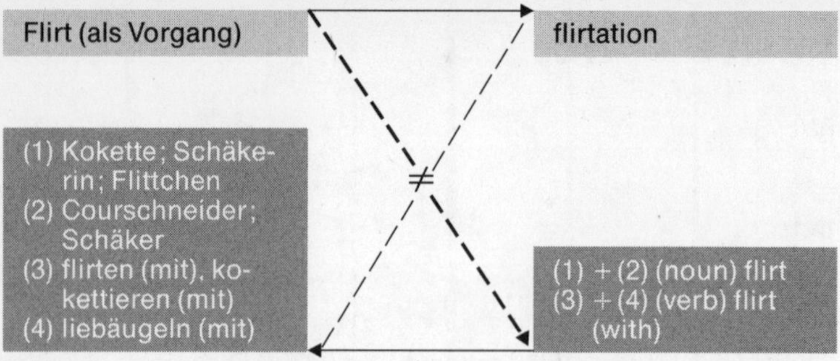

FALSE FRIENDS IN CONTEXT

Dealing with Office Romeos

Personnel Manager (addressing Mr. Webster in the company director's office): You're our transport manager. One of our secretaries has been complaining for some time about the suggestive comments you apparently keep making.
Mr. Webster: I always tried to be friendly to everybody. When I paid Miss Loveless a compliment the other day, I was just trying to be nice to her. There was not the slightest ________ (1) behind it.
Company Director: But I've evidence from two other colleagues who watched you knee-patting and bottom-pinching her.
Mr. Webster: Everyone knows Miss Loveless has always been a ________ (2). Secretaries like her can't tell the difference between an office ________ (3) and sexual harassment.
Personnel Manager: So you admit you've had a ________ (4) with one of our staff members.
Company Director: We can't tolerate any form of ________ (5) in the office. We are giving you the chance to hand in your resignation, but if you don't we'll be forced to give you your notice of dismissal before you leave this office!

SOLUTION

(1) flirtation (2) flirt (3) office **flirtation** (4) flirtation (5) flirtation

GIFT ≠ gift

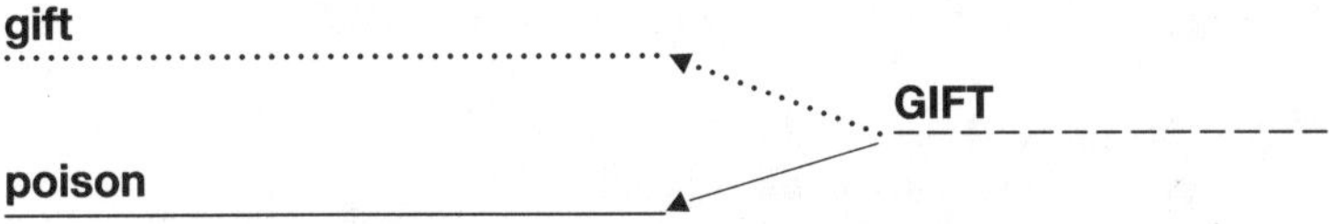

GIFT: (1) poison
(2) in combinations such as '**poison** gas', 'rat **poison**'
(3) (Tier-, besonders Schlangen**gift**) venom
(4) ('**Gift-**') in combinations such as '**toxic** waste' (der Fachbegriff in der Medizin, Pharmazie und neuerlich in der Umweltdiskussion ist '**toxin**')

(1) Dieses Schädlingsbekämpfungsmittel enthält ein gefährliches **Gift** für den Menschen, auch in relativ geringen Mengen.
This pesticide contains a dangerous **poison** for man, even in relatively small amounts.
(2) "Der **Gift**schrank sollte stets abgeschlossen sein", sagte der Apotheker zu der Verkäuferin.
"The **poison** cupboard should always be kept locked," the chemist told his assistant.
(3) Das **Gift** der Kobra tötete beinahe den Missionar.
The cobra's **venom** nearly killed the missionary.
(4) Ein deutsches Schiff versuchte in Großbritannien mit einer Ladung **Gift**müll zu landen.
A German ship was trying to land in Britain with a cargo of **toxic** waste.

gift: (1) (formelles) Geschenk
(2) '**Geschenk-**', '**-geschenk**' (in combinations)
(3) Talent, Begabung

(1) "These carnations are a **gift** for my landlady," she mentioned.
"Diese Nelken sind ein **Geschenk** für meine Zimmerwirtin", erwähnte sie.
(2) Christmas was only three weeks away, so he rang the **gift** shop and asked, "Could you send me your Xmas **gift** guide?"
Weihnachten war nur noch drei Wochen entfernt; daher rief er das **Geschenk**artikel-Geschäft an und fragte: "Könnten Sie mir Ihren Weihnachts**geschenk**katalog zusenden?"

(3) Her sister has a real **gift** for embroidery.
Ihre Schwester hat ein wirkliches **Talent** für Stickereien.
Our eldest daughter has a **gift** for mathematics.
Unsere älteste Tochter hat eine **Begabung** für Mathematik.

Note: farewell **gift** = Abschieds**geschenk**
gift token = **Geschenk**gutschein
have a **gift** for languages = sprachbegabt sein
but: dowry = Mit**gift**

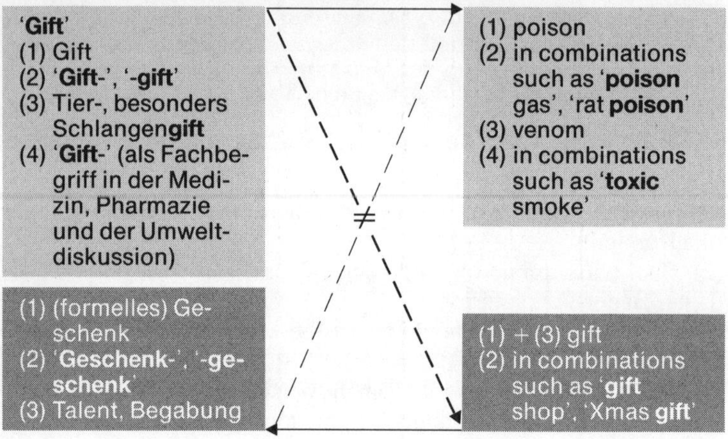

'Gift'
(1) Gift
(2) 'Gift-', '-gift'
(3) Tier-, besonders Schlangengift
(4) 'Gift-' (als Fachbegriff in der Medizin, Pharmazie und der Umweltdiskussion)
(1) poison
(2) in combinations such as 'poison gas', 'rat poison'
(3) venom
(4) in combinations such as 'toxic smoke'
≠
(1) (formelles) Geschenk
(2) 'Geschenk-', '-geschenk'
(3) Talent, Begabung
(1) + (3) gift
(2) in combinations such as 'gift shop', 'Xmas gift'

FALSE FRIENDS IN CONTEXT

Business as Usual?

Mr. Fawcett: Have you heard about the ship carrying ________ (1) waste?
Mr. Corrigan: No, I haven't.
Mr. Fawcett: A ship with a 2,100 ton cargo of ________ (2) waste has sailed from West Germany to Africa. The crew of the German-owned ship has simply dumped the ________ (3)-waste drums in the bush on the banks of the River Niger.
Mr. Corrigan: What's that got to do with us?
Mr. Fawcett: Nothing, or rather, it didn't have until last week. The

Nigerians forced the crew of the Karin B to take the ________ (4) waste on board the ship again. It's now down at the harbour after having been refused permission to land in Italy. What's more, there's even a British hazardous waste company wanting to deal with it.
Mr. Corrigan: It's a scandal!
Mr. Fawcett: The local people read the word GIFT on the barrels. But it was in fact ________ (5)!
Mr. Corrigan: Let's organize a demonstration, inform the local press and invite the TV people.

SOLUTION

(1) **toxic** waste (2) **toxic** waste (3) **toxic**-waste drums (4) **toxic** waste
(5) poison

In for a Penny, in for a Pound

Outside the bargain shop the price for each item was at £ 1. So I went inside and bought one and was asked £ 1.50.
When I complained, the assistant explained, "That's because each item contains a free ________ (6)."

SOLUTION

(6) gift

HAUSMEISTER ≠ housemaster

housemaster

HAUSMEISTER

caretaker

HAUSMEISTER(IN): (woman) caretaker (BE); janitor (AE)

Die **Hausmeisterin** von Björn Borgs Mailänder Luxuswohnung berichtete: "Er hatte seine Wohnungsschlüssel verloren. Daher bat er mich, die Eingangstür zu öffnen."
The **woman caretaker** of Björn Borg's luxury Milan flat reported, "He had lost the keys to his flat, so he asked me to open the front door."
Wieder einmal hatte der Direktor vergeblich nach Scrodd, dem Ober-**Hausmeister**, gesucht. Man fand ihn im Keller. "Beim nächsten Mal werde ich den **Hausmeister** entlassen. Er ist viel zu langsam", schwor er sich.
Once again the Headmaster had looked for Mr. Scrodd, the senior **caretaker**, in vain. They found him in the cellar. "Next time I'll sack the **caretaker**. He's much too slow," he swore to himself.

Note: '**Interims-**', '**Übergangs-**' = **caretaker** (in combinations)
Interim-Premierminister = **caretaker** prime minister
Interimspräsident = **caretaker** president (of a club)
Übergangsregierung = **caretaker** government
Interimsvorsitzender = **caretaker** chairman
Sir Neil Shields has taken over as **caretaker** chairman of London Regional Transport after the Clapham train disaster (cf. *Daily Telegraph* Nov. 11, 1988, p. 13).

housemaster/housemistress: Hausleiter(in) (an Internatsschulen); verantwortliche(r) Lehrer(in) für eine Internatseinheit ('**house**')

Note: A **housemaster** is a teacher in charge of one of the houses in a **private school**. The British do, however, also have houses in **day schools** for the purpose of organization and competition, and the person in charge of such a unit is usually called **head of house**.

Tom's parents wanted to know how he was settling down in his new boarding school, so they rang up his **housemaster** to find out.

Toms Eltern wollten wissen, wie er sich in der neuen Internatsschule eingelebt hatte; daher riefen sie seinen **Hausleiter** an, um sich danach zu erkundigen.

Jane accompanied her son to his prep school only to discover that her new lover was his new **housemaster** – respectfully married of course.

Jane begleitete ihren Sohn zur privaten Grundschule, um festzustellen, daß ihr neuer Liebhaber sein neuer **Hausleiter** ist – natürlich achtbar verheiratet.

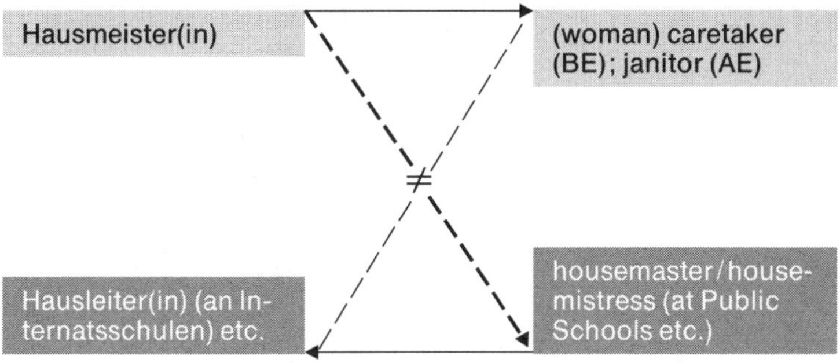

FALSE FRIENDS IN CONTEXT

When the Cat is Away . . .

The Headmaster had returned to his school one day earlier from the Headmasters' Conference in Eastbourne. He had asked to see Mr. Scrodd, the ________ (1), but the ________ (2) didn't turn up. The school secretary had looked everywhere in the school building. She had even looked in the school grounds. When she asked some of the older boys, they had only laughed and left her wondering. They couldn't find the ________ (3). The Headmaster swore he would find him and asked one of the ________ (4) and the Deputy Head to accompany him.

The three went straight down to the cellar. They found Scrodd fast asleep on a sofa surrounded by empty beer bottles. "I would like you to write a report for me on what you've just seen," the Headmaster told his colleagues. "Don't tell anyone, I'll ask him to come and see me in my study tomorrow morning and then give him the sack," he said, hurrying away.

SOLUTION

(1) caretaker (2) caretaker (3) caretaker (4) housemasters

"He is the caretaker and he really takes care of the female inhabitants..."

HELM ≠ helm

helm [helm]

HELM

helmet [ˈhelmɪt]

HELM: (1) helmet
(2) in combinations such as 'crash **helmet**'

(1) Der **Helm** des Polizisten fiel während des Gedenkgottesdiensts laut zu Boden.
The policeman's **helmet** clattered to the ground during the memorial service.
Um 1860 entschied sich die Polizei von Brighton für weiße **Helme** im Sommer als lokale Note.
About 1860 Brighton police decided on white **helmets** for summer as a local touch.
(2) Den Friedenstruppen der Vereinten Nationen – besser bekannt als Blau**helme** – ist der Friedens-Nobelpreis für 1988 zuerkannt worden.
The Peace Forces of the United Nations, better known as the Blue **Helmets**, have been awarded the Nobel Peace Prize for 1988.
“Bitte trage beim Motorradfahren einen Sturz**helm**. Ich kann sonst nicht schlafen”, bat ihn Johns Frau.
“Please wear a crash **helmet** when you ride your motor bike. Otherwise I can't get to sleep,” John's wife asked him.

Note: Astronauten-**Helm** = space **helmet**
Tropen**helm** = pith **helmet** (or topee, also topi)
One of the best things about polo is the hat you get to wear – a sort of a pith **helmet** with a visor at the front.
Sicherheits**helm** = safety **helmet**
Simon Houlton was the first man in Britain to be fined £ 100 for failing to wear a safety **helmet** on a local building site.

but: Kapuzenmütze = balaclava **helmet**
Police later found the bank robbers' **balaclava helmets** buried in the ground.

helm: (1) Steuer (auf dem Schiff)
(2) Ruder (fig.)

(1) In spite of the storm the captain remained at the **helm** of the ship all night.
Trotz des Sturms blieb der Kapitän die ganze Nacht am **Steuer** des Schiffs.
Murdo MacKenzie handed over the **helm** after 31 years as skipper of the ferry across the Sound of Sleat to the Isle of Skye.
Nach 31 Jahren gab Murdo MacKenzie das **Steuer** als Kapitän der Fähre über den Sleat-Sund zur Insel Skye ab.
(2) On May 13, 1940 Churchill took over the **helm** of government.
Am 13. Mai 1940 übernahm Churchill das **Ruder** der Regierung.
With the new managing director at the **helm** of the company, we'll be successful.
Mit dem neuen Manager am **Ruder** unserer Gesellschaft werden wir erfolgreich sein.

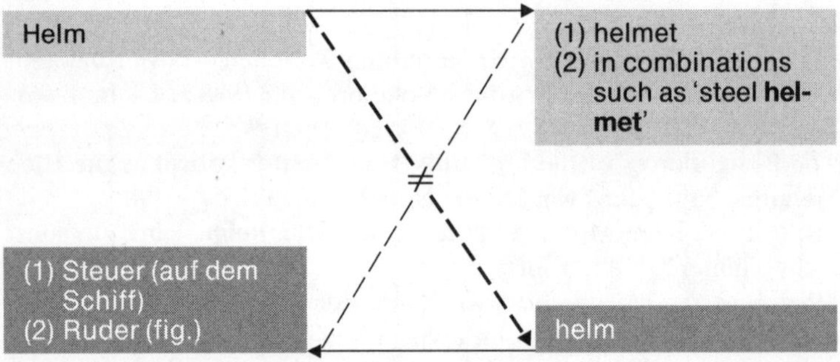

FALSE FRIENDS IN CONTEXT

Going on Holiday

Beverley, aged 15, had told her parents she wanted to go on a fortnight's sailing holiday with Keith, her boyfriend.
When Beverley met Keith again he asked her, "What did they say?"
"Dad said it's all right as long as I stay at the ________ (1) of the boat. And Mum said it's all right with her as long as I wear a crash ________ (2)."

SOLUTION

(1) helm (2) crash **helmet**

"I am saving for my own yacht. I've already bought the helm for a start."

HOSE ≠ hose

hose [həʊz]

HOSE
(für Männer)

trousers etc.

HOSE: (1) (für Männer) (a pair of) trousers (BE), (a pair of) pants (mainly AE)
(2) (kurze Freizeit-**Hose**) shorts

Note: '**Trousers**', '**pants**' and '**shorts**' are plural nouns even if the singular 'eine **Hose**' may be meant in German. '**Slacks**' may also be found, but it is now somewhat old-fashioned.

(1) "Du siehst komisch in der Kord**hose** aus", befand die Freundin des Managers. "Sie ist zu ausgebeult."
"You look odd in those corduroy **trousers**," the manager's girlfriend remarked. "They are too baggy."
"Zieh zunächst die **Hose** aus", befahl der Arzt dem Jungen, den er im Begriff war zu untersuchen.
"Take off your **pants** first," the doctor told the young boy he was going to examine.
(2) "Zieh doch deine Freizeit-**Hose** an. Wir sind in den Ferien", drängte ihn seine Frau.
"Put on your **shorts**, we're on holiday," his wife urged him.

Note: Strumpf**hose** = (a pair of) tights
Nylon-Strumpf**hose** = panty **hose** (mainly AE)
"Barbara Bush is real lady, a sort of a Harry Truman in **panty hose**," the show host described her in 'Tonight'.
'die **Hosen** anhaben' (koll.) = wear the **pants**
You can tell that she **wears the pants** in the Hogan family.

but: kleine Wind**hose** (nur auf dem Land) = dust whirl, dust devil
mittlere Wind**hose** (über Land oder Wasser) = whirlwind
starke Wind**hose** (auf dem Land) = tornado

hose: (1) (Wasser- etc.) Schlauch
(2) '-**schlauch**' (in combinations)

Note: '**Hose**pipe' is also used for '**hose**'.

(1) "I'll take out the **hose** and give everything a rinse," said the mechanic.
"Ich hole den **Schlauch** heraus und spüle alles ab", sagte der Monteur.
(2) The firemen used all their water-**hoses** to fight the forest fire, but they didn't get it under control.
Die Feuerwehrleute benutzten alle ihre Wasser**schläuche**, um den Waldbrand zu bekämpfen, aber sie bekamen ihn nicht in den Griff.
"I'll get the plastic **hose** from the garage and water the garden," her husband announced after dinner.
"Ich hole den Plastik**schlauch** aus der Garage und wässere den Garten", kündigte ihr Mann nach dem Essen an.

Note: fire **hose** = Feuerwehr**schlauch**
but: rubber dinghy = **Schlauch**boot

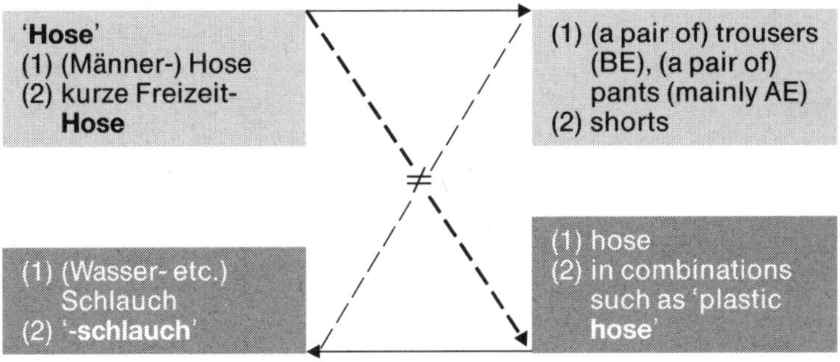

FALSE FRIENDS IN CONTEXT

A Clever Solicitor – Caught Out

Fred (reads out a newspaper headline):
"Clever Solicitor Obtains £ 10 Million by Fraud". Really!
Pat: How did he manage that?
Fred: He dealt in property and investments and over ten years managed to fiddle the money from his clients.
Pat: How did they catch him then?

Fred: Believe it or not, by his ________ (1). In addition to being a solicitor he was on the board of 14 companies, and he had the habit of wearing the same type of ________ (2) wherever he was.
Pat: Really?
Fred: One day a business competitor, recognising his ________ (3), realised that the man was both a solicitor and a director of a rival firm. And his wife confirmed that he always wore the same type of ________ (4).
Pat: Was the solicitor put behind bars?
Fred: When the net began to close he bought a length of ________ (5), attached it to his car exhaust and gassed himself – as usual wearing the same type of ________ (6).
Pat: How amazing!
Fred: Even in the last deal of his life he cheated. He paid for the ________ (7) pipe with a credit card – and the payment bounced.

SOLUTION

(1) trousers (2) trousers (3) trousers (4) trousers (5) length of **hose**
(6) type of **trousers** (7) **hose** pipe

ISOLIERT ◑ isolated

isolated [ˈaɪsəleɪtɪd] .... **ISOLIERT** (gegen Hitze, Kälte etc.)

insulated [ˈɪnsjulertɪd] ——— **ISOLIERT** (gegen Hitze, Kälte etc.)

ISOLIERT: (1) (Elektr.: abisoliert gegen) insulated (against)
(2) (gegen Hitze, Kälte etc. isoliert) insulated (against)

(1) Das Elektrokabel Ihres Rasenmähers war an einer Stelle schlecht **isoliert**; deshalb lief er manchmal nicht richtig.
The electric cable of your lawn-mower was badly **insulated** in one place, and that's why it sometimes didn't work properly.
(2) Viele Häuser sollten besser **isoliert** werden, da viel Heizwärme durch die Fenster, Wände und das Dach verloren geht.
Many houses need to be better **insulated**, as much of the heat escapes through the windows, walls and roof.

Note: The noun is **insulation**.
The first floors of the new houses are built of concrete, which is expensive but good for sound **insulation**.

isolated: (1) (verb) feel isolated: sich isoliert fühlen
(2) (verb) be isolated: isoliert sein, isoliert leben
(3) (med.) be isolated (from): isoliert werden (von)
(4) (adj.) abgelegen
(5) '**Einzel-**' (in combinations)

(1) The couple had felt too **isolated** in the anonymous city, so they decided to move to a small town.
Das Ehepaar hatte sich in der anonymen Großstadt zu **isoliert** gefühlt; aus diesem Grunde entschlossen sie sich, in eine Kleinstadt zu ziehen.
(2) The former actor had been too **isolated** since his wife's death.
Der frühere Schauspieler hatte seit dem Tode seiner Frau zu **isoliert** gelebt.
(3) The patient had to be **isolated** from the others because he had jaundice.

Der Patient mußte von den anderen **isoliert** werden, weil er Gelbsucht hatte.
(4) Gordon was frogmarched to an **isolated** spot and then murdered.
Gordon wurde an einen **abgelegenen** Ort im Polizeigriff abgeführt und dann ermordet.
(5) The air raid was an **isolated** operation.
Der Luftangriff war eine **Einzel**aktion.

Note: The noun is **isolation**.
The cancer patient had to spend the last few weeks in utter **isolation**.

but: (weather) **isolated** = vereinzelt
The weather in England will be bright at first with **isolated** showers later which will be mainly in the west.

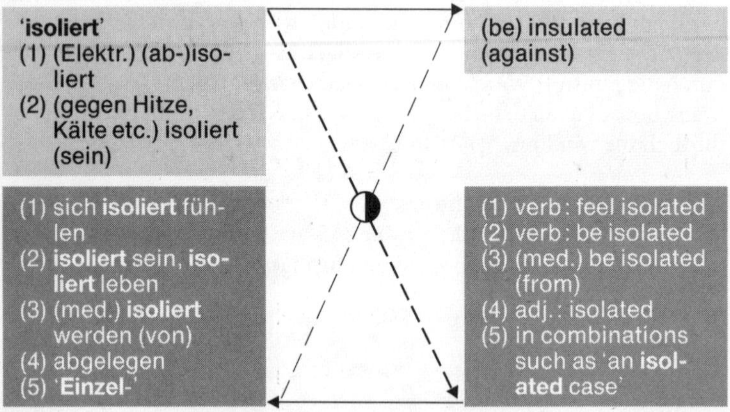

FALSE FRIENDS IN CONTEXT

How do you Stop it?

Mr. Parkin, a widower, had been ________ (1) for the last thirty years or so. At first he enjoyed living on his own on the ________ (2) cliff-top. But over the years he began to feel lonely in his ________ (3) cottage. And in the winter he felt the cold as the walls were badly ________ (4).

But one day Old Parkin decided to go to the nearest town to have a look round. He was surprised when a car driver stopped to give him a lift into town. It was the first time he had been in a car, and he was astonished how fast the car could go – 20 miles an hour. He was also surprised when the car suddenly left the road and crashed into an oak tree.
As the driver and the car did not move, he got out of the car after a while. "Thank you for the lift," he said to the driver after climbing out. "But how do you stop when there are no oak trees about?"

SOLUTION

(1) isolated (2) isolated (3) isolated (4) insulated

MAJOR ≠ mayor

mayor [meə]

major [ˈmeɪdʒə]

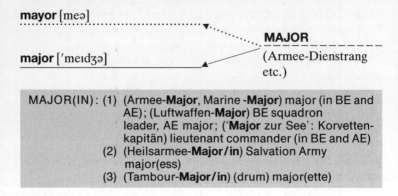

MAJOR
(Armee-Dienstrang etc.)

MAJOR(IN): (1) (Armee-**Major**, Marine -**Major**) major (in BE and AE); (Luftwaffen-**Major**) BE squadron leader, AE major; ('**Major** zur See': Korvettenkapitän) lieutenant commander (in BE and AE)
(2) (Heilsarmee-**Major/in**) Salvation Army major(ess)
(3) (Tambour-**Major/in**) (drum) major(ette)

(1) Ein umherfliegender Eisbrocken einer Lawine tötete **Major** Hugh Lindsay, einen Freund von Prinz Charles, während eines Skiurlaubs in Klosters.
A flying lump of ice from an avalanche killed **Major** Hugh Lindsay, a friend of Prince Charles, on a skiing holiday at Klosters.
Während der Golfkrise wurde der Luftwaffen-**Major** nach Saudi-Arabien versetzt.
During the Gulf crisis our **squadron leader** was stationed in Saudi Arabia.
Er war sechs Jahre '**Major** zur See' (= Korvettenkapitän) auf einem Zerstörer.
He was **lieutenant commander** on a destroyer for six years.
(2) Mrs. Birtles, 68, ist eine ehemalige Heilsarmee-**Majorin**.
Mrs. Birtles, 68, is a former Salvation Army **majoress**.
(3) Helen ist seit einem halben Jahr Tambour-**Majorin** beim neuen Musikkorps; sie ist äußerst erfolgreich gewesen.
Helen has been a **majorette** with the new band for six months; she has been extremely successful.

Note: A British **major** is an army officer ranking above a captain (= Hauptmann) and below a lieutenant-colonel (= Oberstleutnant); the same applies to the Royal Marines and the US Marine Corps as well as the US Army and the US Air Force (but **not** the Royal Air Force).

A Royal Air Force **squadron leader** (= Luftwaffen-**Major**) corresponds to the rank of **major** in the US Air Force. In the Royal Air Force a **squadron leader** is an officer ranking above a **flight lieutenant** (= Hauptmann der Luftwaffe) and below a **wing commander** (= Oberstleutnant der Luftwaffe).

Compare: The term **major** exists neither in the Royal Navy nor in the US Navy. The corresponding rank in the Royal Navy as well as US Navy is **lieutenant commander** (= Korvettenkapitän). It is an officer ranking above a **lieutenant** (= Kapitänleutnant) and below a **commander** (= Fregattenkapitän).

A **major(ess)** in the Salvation Army is an officer ranking above a **senior captain** and below a **senior major(ess)**.

but: '**major**' may also be used as an adjective meaning '**Haupt-**'; **bedeutend**; **größer**

major road ahead = Achtung **Haupt**verkehrsstraße
a **major** composer = ein **bedeutender** Komponist
a **major** obstacle = ein **größeres** Hindernis

mayor(ess): Bürgermeister(in)

To people's general surprise David Dinkins became New York's first black **mayor**.
Zur allgemeinen Überraschung wurde David Dinkins New Yorks erster schwarzer **Bürgermeister**.
The **Mayoress** of Cambridge visited Heidelberg during the 600th anniversary celebrations of the University; she came as a representative of Heidelberg's twin town.
Die **Bürgermeisterin** von Cambridge besuchte Heidelberg während der 600-Jahr-Feierlichkeiten der Universität; sie kam als Abgesandte von Heidelbergs Partnerstadt.
The President of the Republic of India was entertained at a banquet by the Lord **Mayor** of London at the Guildhall.
Der Präsident der Republik Indien wurde vom Ober**bürgermeister** von London in der Guildhall zu einem Bankett empfangen.
The acting **mayor** said, "Now the suspended **mayor** can begin to clear his name."
Der stellvertretende **Bürgermeister** sagte: "Jetzt kann der amtsenthobene **Bürgermeister** beginnen, gegen die Anschuldigungen vorzugehen."

Note: lady **mayoress** = offizielle Begleiterin des '**mayor**'
At the reception the **lady mayoress** welcomed the guests.
A mayor may choose a female companion who may or may not be his wife as '**lady mayoress**'.

Compare: Unlike Germany where the **mayor** of a city receives a regular income, in England it is a position of honour which carries no salary.

but: A mayor in Scotland is called **provost**.

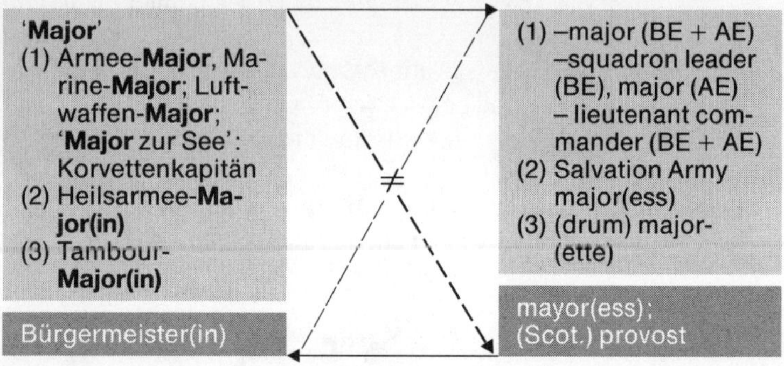
'Major'
(1) Armee-Major, Marine-Major; Luftwaffen-Major; 'Major zur See': Korvettenkapitän
(2) Heilsarmee-Major(in)
(3) Tambour-Major(in)
Bürgermeister(in)
≠
(1) –major (BE + AE) –squadron leader (BE), major (AE) – lieutenant commander (BE + AE)
(2) Salvation Army major(ess)
(3) (drum) major-(ette)
mayor(ess); (Scot.) provost

FALSE FRIENDS IN CONTEXT

Forms of Identity

Mistaken Identity

The inevitable happened. The ________ (1) suddenly appeared in the guardroom. He found it empty except for a private, who, in shirt and jeans, was smoking a cigar in one corner.
"Where is the officer on duty?" demanded the ________ (2).
"He went across to the officers' mess, sir," replied the private.
"And where are the other sentries?" he continued.
"They went across to the canteen, sir."
"Then what are you here for?" shouted the ________ (3).
"I'm here because I'm the prisoner," was the answer.

SOLUTION

(1) major (2) major (3) major

Black Identity

A young black man in a jogging suit called out, "Norm Rice for ________ (4)? What a joke. No black man can ever be elected ________ (5) in this city." "Why not? You wait and see," was all the black candidate was able to answer.
The young black man was wrong – Rice won easily, becoming the first black ________ (6) of Seattle.

SOLUTION

(4) mayor (5) mayor (6) Mayor

"Slow down, darling. Major obstacle ahead!!"

MORAL ◑ moral

moral [ˈmɒrəl]

MORAL
(innere Einstellung)

morale [məˈra:l]

MORAL: (1) (innere Einstellung einer Truppe etc.; Geist einer Mannschaft etc.) morale
(2) in combinations such as '**morale** booster', 'troop **morale**'
(3) (**Moral**prinzipien, **Moral**vorstellungen) morals (pl.)

(1) Am dritten Tag, nachdem unser Schiff gekentert war, fingen wir acht Fische, und unsere **Moral** begann gegen alle Vernunft zu steigen.
On the third day after our ship had capsized we caught eight fish and our **morale** began, against all logic, to rise.
"Sechs Niederlagen in Folge haben die **Moral** unserer Mannschaft untergraben", gestand der Trainer von Blackpool ein.
"Six defeats in a row have undermined the **morale** of our team," the Blackpool coach admitted.
(2) Die Kampf**moral** der britischen Gurkha-Einheiten ist stets hoch gewesen.
The battle **morale** of the British Gurkha troops has always been high.
Die Zeitungsanzeige soll der **Moral**- und Motivationssteigerung dienen.
The advertisement in the paper will be used as a **morale** and motivation booster.
(3) Public **morals** have declined since the last war.
Die öffentliche **Moral** ist seit dem letzten Krieg gesunken.
"She hasn't got any **morals** herself, but keeps criticising others," said my father.
"Sie hat selbst keine **Moral**, kritisiert aber in einem fort die anderen", sagte mein Vater.

Note: '**morale**' is always positive referring to people's discipline, courage and confidence as in 'public **morale**'.
'**Morals**', on the other hand, is neutral or negative referring to standards of behaviour as in 'public **morals**' or a person who does not mind doing wrong as in 'loose **morals**'.

but: schlechte Zahlungs**moral** = be slow in payment
"Some of my customers **are slow in payment** after the summer holidays," the businessman complained.

moral: (1) Moral (im Sinne von 'Lehre')
(2) (Adj.) moralisch, sittlich

Note: The term '**moral**' can be used as an adjective or a noun.

(1) The **moral** behind the fairy tale should be obvious to everyone.
Die **Moral** dieses Märchens dürfte für jeden offenkundig sein.
(2) The first bra-and-briefs combination seen outside the bedroom caused a **moral** outrage. It was the first Réard bikini on June 5, 1946.
Die erste BH/Höschen-Kombination, die außerhalb des Schlafzimmers getragen wurde, rief einen Sturm **moralischer** Entrüstung hervor. Es war der erste Bikini von Réard am 5. Juni 1946.
The priest had tried to raise the **moral** standards, but had realized how little he could do.
Der Priester hatte versucht, die **sittlichen** Maßstäbe zu heben, erkannte aber, wie wenig er ausrichten konnte.

Note: a **moral** victory = ein **moralischer** Sieg
He was sure to have won a **moral** victory.
but: **moral** courage = Zivilcourage
double standards = doppelte **Moral**

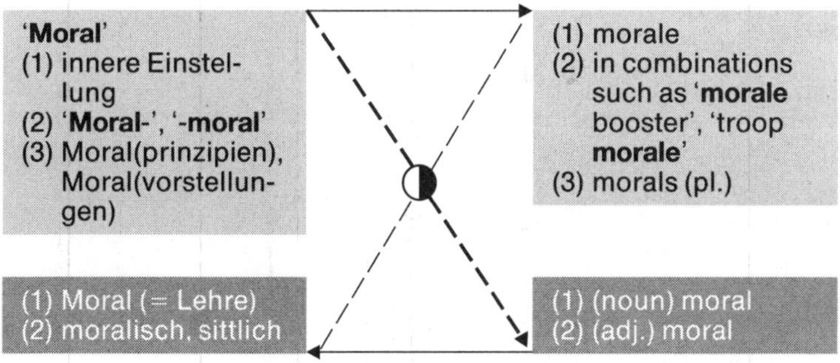

FALSE FRIENDS IN CONTEXT

Getting One's Way on Grammar

Education Secretary (during an interview): Quite frankly, staffroom ________ (1) is low at most schools at present. No positive lead from head teachers, complaints everywhere from teachers.
Education Reporter: An opinion poll showed that a third of teachers are disheartened by low pay and status and, what's more, are thinking of leaving the profession.
Education Secretary: No doubt the ________ (2) among teachers is low these days. It would be folly to suggest otherwise. However, we are in danger of lowering ________ (3) standards still further and creating a negative public opinion.
Education Reporter: But how can teachers be given ________ (4) support in the future?
Education Secretary: Obviously, talking about low ________ (5) in the staffrooms makes it worse. Better pay does not mean better teachers. Accepting trendy teaching ideas without testing them first does not mean better teaching. ________ (6) indignation does in no way support educational reform.

SOLUTION

(1) staffroom **morale** (2) morale (3) **moral** standards (4) **moral** support (5) morale (6) **moral** indignation

PENSION ◑ pension

pension ['penʃn] ··········▸ **PENSION**

guest-house ['gesthaʊs] ——▸ (= kleines Privathotel etc.)

PENSION: (1) (Gästehaus, kleines Privathotel) guest-house
(2) (kleines Privathotel etc.) pension ['pɑ̃:ŋsɪɔ̃:ŋ] (especially on the Continent and Latin America, mostly with French pronunciation)

Note: '**boarding-house**' is generally very down-market – for poor commercial travellers for example – as opposed to **guest-house**, which is more like a small hotel.

(1) Den letzten Sommer verbrachten wir in einer herrlichen **Pension** in Torquay.
Last summer we spent in a delightful **guest-house** in Torquay.
(2) Die Browns sind schon zum zweitenmal in eine kleine **Pension** im Schwarzwald gefahren.
The Browns have gone to a small '**pension**' in the Black Forest for the second time.
Diesen Sommer werden unsere Freunde ihren Urlaub in derselben **Pension** bei Avignon verbringen wie im letzten Jahr.
This summer our friends are going to spend their holidays in the same **pension** near Avignon as last year.

Note: The English term **guest-house** should not be confused with the German word '**Gasthaus**' which is '**inn**' (**mit** Zimmervermietung) or '**restaurant**' (**ohne** Zimmervermietung).

pension: (1) Rente, Pension
(2) '**Pensions-**'; '**Renten-**', '**-rente**' (in combinations)
(**see** Rente ≠ rent)

(1) Since his retirement my brother-in-law gets only a small **pension**.
Seit seiner Pensionierung bekommt mein Schwager nur eine kleine **Rente**.
The Thompsons couldn't have bought their new car from their **pension**. They must have been lucky in the pools.

Die Thompsons können ihren neuen Wagen nicht von ihrer **Pension** gekauft haben. Sie müssen im Lotto Glück gehabt haben.
(2) "The Swiss **pension** scheme was a good investment," the broker commented.
"Der schweizerische **Pensions**plan war eine gute Anlage", merkte der Makler an.
As a Falkland's War veteran he receives an invalidity **pension** on top of his basic **pension**.
Als Teilnehmer am Falkland-Krieg bekommt er zur Grund**rente** noch eine Erwerbsunfähigkeits**rente**.

Note: early retirement **pension** = vorgezogene Alters**rente**
pension age/retirement age = **Renten**alter
pension scheme = Pensionsplan, Pensionskasse; Altersversorgungswerk

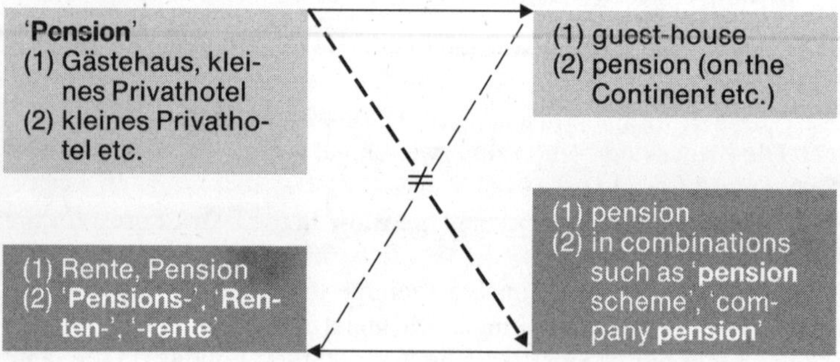

FALSE FRIENDS IN CONTEXT

Avoiding the Cops

Ronny: They're looking for the murderer of a 13-year-old girl.
Julie: The police have issued an identikit picture of the man in the morning paper.
Ronny: More than fifteen officers are combing local hotels, restaurants and ________ (1).
Julie: Your friend Nigel from the ________ (2) in Brighton rang me to say the cops are asking for guest lists. And we haven't kept any records!

Ronny: They'll fine us and close down this ________ (3).
Julie: Listen, I'll replace our sign outside by my antique sign from the last exhibition.
Ronny: Quick, then Julie! I'll put a 'CLOSED' notice with a Wedgwood vase in the front window.
Julie (coming in again): Now slip out the back way, Ronny. Take your ________ (4) book with you. I'll ring you at the pub when the cops are no longer around.

SOLUTION

(1) guest-houses (2) guest-house (3) guest-house (4) **pension** book

FALSE FRIENDS TRAPS TEST 6

NOT SO EASY FALSE FRIENDS

1.a. My girlfriend, looking like an astronaut in her ________, was riding her motorbike (**Helm ≠ helm**).
1.b. With the new manager at the ________, the company has got the right man, at the right time in the right place (**Helm ≠ helm**).
2.a. "I've been working in that ________ for twelve years (**Fabrik ≠ fabric**), but I'm not putting up with the conditions there any longer," one of the workers confirmed his position.
2.b. Terrorism may threaten the ________ of a democracy and its laws (**Fabrik ≠ fabric**).
3.a. Sometimes a busy mother with five children has to expect a little ________ from her husband (**Flirt ≠ flirt**).
3.b. "Don't ________ at the office party (**Flirt ≠ flirt**)," she advised me. But she turned out to be a cheap ________ herself (**Flirt ≠ flirt**).
4.a. Fidel Castro has set up a colony for AIDS sufferers to keep them ________ from the rest of Cuban society (**isoliert ◑ isolated**).
4.b. Each hot water heater comes fully ________ to keep your water hotter for longer (**isoliert ◑ isolated**).
5.a. It wasn't a secret what ________ the Gorbachevs had picked out for the American president (**Gift ≠ gift**).
5.b. "Don't touch the white powder over there. It's ________ that might kill you," the old woman warned me (**Gift ≠ gift**).
6. "The school ________ (**Hausmeister**) will have to watch what's going on in the school building," said the headmaster.
7. To everyone's surprise, the club's president withdrew from office for ________ (**familiär**) reasons.
8. It is very noticeable how my daughter's ________ (**Moral**) has improved since she returned home.
9. When the ________ (**Bürgermeister**) of Torquay appeared on the balcony of the town hall, the crowd began to cheer.
10. "I don't think I need a pair of ________ (**Hose**), all I want is a plastic ________ (**Schlauch**) for the garden," said my uncle, looking at the shop assistant.

ANSWER SHEET: TRUE FRIENDS TEST 6

NOT SO EASY FALSE FRIENDS

1.a. My girlfriend, looking like an astronaut in her **helmet**, was riding her motorbike.
1.b. With the new manager at the **helm**, the company has got the right man, at the right time in the right place.
2.a. "I've been working in that **factory** for twelve years, but I'm not putting up with the conditions there any longer," one of the workers confirmed his position.
2.b. Terrorism may threaten the **fabric** of a democracy and its laws.
3.a. Sometimes a busy mother with five children has to expect a little **flirtation** from her husband.
3.b. "Don't **flirt** at the office party," she advised me. But she turned out to be a cheap **flirt** herself.
4.a. Fidel Castro has set up a colony for AIDS sufferers to keep them **isolated** from the rest of Cuban society.
4.b. Each hot water heater comes fully **insulated** to keep your water hotter for longer.
5.a. It wasn't a secret what **gift** the Gorbachevs had picked out for the American president.
5.b. "Don't touch the white powder over there. It's **poison** that might kill you," the old woman warned me.
6. "The school **caretaker** will have to watch what's going on in the school building," said the headmaster.
7. To everyone's surprise, the club's president withdrew from office for **personal** reasons.
8. It is very noticeable how my daughter's **morale** has improved since she returned home.
9. When the **Mayor** of Torquay appeared on the balcony of the town hall, the crowd began to cheer.
10. "I don't think I need a pair of **trousers**, all I want is a plastic **hose** for the garden," said my uncle, looking at the shop assistant.

PHYSIKER ≠ physician

physician [fɪ'zɪʃn]

PHYSIKER

physicist ['fɪzɪsɪst]

PHYSIKER(IN): (1) physicist
(2) in combinations such as 'nuclear **physicist**'

(1) Sie wurde eine der führenden **Physikerinnen** am Max-Planck-Institut.
She became one of the leading **physicists** at the Max Planck Institute.
Friedrich Dürrenmatts Theaterstück **'Die Physiker'** wird von vielen Fachleuten als sein bestes Werk angesehen.
Friedrich Dürrenmatt's play **'The Physicists'** is considered by many experts to be his best work.
(2) Die neue schall-isolierende Farbe wurde von Atom**physikern** erfunden.
The new soundproof paint has been invented by nuclear **physicists**.

physician: (1) Ärztin/Arzt
(2) Mediziner(in) (in AE mainly used for a doctor)

Note: '**Physician**' is still used in BE within the medical profession; 'doctor' is a more general term.

(1) Dr. Davey, who has been the Queen's homoeopathic **physician**, treats nosebloods and thrombosis with sweet clover.
Dr. Davey, der am Königlichen Hof **Arzt** für Homöopathie war, behandelte Nasenbluten und Thrombose mit süßem Klee.
(2) Professor Edward Wayne, a general **physician** at heart, became Physician to the Queen in Scotland.
Prof. Edward Wayne, von Hause aus Allgemein-**Mediziner**, wurde Leibarzt der Königin in Schottland.

Note: consultant (mainly at a hospital, often = Facharzt in a senior position)
The abbreviation **GP** or G. P. (always in capitals) is still quite

common for **g**eneral **p**ractitioner (normally in small letters) = (praktischer) Arzt

"I was worried after the smear test, so I rang my **GP**," she said.

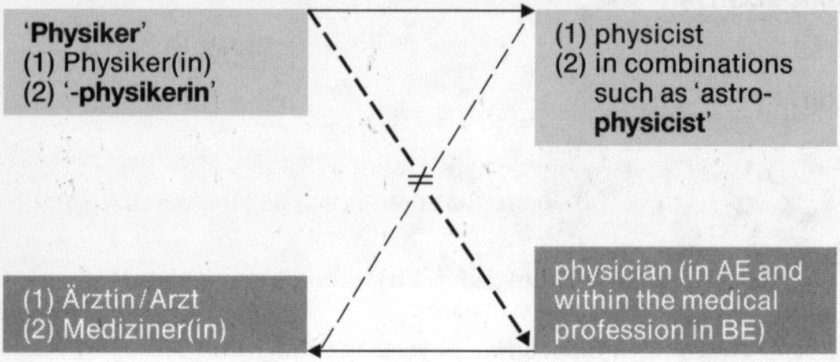

FALSE FRIENDS IN CONTEXT

Two Incidents – Same Profession

A consultant at a leading London hospital was appointed an honorary ________ (1) to the Queen. He announced it by putting up a note on the noticeboard: "Professor *Harmsworth* is happy to announce his appointment as honorary ________ (2) to Her Majesty the Queen." The next day he found a little handwritten note below it: "God save the Queen. Don't **harm** her; she'**s worth** it!"

* * *

The coroner had called in a ________ (3) to state whether a generator could have produced a sufficient electrical charge to have caused the victim's death. After the judge had sent him away he asked the doctor, "Why do you want to change the death certificate?" – "The thing is," the pathologist replied, "I signed my name in the space marked 'cause of death'."

SOLUTION

(1) physician (2) physician (3) physicist

PLASTIK ◑ plastic

plastic ····· **PLASTIK**

sculpture [ˈskʌlptʃə] ← (als Kunstgegenstand)

PLASTIK: (1) (als Kunstgegenstand) sculpture
(2) in combinations such as 'bronze **sculpture**'

(1) "Jede **Plastik** ist handgearbeitet und einzeln vom Künstler signiert", bestätigte der Bildhauer.
"Each **sculpture** is made by hand and individually signed by the artist," the sculptor confirmed.
(2) Der Schauspieler Alain Delon wandte ein Leben darauf, eine Sammlung von Bugatti-Tier**plastiken** aufzubauen, die wenigstens 3 Millionen Pfund wert ist.
The actor Alain Delon spent a lifetime building up a collection of Bugatti animal **sculptures** worth at least £ 3 million.
"Ich mag blank polierte Bronze-**Plastiken** und sammle sie", erläuterte der Kunsthändler seinen Gästen.
"I like polished bronze **sculptures** and collect them," the art dealer explained to his guests.

plastic: (1) Plastik, Kunststoff
(2) '**Plastik**-' (in combinations)

(1) **Plastic**, in my opinion, is one of the curses of modern times.
Plastik ist meiner Meinung nach ein Fluch der Moderne.
Look at the house over there. The window frames are made of **plastic**.
Schau dir das Haus dort drüben an. Die Fensterrahmen sind aus **Kunststoff** gemacht.
(2) "**Plastic** bottles, **plastic** bags and, more recently, **plastic** lemons are gradually becoming an environmental problem," said my friend, criticising the disposal of refuse.
"**Plastik**flaschen, **Plastik**tüten und, seit neuerem, **Plastik**-Zitronen stellen langsam ein Umweltproblem dar", kritisierte mein Freund die Abfallbeseitigung.
The Cambridge crew lost the 1989 Boat Race because they were using **plastic** oars.

Die Mannschaft von Cambridge verlor 1989 die Themse-Regatta, weil sie **Plastik**ruder benutzte.

Note: **plastic** sheeting = **Plastik**folie

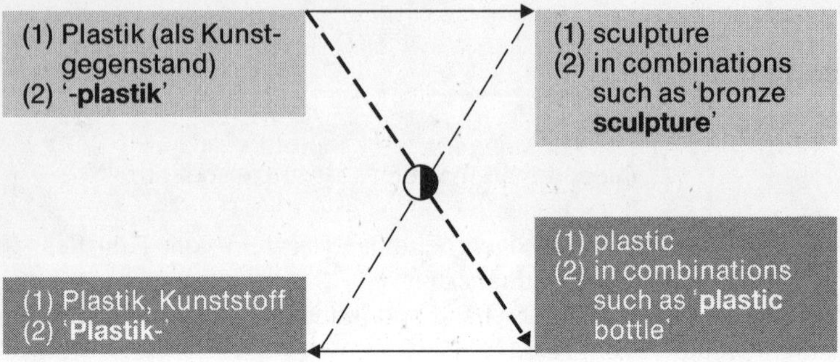

FALSE FRIENDS IN CONTEXT

ID Card Scheme

John: We live in the ________ (1) age and, just imagine, the Tory M. P. for Norfolk North argues he could reduce crime in this country if...
Robert: There's always an 'if'.
John: The wartime ID card was abolished in 1952. Since then crime has risen sevenfold. If...
Robert: Oh, John, not 'if' again.
John (This time without being bothered): every Briton carried a ________ (2) card showing his name, sex, date of birth, address, crimes would be much easier to clear up.
Robert: Would that be the same as a National Identity Card?
John: If the ________ (3) card scheme becomes law, I'm sure they will erect a monument to that M. P., a ________ (4) of him perhaps.
Robert: Unfortunately, this is contrary to my notion of democracy and I'm against it.

SOLUTION

(1) **plastic** age (2) **plastic** card (3) **plastic** card scheme (4) sculpture

POLITIK ◑ politics

politics ['pɒlətɪks]

POLITIK
(= praktische Politik)

policy ['pɒləsɪ]

POLITIK: (1) (praktische Politik, konkretes Vorgehen etc.) policy
(2) in combinations such as 'foreign **policy**'

(1) Intelligenz ist erwünscht, um **Politik** schlüssig darzustellen.
Intelligence is desirable in order to present **policy** coherently.
(2) "Ich stimme mit der Außen- und Wirtschafts**politik** der neuen Regierung nicht überein", verdeutlichte der Parlamentsabgeordnete seinen Standpunkt.
"I don't agree with the new government's foreign and economic **policies**," said the M. P., clarifying his position.
"Mir geht es darum, eine aktive Umwelt**politik** zu betreiben", unterstrich der Politiker seine Haltung.
"The point is I want to pursue an active environmental **policy**," the politician stated, emphasizing his attitude.

Note: The German term '**Politik**' (in the singular) may be rendered '**policies**' (in the plural) into English.
British farmers blame Government **policies** for many of their economic ills.

but: Versicherungsschein, (Versicherungs-)Police = **policy**
Prospero Home Contents is a new, simpler type of **policy** which gives you a greater degree of cover for a lower premium.

politics: (1) (Politik, allgemein oder theoretisch) Politik
(2) '**Politik-**', '**-politik**' (in combinations)

(1) My son is studying **politics** and later on he wants to go into **politics**.
Mein Sohn studiert **Politik**, und später möchte er in die **Politik** gehen.
Politics is a game for pragmatists.
Die **Politik** ist ein Spiel für Pragmatiker.
(2) "Some things should be above party **politics**," stated the Environment Secretary.

"Einige Dinge sollten über der Partei**politik** stehen", stellte der Umweltminister fest.

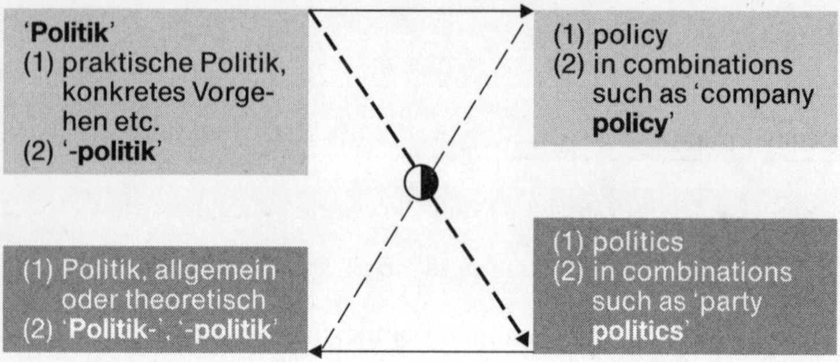

FALSE FRIENDS IN CONTEXT

Mrs. T's Ivory Tower

Member of Parliament: Conservative ________ (1) has failed to address the major structural problems of Britain.
Constituent: I don't agree there. ________ (2) is a game for pragmatists who know that in order to win some you have to lose some.
Member of Parliament: This sort of argument does nothing to improve our national ________ (3). As you know, since the 1987 election British centre ________ (4) has lost its sense of direction. What we need is a strong coordinated ________ (5).
Constituent: Who is strong enough to put Britain's centre back on the map? And who is that strong politician?
Member of Parliament: The answer is quite simple. Owen is the best man centre ________ (6) in Britain has. In the future the SDP will become a strong centre party.
Constituent: Hear! Hear! You'd better tell that first of all to your party's home ________ (7) committee. The trouble is there's no common ground between the extreme centre and the moderate centre.

SOLUTION

(1) policy (2) politics (3) politics (4) politics (5) policy (6) politics
(7) policy

PREIS ◑ price

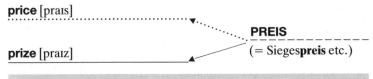

price [praɪs] ········ **PREIS**

prize [praɪz] ———— (= Siegespreis etc.)

PREIS: (1) (Gewinn-, Siegespreis) prize
(2) in combinations such as '**prize** draw'

(1) Es gibt einen ersten **Preis** von 50 Pfund und zwei weitere **Preise** von 10 Pfund für die Einsender der ersten drei richtigen Kreuzwort-Lösungen.
There is a first **prize** of £ 50 and two runners-up **prizes** of £ 10 for the senders of the first three correct crossword solutions.
Die **Preise** wurden den Siegern im Barbican Center in London überreicht.
The **prizes** were presented to the winners in the Barbican Centre in London.
(2) Steffi Graf gewann im Jahre 1988 mehr als 1,5 Millionen Dollar an **Preis**geld.
Steffi Graf won more than $ 1.5 million in **prize** money in 1988.
Den Trost**preis** erhielt die Mannschaft von Luxemburg.
The consolation **prize** went to the team from Luxembourg.

Note: **Preis**richter (bei Musik-, Schönheits- und bestimmten Sportwettbewerben, z. B. beim Eiskunstlauf) = judge(s)
Preisskat = competition skat
ein **preis**gekrönter Autor = a **prize**-winning author

price: (1) (Verkaufs-, Laden-) Preis
(2) '**Preis-**', '**-preis**' (in combinations)

(1) The **prices** of small cars have gone up in the last few years.
Die **Preise** für Kleinwagen sind in den letzten Jahren gestiegen.
(2) Designer clothes are out of my **price** range at the moment.
Modellkleider sind für mich in dieser **Preis**lage im Augenblick unerschwinglich.
The last **price** freeze led to cut-**price** flights across the Atlantic.
Der letzte **Preis**stopp führte zu Billig**preis**-Flügen über den Atlantik.

Note: fare = Fahr**preis** (Bus-, Flug**preis** etc.)
"London's bus and Tube **fares** went up by more than 12 per cent last January. Train **fares** went up in February and air **fares** in May, but there's been no pay rise," grumbled a man in the queue.
at cost **price** = zum Selbstkosten**preis**
drop in **prices** = **Preis**senkung
slump in **prices** = **Preis**sturz
but: bargain offer = **Preis**schlager

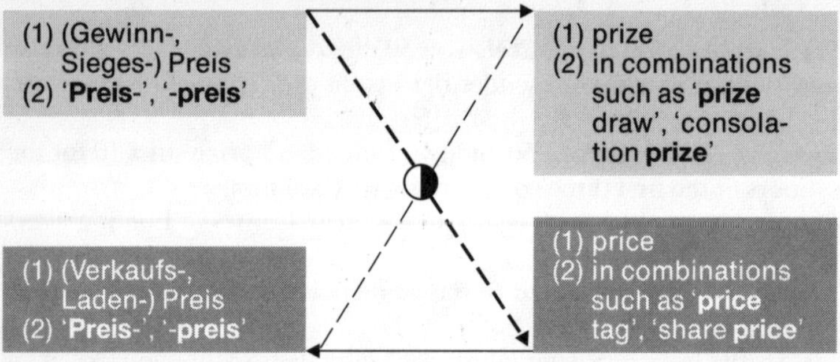

FALSE FRIENDS IN CONTEXT

Value for Money

Mr. Atkin was walking down the main street in Doncaster when a beggar came up to him and asked, "Got a quid for me? Haven't had anything to eat since yesterday morning."
To get rid of him, Mr. Atkin gave him a pound and went away. The following week Mr. Atkin happened to walk down the main street in Doncaster on the same day and at the same time. Again, someone came up to him and asked in a familiar voice, "Got two quid for me? Haven't had anything to eat since yesterday morning."
It was the same beggar he had given a pound to a week before. "Wasn't it last week I gave you a pound, and now you want two. Why's that?" Mr. Atkin wanted to know.
"Well, ________ (1) have gone up since then. Bus ________ (2), too," the beggar replied.

SOLUTION

(1) prices (2) bus **fares**

"The bus fares went up – and so did I!!"

PROSPEKT ≠ prospect

prospect [prɒspekt]

PROSPEKT

prospectus [prəˈspektəs]

PROSPEKT: (1) (meist: kurzer Informations-, Werbeprospekt) leaflet
(2) (meist: längerer Informations-, Werbeprospekt) brochure
(3) (meist: detaillierter Verkaufsprospekt) prospectus

(1) In der Post waren heute so viele **Prospekte**. Ich habe sie alle bis auf einen **Prospekt** von der Olympiastadt Barcelona weggeworfen.
There were so many **leaflets** in the post today. I threw all of them away except one **leaflet** from the Olympic city of Barcelona.
(2) Leider ist unser Reise**prospekt** für nächsten Sommer noch nicht erschienen, aber es steht hier ein Informations**prospekt** zur Verfügung.
Unfortunately our holiday **brochure** for next summer is not yet available, but we have an information **brochure** here.
(3) In dem **Prospekt** wurde Anlegern 60% des Brutto-Gewinns angeboten.
In the **prospectus** investors were offered 60 p. c. of the gross profits.

prospect: (1) Aussicht, Chance
(2) (aussichtsreicher) Kandidat, Mitbewerber (im Sport)

(1) He was 55 now. He knew he had no **prospect** of finding a new job at his age.
Er war jetzt 55. Er wußte, er hatte keine **Aussichten**, in seinem Alter eine neue Stellung zu finden.
"Your **prospects** of leaving court with any liberty are extremely slight," threatened the judge.
„Ihre **Chancen**, den Gerichtssaal in Freiheit zu verlassen, sind äußerst gering", drohte der Richter.
(2) Glasgow Rangers is a likely **prospect** for the UEFA Cup this year.
Glasgow Rangers ist ein aussichtsreicher **Kandidat** für den UEFA-Pokal in diesem Jahr.

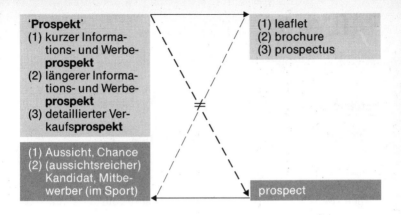

'Prospekt'
(1) kurzer Informations- und Werbe**prospekt**
(2) längerer Informations- und Werbe**prospekt**
(3) detaillierter Verkaufs**prospekt**

(1) leaflet
(2) brochure
(3) prospectus

(1) Aussicht, Chance
(2) (aussichtsreicher) Kandidat, Mitbewerber (im Sport)

prospect

FALSE FRIENDS IN CONTEXT

An Environmental Outlook

Before their holiday they had studied a lot of ________ (1) at home. Now Gladys and Gary are spending their first night in their holiday cottage. Suddenly Gladys wakes up feeling uncomfortable. She puts on the bedside lamp.
Gladys: Oh no, Gary, the rain is dripping down from the ceiling! Nice ________ (2), I must say.
Gary (sleepily): Never mind, Gladys. The ________ (3) said there's running water in all the rooms...
Next morning they happen to look out of the window at the wet street and overhear two street sweepers who are standing there:
First Sweeper: Where has all the paper come from? It wasn't here yesterday.
Second Sweeper (looking down at the litter): Oh, they are ________(4) asking holidaymakers not to throw any paper in the streets.

SOLUTION

(1) brochures (2) prospect (3) brochure (4) leaflets

RATE ◑ rate

rate

RATE

instalment

(Abzahlungs**rate**)

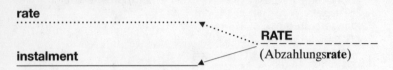

RATE: (Abzahlungs**rate**) instalment, hire purchase

"Wenn Sie die erste **Rate** gezahlt haben, können Sie das Auto abholen", bestätigte der Autohändler nochmals.
"When you've paid the first **instalment**, you can collect the car," the car dealer stated once again.
"Ich hätte gerne den Geschirrspüler auf **Raten** gekauft", sagte der neue Kunde.
"I'd like to buy the dishwasher on **hire purchase**," said the new customer.

rate: (1) Quote
(2) Tempo
(3) Zins**satz**
(4) Zahl, Ziffer
(5) Bezahlung, (geldlicher) Satz
(6) Gebühr
(7) (lokale) Steuer

(1) Towervier Primary School, Bangor, has a good **rate** of success for 11-plus passes.
Die Towervier Grundschule in Bangor hat eine gute Erfolgs**quote** bei den Prüfungen zu den weiterführenden Schulen.
"Why was there such a high failure **rate** in your constituency?" asked the party leader.
"Warum gab es in Ihrem Wahlkreis eine solch hohe Ausfall**quote**?" fragte der Parteivorsitzende.
(2) If the killing of elephants goes on at the present **rate**, World Life Fund will take action.
Wenn die Tötung von Elefanten im gegenwärtigen **Tempo** weitergeht, wird die Welttierschutz-Organisation Maßnahmen ergreifen.
(3) Interest **rates** have been lower in Germany than in England for many years. The hope is that interest **rates** will fall.

Die Zins**sätze** sind in Deutschland über viele Jahre niedriger gewesen als in England. Es besteht Hoffnung, daß die Zins**sätze** fallen werden.
(4) Her normal pulse **rate** was 70 beats per minute, but her pulse **rate** soared to more than 180 after her second kiss.
Ihre normale Puls**zahl** betrug 70 Schläge pro Minute, aber ihre Puls**zahl** stieg auf mehr als 180 nach dem zweiten Kuß.
The birth **rate** in third world countries is considerably higher than in European countries.
Die Geburten**ziffer** in Ländern der Dritten Welt ist beträchtlich höher als in europäischen Ländern.
(5) "We offer top **rates**, career progression and full training," the advertisement promised.
"Wir bieten Spitzen**bezahlung**, berufliche Aufstiegsmöglichkeiten und volle Einarbeitung", versprach die Anzeige.
(6) Postal **rates** will have to go up next year as well as the advertising **rates**.
Die Post**gebühren** werden im nächsten Jahr steigen müssen, aber auch die Anzeigen**gebühren**.
(7) "The council had no legal right to bet with **rate**payers' money," the judge said.
"Der Stadtrat besaß kein gesetzlich verbrieftes Recht, mit Geldern der **Steuer**zahler zu wetten", sagte der Richter.
"Instead they've raised the **rates** recently," several villagers complained.
"Statt dessen haben sie kürzlich die Gemeinde**steuern** angehoben", beschwerten sich einige Dorfbewohner.

Note: In the case of compounds the English word '**rate**' and the German term '**Rate**' often overlap in meaning.
divorce **rate** = Scheidungs**rate**
inflation **rate** = Inflations**rate**
marriage **rate** = Heirats**rate**
Britain has the second highest divorce **rate** in the EC behind Denmark, although, with Portugal, it also has the highest marriage **rate**.

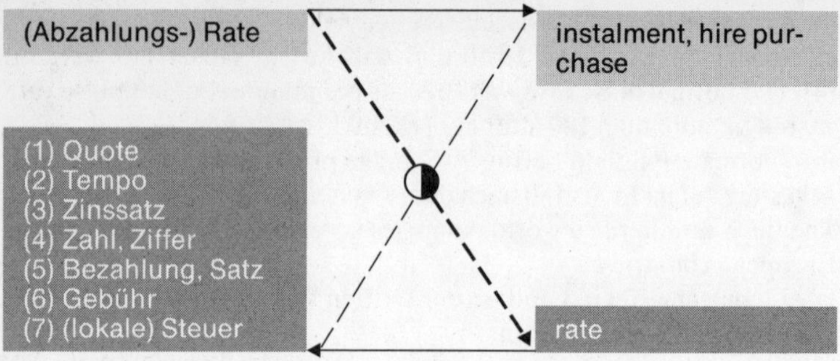

FALSE FRIENDS IN CONTEXT

First-Time Buyers

Anthony: Have you heard about Britain's newest bank?
Paul: You mean the Abbey National?
Anthony: It sold £ 75 million worth of cheap ________ (1) home loans in only 48 hours. That's a record. Our soaring interest ________ (2) are a scandal! Are we to live in mud huts?
Paul: That's right. People are getting used to high interest ________ (3). What's more ...
Anthony: Mind you, the Abbey National has held its mortgage ______ (4) at 13.5 per cent in spite of a 14 per cent base ______ (5).
Paul: Still. The inevitable will happen in the near future. Most borrowers will forget they've bought their new furniture or cars on monthly ________ (6). When interest ________ (7) go up in two years's time many first-time home-buyers will not be able to make both ends meet.
Anthony: Look at other countries! In West Germany mortgage ________ (8) are at 7.5 per cent.
Paul: That's what I keep saying. The government has done next to nothing to help new home-owners in this country.

SOLUTION

(1) rate (2) rates (3) rates (4) rate (5) rate (6) instalments (7) rates
(8) rates

SALAT ◑ salad

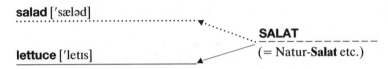

salad ['sæləd] .... **SALAT** (= Natur-**Salat** etc.)

lettuce ['letɪs]

SALAT: (Natursalat, grüner Kopfsalat) lettuce

Du könntest noch etwas **Salat** auf dem Markt kaufen.
You could buy some more **lettuce** on the market.
"Wenn wir **Salat** kaufen, kaufen wir immer Iceberg-**Salat**, auch wenn wir ihn aus Australien holen müssen", lautete die Anzeige von McDonald's.
"When we buy **lettuce**, we always buy Iceberg **lettuce**, even if we have to go to Australia to get it," it said in the McDonald's advertisement.

Note: The plural of '**lettuce**' is simply '**lettuces**'.
Lettuces take up less space and are not so easily spoiled by rain.

salad: (1) (zubereiteter) Salat (als Gericht)
(2) '**Salat-**', '**-salat**' (in combinations)

(1) A tossed **salad** would go well with this," added my girlfriend.
Ein angemachter **Salat** würde gut dazu passen", fügte meine Freundin hinzu.
Why don't you have some more **salad**, Diana? It's so delicious.
Warum nimmst du nicht noch etwas **Salat**, Diana? Er ist so köstlich.
(2) There's also some **salad** dressing, if you like.
Wenn du möchtest, da ist auch noch etwas **Salat**sauce.
For dessert we'll have fruit **salad**.
Zum Nachtisch gibt es Obst**salat**.

Note: cucumber **salad** = Gurken**salat**
endive **salad** = Endivien**salat**
lobster **salad** = Hummer**salat**
potato **salad** = Kartoffel**salat**
tomato **salad** = Tomaten**salat**
ham **salad** = Schinken**salat**

side **salad** = **Salat** (als Beilage)
crispy **salad** = knackiger **Salat**

but: green **salad** = zubereiteter Kopf**salat**
The main course was cold lobster tossed in mayonnaise served with a **green salad**.

Compare: We prepare or eat **salads**, but we sow or grow **lettuce**.
The kidney bean **salad** was lined with spring onions and shredded **lettuce**.

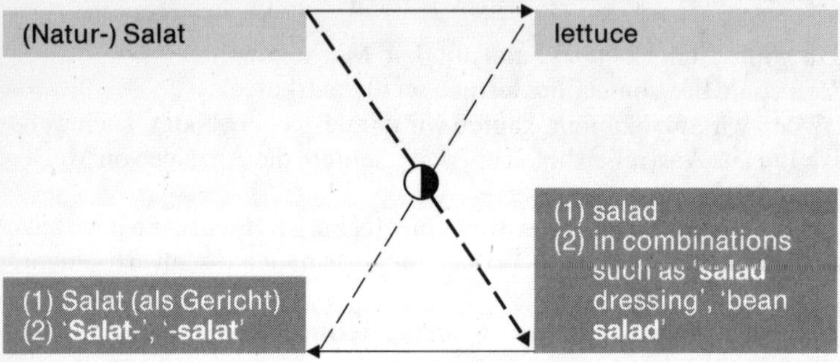

FALSE FRIENDS IN CONTEXT

Taking your Girlfriend out

A German undergraduate had invited a beautiful girl to a first-class restaurant to impress her. When he looked at the prices on the menu his heart sank. "I must make sure she doesn't order one of these expensive dishes," he thought quickly. So he turned to his new girlfriend, saying jokingly, "What will you have, my plump little doll?" and without waiting for an answer added, "Wouldn't you like a ________ (1)? What about some crispy ________ (2)?"

SOLUTION

(1) salad (2) crispy **salad**

SCHAL ≠ shawl

shawl .... **SCHAL** (= Umlege**schal** für den Hals)

scarf etc.

SCHAL: (1) (Umlege**schal** für den Hals) scarf (pl. scarves BE)
(2) in combinations such as 'silk **scarf**'
(3) (Gardinen**schal**) curtain

(1) "Der bunte **Schal** steht dir gut", meinte seine Freundin anerkennend.
"Your coloured **scarf** looks nice", his girlfriend said with approval.
(2) Die meisten Studenten trugen auch im Frühjahr die weiß-roten College-**Schals**.
Most undergraduates wore the white-and-red college **scarves** even in spring.
Mehr als sieben Millionen Seiden**schals**, von Hermes entworfen – jeder mißt 90 cm im Quadrat –, wurden in der ganzen Welt verkauft.
More than seven million silk **scarves** created by Hermes – each measures 90 cm square – have been sold throughout the world.
(3) "Die neuen Gardinen**schals** in deiner Wohnung gefallen mir", sagte meine Mutter.
"I like the new **curtains** in your flat," said my mother.

Note: Kopf**tuch** = headscarf (of finer material)
When it started to drizzle Helen put on her **headscarf** to protect her from the rain.

shawl: (1) (Umhänge-) Tuch
(2) Dreieckstuch

(1) The new fashion this spring is to wear big Indian-style **shawls** sprinkled with glitter dust.
Nach der neuen Frühjahrsmode werden große **Tücher** im Indianer-Stil, besät mit Glitzerstaub, getragen.
The model wore the shiny swimming costume with a net **shawl**.
Das Mannequin trug den glänzenden Badeanzug mit einem **Tuch** aus Tüll.

(2) The old woman wrapped her **shawl** round her shoulders to protect her from the biting wind.
Die alte Frau wickelte das **Dreieckstuch** um die Schultern, um sich vor dem beißenden Wind zu schützen.

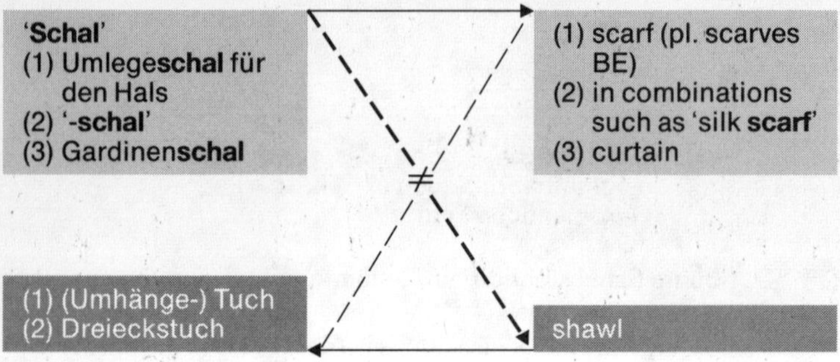

FALSE FRIENDS IN CONTEXT

Caught in Shorts

Personnel Manager: . . . Last week he turned up with a silk shirt and a college ________ (1) round his neck. Small wonder our company director saw red. And now this.
Trade Unionist: What do you mean?
Personnel Manager: Your member, Mr. Baker, reported twice for work in Bermuda shorts in bright green, orange and shocking pink. What if everyone came to work in trendy clothes?
Trade Unionist: I don't see the point of what you're saying. You can't sack him for wearing clothes you dislike.

* * *

Newspaper Reporter: What did your boss tell you to wear?
Mr. Baker: He told me to wear overalls over my Bermuda shorts at work to which I had to agree.
Newspaper Reporter: So they want you to turn up for work in clogs and ________ (2).
Mr. Baker: It was you who said that.

SOLUTION

(1) college **scarf** (2) shawls

No Royal Comfort

On her visit to victims of the North Wales flood disaster in 1990 wind-swept Princess Diana turned her ________ (3) into a head________ (4). She brought comfort to families forced from their homes.

SOLUTION

(3) shawl (4) headscarf

"Unbelievable how you manage to attract attention with a simple shawl..."

SCHATTEN ◑ shade

shade [ʃeɪd] ······▸ **SCHATTEN**

shadow [ˈʃædəʊ] ——◂ (**Schatten**bild, -umriß)

SCHATTEN: (1) (Schattenbild, Schattenumriß) shadow
(2) shadow (fig.)

Note: A '**shadow**' can be cast by people, animals etc. or any bright object, such as a candle, a fire, a spotlight etc. A '**shadow**' usually has a clear shape.

(1) Unser Hund sah seinen **Schatten** vor sich, aber jedes Mal, wenn er seinen eigenen **Schatten** zu fangen versuchte, war er weg.
Our dog saw his **shadow** in front of him, but whenever he wanted to catch his own **shadow** it was gone.
(2) Nach drei Jahren Gefängnis war der Ex-Präsident nur noch ein **Schatten** seiner selbst.
After three years in prison the ex-president was only a **shadow** of his former self.
Frankreichs erste Dame, Danielle Mitterand, trat aus dem **Schatten** ihres Mannes, als sie größere Anerkennung verlangte.
France's First Lady, Danielle Mitterand, emerged from her husband's **shadow** to demand greater recognition.

Note: Lid**schatten** = eye **shadow**
The eye**shadow** went well with her blue eyes.
Schattenkabinett = **shadow** cabinet
but: **Schatten**dasein = **shadowy** existence

shade: (1) (schattiger Ort als Schutz vor der Sonne) Schatten
(2) Schatten (fig.)
(3) Schattierung, Nuance, Farbton

Note: '**Shade**' refers to the light of the sun and protects from strong light or heat; it has no particular shape.

(1) I can't work when it's more than forty degrees in the **shade**.
Ich kann nicht arbeiten, wenn mehr als vierzig Grad im **Schatten** herrschen.
This plant grows well in ordinary soil in sun or partial **shade**.
Diese Pflanze wächst gut auf normalem Boden in der Sonne oder im Halb**schatten**.
(2) Claudia Leistner's performance during the world figure-skating championships put everyone else in the **shade**.
Claudia Leistner stellte mit ihrer Leistung während der Weltmeisterschaften im Eiskunstlauf alle anderen in den **Schatten**.
(3) This word has many different **shades** of meaning.
Dieses Wort hat viele verschiedene Bedeutungs**schattierungen**.
"I'd like a jumper in a lighter **shade** of brown," she said to her daughter.
"Ich hätte gerne einen Pullover in einem helleren Braun-(**Farb-)** **Ton**", sagte sie zu ihrer Tochter.
Eventually she chose a darker **shade** of blue.
Schließlich wählte sie eine dunklere Blau-**Nuance**.

Note: eye**shade** = Augenschirm, -blende
The spectator at the cricket match put on an eye**shade** against the glare of the sun.
light and **shade** = Licht und **Schatten**
but: lamp**shade** = Lampen**schirm**
sun**shade** = Sonnen**schirm**; Markise
Compare: the **shady** side (of a building) = die **Schatten**seite (eines Gebäudes)
the dark (or seamy) side (of life) = die **Schatten**seite (des Lebens)

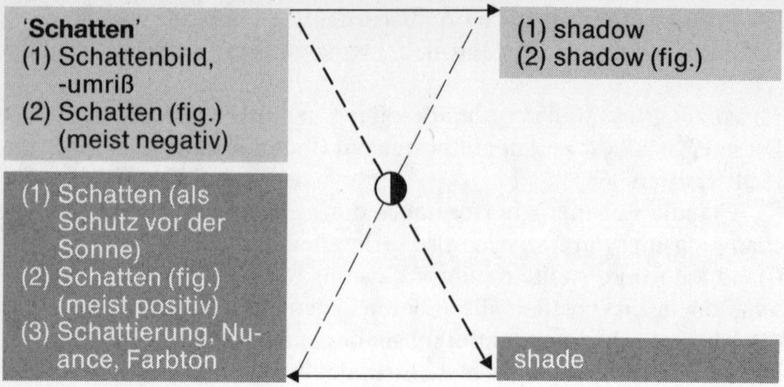

FALSE FRIENDS IN CONTEXT

Trail of Terror

Political TV Correspondent: What impressed you most during your visit to Malawi?
British Prime Minister: I had expected to be confronted with the refugee problem in Malawi, but I hadn't expected between 10,000 and 20,000 Mozambique refugees every month. What's cast a ________(1) over my visit is the terror of Renamo's butchering bandits who call themselves 'freedom fighters'.
Political TV Correspondent: Did you come face-to-face with Renamo's trail of terror?
British Prime Minister: I did. Only yesterday I walked along in the ________ (2) of some ruined buildings. Under the ________ (3) of a Nkuyu tree lay a frightened youth. It was about the only spot offering ________ (4) from the searing heat. I talked to him. It turned out he had been forced to flee because he was certain to be conscripted into Renamo's army. He had told no-one of his intention to flee, not even his own family.
Political TV Correspondent: There are doubts whether the total number of refugees does in fact amount to a ________ (5) over 650,000 in a population of seven million.
British Prime Minister: From what we know the figure is correct as one of the members of the ________ (6) Cabinet who has also been to

Malawi will confirm. It's the result of the trail of terror by Renamo's 'freedom fighters'.

SOLUTION

(1) shadow (2) shadow (3) shade (4) shade (5) shade (6) **Shadow** Cabinet

SCHELLFISCH ≠ shellfish

shellfish ·········· **SCHELLFISCH**

haddock [ˈhædək]

SCHELLFISCH: (1) haddock
(2) in combinations such as '**haddock** fillet'

(1) Das Ramsden Restaurant in Guiseley, Yorkshire, fertigt eine Million Menschen im Jahr ab und hat einen Umsatz von 241 000 Pfund **Schellfisch**.
Ramsden's restaurant in Guiseley, Yorkshire, serves one million people a year and gets through 241,000 pounds of **haddock**.
Wegen verbesserter Fisch-Aufzuchtmethoden kann Lachs bald billiger sein als **Schellfisch**.
Due to improved fish-farming techniques salmon may soon be cheaper than **haddock**.
(2) In Yorkshire besteht Harrys Spezialgericht aus einem **Schellfisch**-Filet und einer Tasse Tee.
In Yorkshire, Harry's Special is a **haddock** fillet and a cup of tea.

shellfish: (eßbare) Meeresfrüchte (= eßbare Krebs- und Schalentiere)

Lobsters, shrimps, crayfish, but also oysters, are all **shellfish**.
Hummer, kleine Garnelen, Langusten, aber auch Austern sind alles **Meeresfrüchte**.
Shelled prawns and other **shellfish** in cheese sauce make a splendid first dish for a supper party.
Entschalte Garnelen und andere **Meeresfrüchte** in Käsesauce bilden einen hervorragenden ersten Gang für eine Abendgesellschaft.

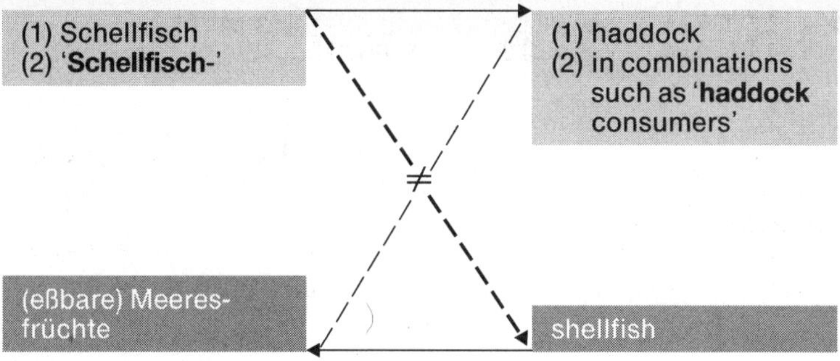

FALSE FRIENDS IN CONTEXT

Keeping the Doctor Away

Helen: Why do women often have goitres?
Doctor: That's a good question. It is often a sign of iodine deficiency and may become serious for people who live a long way from the sea.
Helen: So what do you suggest? Is there anything I could do about it?
Doctor: You simply eat some ________ (1) once or twice a week.
Helen: ________ (2)? But that's not a medicine. That's a fish!
Doctor: That's right. In fact ________ (3) is one of the best remedies for any kind of iodine deficiency. One hundred grams of ________ (4) contains 320 micrograms of iodine. And that's a lot. By the way, ________ (5) such as shrimps and lobsters do not help.
Helen: Thank you for the tip. I'll go and buy some now.

SOLUTION

(1) haddock (2) haddock (3) haddock (4) haddock (5) shellfish

FALSE FRIENDS TRAPS TEST 7

NOT SO EASY FALSE FRIENDS

1.a. "We don't catch as much ________ as we used to," the fishermen told the TV reporter (**Schellfisch ≠ shellfish**).
1.b. "I'd like to have some ________ at the seaside restaurant tonight," she said (**Schellfisch ≠ shellfish**). "Shrimps and oysters are always so delicious there."
2.a. The ________ for that old car was too high, so he didn't buy the Jaguar (**Preis ◑ price**).
2.b. Sakharov became the first Soviet winner of the Nobel Peace ________ (**Preis ◑ price**).
3.a. "The aim of our ________ must be to contribute to development in East Germany," the West German Chancellor stated, facing the TV cameras (**Politik ◑ politics**).
3.b. Actor Michael Douglas intends to follow President Ronald Reagan and abandon the screen for a career in ________ (**Politik ◑ politics**).
4.a. "Could I have a ________ about Bodiam Castle in Sussex?" he asked on the phone (**Prospekt ≠ prospect**).
4.b. If he went to London, his career ________ would be brighter and his social life better (**Prospekt ≠ prospect**).
5.a. "I had ham ________ on the flight from Madrid to London," Mary informed her doctor. "And now I feel ill." (**Salat ◑ salad**)
5.b. In spring our neighbours grow ________ in the back part of their garden (**Salat ◑ salad**).
6. The new professor wore the college ________ (**Schal**) like most of the undergraduates.
7. She would have liked a ________ (**Plastik**) in the garden in front of the French window, but she couldn't afford it.
8. "This type of rose can't grow in the ________ (**Schatten**)," the old gardener told me.
9. Leading ________ (**Physiker**) signed a memorandum in 1945 warning politicians against a nuclear war.
10. Those who work overtime will get increases in overtime ________ (**Bezahlung**, **Sätze**) by over 20 per cent.

ANSWER SHEET: TRUE FRIENDS TEST 7

NOT SO EASY FALSE FRIENDS

1.a. “We don’t catch as much **haddock** as we used to,” the fishermen told the TV reporter.
1.b. “I’d like to have some **shellfish** at the seaside restaurant tonight,” she said. “Shrimps and oysters are always so delicious there.”
2.a. The **price** for that old car was too high, so he didn’t buy the Jaguar.
2.b. Sakharov became the first Soviet winner of the Nobel Peace **Prize**.
3.a. “The aim of our **policy** must be to contribute to development in East Germany,” the West German Chancellor stated, facing the TV cameras.
3.b. Actor Michael Douglas intends to follow President Ronald Reagan and abandon the screen for a career in **politics**.
4.a. “Could I have a **leaflet** about Bodiam Castle in Sussex?” he asked on the phone.
4.b. If he went to London, his career **prospects** would be brighter and his social life better.
5.a. “I had ham **salad** on the flight from Madrid to London,” Mary informed her doctor. “And now I feel ill.”
5.b. In spring our neighbours grow **lettuce** in the back part of their garden.
6. The new professor wore the college **scarf** like most of the undergraduates.
7. She would have liked a **sculpture** in the garden in front of the French window, but she couldn’t afford it.
8. “This type of rose can’t grow in the **shade**,” the old gardener told me.
9. Leading **physicists** signed a memorandum in 1945 warning politicians against a nuclear war.
10. Those who work overtime will get increases in overtime **rates** by over 20 per cent.

SELBSTBEWUSST ≠ self-conscious

self-conscious [ˌselfˈkɒnʃəs]

SELBSTBEWUSST

self-confident [ˌselfˈkɒnfɪdənt]

SELBSTBEWUSST: (1) (allgemein) self-confident
(2) (**negativ** besetzt: zu selbstbewußt, von sich eingenommen) self-assertive
(3) (**positiv** besetzt: gesundes Selbstbewußtsein zeigend) self-assured

(1) Ein Sprecher der britischen Olympia-Mannschaft sagte **selbstbewußt** einem Fernseh-Reporter, er rechne mit mehreren Goldmedaillen.
A spokesman for the British Olympic team told a TV reporter in a **self-confident** manner that he expected several gold medals.
(2) Bob ist ein netter Kerl, aber er tritt ein wenig zu **selbstbewußt** auf, was manchmal seine Freunde verärgert.
Bob's a very good chap, but he's a bit **self-assertive** which sometimes annoys his friends.
(3) "Du hast allen Grund, **selbstbewußter** aufzutreten", riet mir meine Mutter. "Du hast nichts zu verlieren."
"You've every reason to be more **self-assured**," my mother advised me. "You've nothing to lose."

Note: The noun is **self-confidence** = Selbstvertrauen, Selbstbewußtsein.
A Carnegie course will develop your **self-confidence**. You'd better join one.

self-conscious: (1) gehemmt, befangen
(2) verlegen

(1) The young girl didn't reply when spoken to in front of the film camera; she seemed extremely **self-conscious**.
Das junge Mädchen antwortete nicht, als man sie vor der Filmkamera ansprach; sie wirkte ausgesprochen **gehemmt**.

"Singing to such a big audience always makes me a bit **self-conscious**," the new rock star admitted.
"Das Singen vor so einem großen Publikum macht mich immer ein wenig **befangen**", gestand der neue Rockstar ein.
(2) Then came the moment when Jeannie's glance and her **self-conscious** gesture showed me she still loved John.
Dann kam der Augenblick, als mir Jeannies Blick und ihre **verlegene** Geste verrieten, daß sie immer noch John liebte.

Note: The noun is **self-consciousness** = Befangenheit, Gehemmtsein.
Listen. Her **self-consciousness** is a real disadvantage on the catwalk.
but: prejudiced, partial = **befangen** (jur.)
"It wasn't a fair trial. The judges were **prejudiced**," one of the journalists said afterwards.

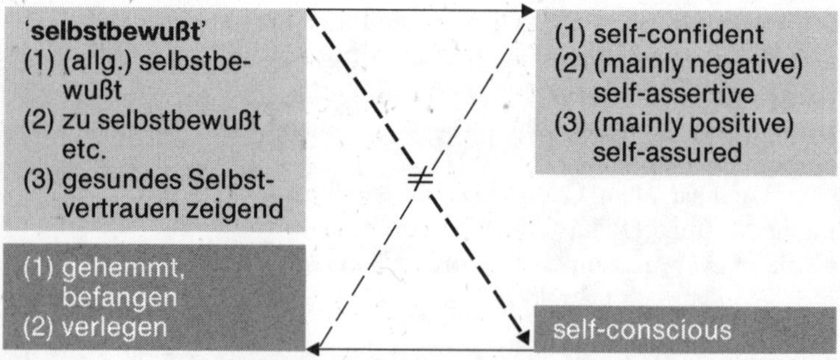

FALSE FRIENDS IN CONTEXT

What about P-Plates?

Young Motorist: I like the idea of introducing P-Plates for drivers who have just passed their test.
Old Motorist: That's certainly a good idea. Certain allowances could be made for them which would make them more ________ (1) as drivers.
Young Motorist: I remember how ________ (2) I was behind the

wheel during the first few months after passing my test. I was always afraid of bumping into the other cars.

Old Motorist: Exactly. A provisional plate would help to create a more a active and ________ (3) driver, unlike the ________ (4) learner who is overawed by the rush-hour traffic. I'm all for the new P-Plates. It would cut down the number of lunatic drivers who should never be allowed on the roads.

SOLUTION

(1) self-confident (2) self-conscious (3) **self-confident** driver (4) **self-conscious** learner

"My husband is still a bit self-conscious while driving his car."

SPENDEN ≠ spend

spend

SPENDEN

donate

SPENDEN (für): (Geld etc. geben für) donate (to), contribute (to)

"Wir haben dieses Jahr schon **für** die 'Gesellschaft für Multiple Sklerose' **gespendet**. Wir wollen daher nicht für den 'Fonds zur Rettung der Seehunde' auch noch **spenden**", wies mein Vater den Mann an der Tür ab.
"We've already **donated to** the 'Multiple Sclerosis Society' this year. So we don't want to **donate** money **to** the 'Save-the-Seals Fund'," said my father, as he turned away the man at the door.
"Aber ich werde am Jahresende noch 200 Pfund **für** die 'Sporthilfe' **spenden**", sagte mein Vater, nachdem der Mann gegangen war.
"But I'll **contribute** another £ 200 **to** 'Sport Aid'," said my father after the man had gone.

spend (on): (1) ausgeben (für)
(2) (Zeit etc.) verbringen (**see** spendieren ≠ spend)

(1) "Even teenagers **spend** a lot of money **on** cosmetics," said the commentator.
"Sogar Teenager **geben** viel Geld **für** Kosmetik **aus**", befand der Kommentator.
(2) We kept separate apartments, but we **spent** a lot of time together.
Wir hatten getrennte Apartments, aber wir **verbrachten** viel Zeit miteinander.

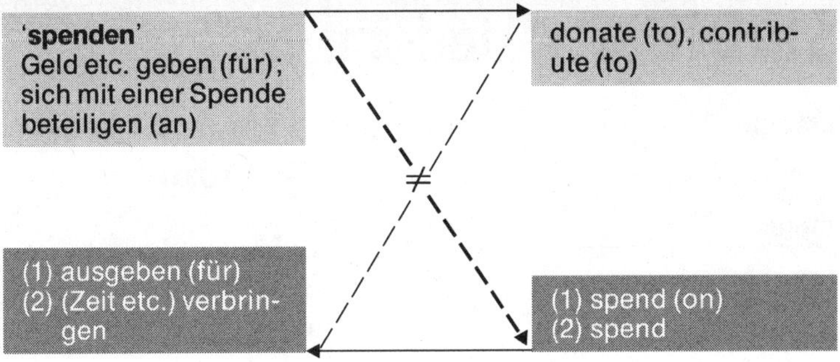

FALSE FRIENDS IN CONTEXT

Knowing the Telephone Directory

Tommy: May I invite you for a drink?
Sandra: No thanks, I'm not interested. ________ (1) the money instead to the Animal Welfare Trust.
Tommy: Look, Sandra, if you give me your telephone number I'll give you a ring.
Sandra: It's in the book. You'll have to look it up.
Tommy: O. K. What's your second name, by the way?
Sandra (calmly): That's in the book as well. You'll just have to ________ (2) some time finding me.

SOLUTION

(1) donate . . . to (2) spend

STADIUM ≠ stadium

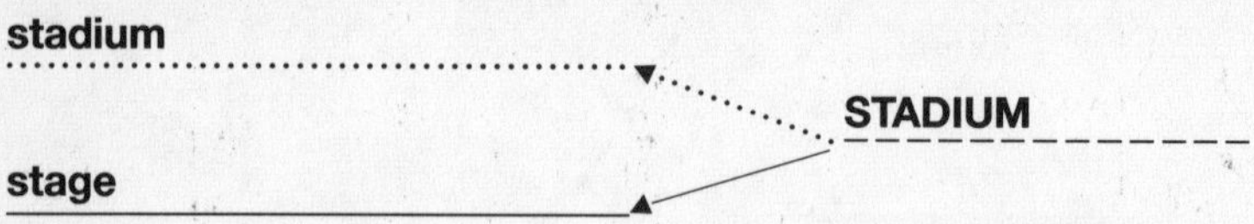

STADIUM: (1) stage
(2) phase (of development etc.)

(1) "Die Verhandlungen befinden sich erst in einem frühen **Stadium**; daher kann man noch nichts über den Erfolg sagen", warnte der Bankier.
"The negotiations are only at an early **stage**; it is premature to say anything about their success," warned the banker.
"In diesem **Stadium** meiner Karriere würde mich nichts mehr völlig umwerfen", gab der Showmaster zu.
"At this **stage** in my career nothing could totally throw me," the presenter admitted.
(2) Die Präsidentschaftswahlen sind jetzt in ihr entscheidendes **Stadium** getreten.
The presidential election has reached its crucial **phase** now.

stadium: (1) (Sport-)Stadion (in AE also **dome**)
(2) '**Stadion-**', '**-stadion**' (in combinations) (**see** Dom ≠ dome)

Note: The plural of **stadium** is **stadia** or **stadiums**.

(1) St. Petersburg, Florida, built a $110 million domed **stadium** without a baseball team to play in it.
St. Petersburg in Florida baute für 110 Millionen Dollar ein **Stadion**, ohne eine Baseball-Mannschaft zu haben, die fest darin spielt.
(2) Fans, who attend **stadium** events spend millions of dollars each year in nearby businesses.
Fans, die zu **Stadion**-Veranstaltungen kommen, geben jedes Jahr Millionen von Dollars in nahe gelegenen Geschäften aus.
When the first marathon runner came into the Olympic **stadium** the spectators received him with a standing ovation.
Als der erste Marathonläufer in das Olympia**stadion** kam, erhielt er von den Zuschauern stürmischen Beifall.

Note: dome = überdachtes Stadion (mainly in the US or Canada)
Georgia is building a £210 million **dome** to keep the 'Falcons' in Atlanta.

Compare: In AE **bowl** is a stadium in which champion football teams play each other such as the Rose **Bowl** in Pasadena.
The world championship games in (American) football are called the Super **Bowl**.
The Rose**bowl** is the Cup Final in American college football.

but: ice **bowl** = Eis(lauf)**stadion** (also used in BE); ice **rink** is the usual word in British English.
"Just ring 0634388477 to find out whether the **Ice Bowl** in Gillingham, Kent, is open," she suggested.

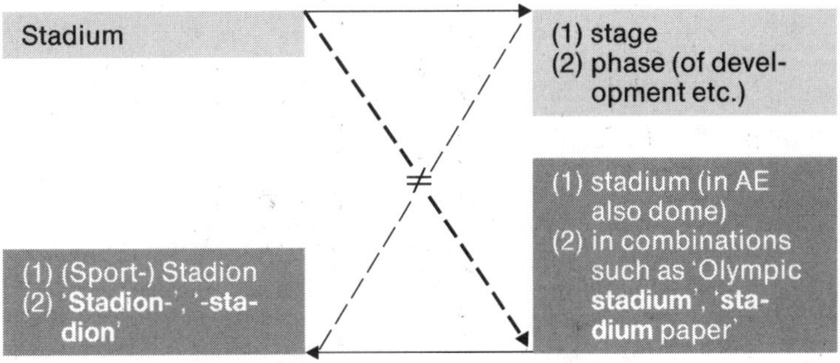

FALSE FRIENDS IN CONTEXT

The Art of Judging

Art student (to art professor): Would you say that I am improving as an artist?
Art professor: Well, at this ________ (1) it is not easy to tell.
Art student: But look at the nude painting I've just finished.
Art professor: If you were to paint a crowd in a football ________ (2) I could tell more easily what your work is like.
Art student: But don't you see, the crowd forms the background to the nude?
Art professor: Well, keep working on it for another three months. At this ________ (3) your technique needs a lot of improvement.

SOLUTION

(1) stage (2) football **stadium** (3) stage

The Texan Dream – An Indoor Country

When Prince Rainier visited the huge indoor sports ________ (4) in Houston, the Astrodome, for the first time, a ten-gallon hatted Texan asked him, "Prince, have you got anything like this in Monaco?" Rainier replied with a smile, "If there was, I would rule the world's only indoor country."

SOLUTION

(4) sports **stadium**

TECHNIK ◑ technique

technique [tek'ni:k]

TECHNIK
(= Technik allgemein)

technology [tek'nɒlədʒɪ]

TECHNIK: (1) (allgemein) technology
(2) in combinations such as 'computer **technology**'

(1) Viele Leute glauben, die moderne **Technik** könne alles bewirken.
Many people believe modern **technology** can do anything.
(2) Das Zeitalter der **Technik** begann mit der neuen Druck**technik**.
The age of **technology** began with the new printing **technology**.

technique: (1) (spezielle) Technik
(2) '-**technik**' (in combinations)
(3) Verfahren, Methode; Arbeitsweise

(1) Dry stone walling is an old **technique** still used in many parts of Britain.
Der Bau von Trockensteinmauern ist eine alte **Technik**, die noch immer in vielen Gegenden Großbritanniens verwendet wird.
(2) This construction **technique** sets a new standard.
Diese Bau**technik** hat neue Maßstäbe gesetzt.
A new relaxation **technique** is now being advertised.
Eine neue Entspannungs**technik** wird gerade wieder angeboten.
(3) In foreign language teaching, advances in teaching **techniques** have been made during the last few decades.
Auf dem Gebiet der Fremdsprachenvermittlung sind während der letzten Jahrzehnte Fortschritte in den Lehr**methoden** erzielt worden.
"Thanks to advances in surgical **techniques** breast enlargement is now a routine matter," the advertisement ran.
"Dank der Fortschritte chirurgischer **Verfahren** ist eine Brust-Vergrößerung jetzt eine Routine-Sache", lautete das Inserat.
The new **technique** appealed to her and she was going to use it in her own company because it was environment-friendly.
Die neue **Arbeitsweise** gefiel ihr, und sie würde sie in ihrer eigenen Firma einsetzen, weil sie umweltfreundlich war.

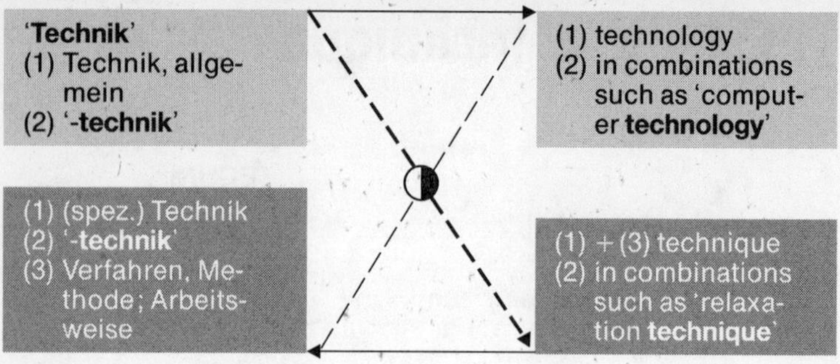

FALSE FRIENDS IN CONTEXT

A Breakthrough in Crime Detection

Scotland Yard Expert: The best way to detect crime is by genetic finger printing. It's the latest achievement of modern ________ (1).
Guardian Law Reporter: I've not heard about it. Can you tell me more about it?
Scotland Yard Expert: More than six months ago a dock worker in the Pepperell case became the first murderer in the world to be trapped by this revolutionary ________ (2). He was jailed for life for having murdered two teenage girls.
Guardian Law Reporter: What kind of ________ (3) do you mean?
Scotland Yard Expert: The pioneer of this new ________ (4) is Dr. Alec Jeffreys from Leicester University. You can detect any crime from the data of genetic finger printing.
Guardian Law Reporter: That sounds fascinating. But what about the cost?
Scotland Yard Expert: A uniformed police officer might help old ladies, but he'll never reduce the crime rate. The cost of that officer is more than £25,000 a year. The cost for genetic finger printing is much lower once the computers are installed. This new ________ (5) is a great breakthrough in crime ________ (6).

SOLUTION

(1) technology (2) technique (3) technique (4) technique (5) technique (6) technology

"Wrong time, wrong place for practising your new relaxation technique! You are fired!"

TRANSPARENT ≠ transparency

transparency [træns'pærənsı] → **TRANSPARENT**

banner ← (= Spruchband)

TRANSPARENT: (Spruchband) banner

Tausende von Bergleuten zogen mit **Transparenten** durch die Straßen Londons und schrien immer wieder ihre Parolen.
Thousands of miners walked with **banners** through the streets of London, shouting their slogans again and again.
"Wir benötigen noch wenigstens zwanzig **Transparente** für die Demonstration", forderte einer der Streikführer.
"We need at least another twenty **banners** for the demonstration," one of the strike leaders demanded.

Note: The word **transparent** [træns'pærənt] does not exist as a noun, but only as an adjective in modern English.
durchsichtig = transparent
"These five cosmetic products are presented in a **transparent** bag," said the marketing manager.

transparency: (1) Folie (für Overhead-Projektor)
(2) Diapositiv (ohne Rahmen)

Note: Ein Diapositiv ist ein 'transparentes, fotografisches Positivbild', das im Gegensatz zum (gerahmten) Dia (**slide**) **ungerahmt** ist.

(1) Our teacher put the **transparency** on the overhead projector and wrote the new words on it with a green felt-tip pen.
Unser Lehrer legte die **Folie** auf den Overhead-Projektor und schrieb die neuen Worte mit einem grünen Filzstift darauf.
(2) The English art dealer Gavin Graham sent a **transparency** of Gilbert Stuart's famous portrait of George Washington to an American art expert, who ruled it was not a painting by Stuart.
Der englische Kunsthändler Gavin Graham schickte ein **Diapositiv**

von Gilbert Stuarts berühmtem Portrait von George Washington an einen amerikanischen Kunstexperten, der feststellte, es sei kein Gemälde von Stuart.

Note: slide = Dia (mit Rahmen)
but: foil = Alu**folie**, Silber**folie**
cooking foil = Back**folie**
kitchen foil = Haushalts**folie**, Alu**folie**
plastic sheeting = Plastik**folie**

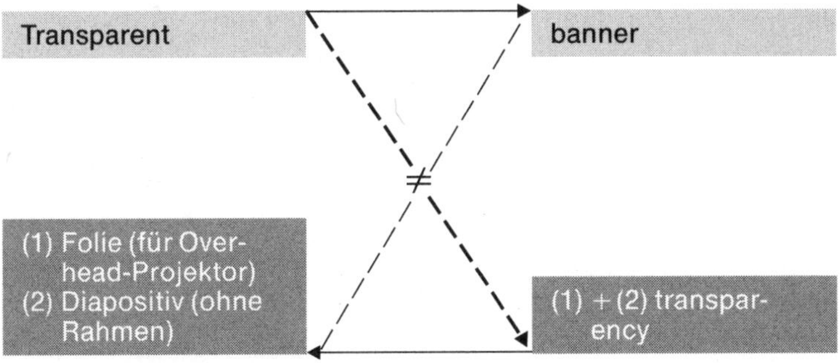

FALSE FRIENDS IN CONTEXT

Washington's Portrait and the Experts

Barry: Did you hear about the art dealer from Notting Hill who bought Washington's portrait in New York in June for £ 1,885 and sold it at Sotheby's in London for £ 302,500 in November?
Mark: How did he manage that?
Barry: After buying the portrait he first made a ________ (1) and sent it to a top art expert in the States, who stated that it was just another copy of the Washington portrait by Gilbert Stuart.
Mark: That's what you'd expect.
Barry: But the dealer traced the last owner of the painting, a Miss Mary Coles, and established that it was a portrait painted by Stuart for one of her ancestors, Judge Coles. It even carried Stuart's original autograph. He kept quiet about his discovery and waited for the November auction at Sotheby's. Once there he insisted on having an

overhead projector in the auction room with a _______ (2) on which the bids for his Washington portrait had to be written down.
Mark: So what happened?
Barry: Washington's portrait fetched a sensational price, £302,500! When he left the auction, his friends put up a _______ (3) with "Three Cheers for Gavin Graham" (that was his name) and "Down with the Art Experts".

SOLUTION

(1) transparency (2) transparency (3) banner

"My husband hates demonstrations..."

VENTILATOR ◑ ventilator

ventilator [ˈventɪleɪtə]

VENTILATOR

fan

VENTILATOR: (1) (electric) fan
(2) in combinations such as '**fan** heater'

(1) Ein **Ventilator** ist die wirksamste Antwort auf Toilettengerüche.
A **fan** is the most effective answer to toilet odours.
(2) Wenn das Wetter heiß ist, kann man Solar-**Ventilatoren** an das Autofenster anklemmen, um die Luft zu kühlen.
If the weather is hot, you can clip solar **fans** to your car window to keep the air cool.

Note: '**fan** heater' ist auch unter den Bezeichnungen 'Schnellheizer' und 'Heizlüfter' bekannt.
Nowadays there are better appliances on the market than **fan heaters**.
but: **Keil**riemen = **fan**belt
Fanpost = **fan** mail

ventilator: (1) (Motor-) Entlüfter, Ventilator
(2) (Ent-) Lüftungsanlage, Lüftungsklappe
(3) (Kühl-) Gebläse
(4) Beatmungsgerät (Med.)

(1) I'm sorry the **ventilator** in the caravan doesn't work. We've got to ring the service engineer.
Der **Entlüfter** im Wohnwagen funktioniert nicht. Wir müssen den Kundendienst-Monteur anrufen.
(2) We'll have to buy a new **ventilator** for the kitchen, the old one has been damaged.
Wir müssen eine neue **Lüftungsklappe** für die Küche kaufen; die alte ist kaputt.
(3) What you hear now is the **ventilator** in the overhead projector.
Was du jetzt hörst, ist das **Gebläse** im Overhead-Projektor.
(4) John's in hospital. After yesterday's accident he can't breathe without the help of a **ventilator**.

John ist im Krankenhaus. Nach dem gestrigen Unfall kann er ohne **Beatmungsgerät** nicht atmen.

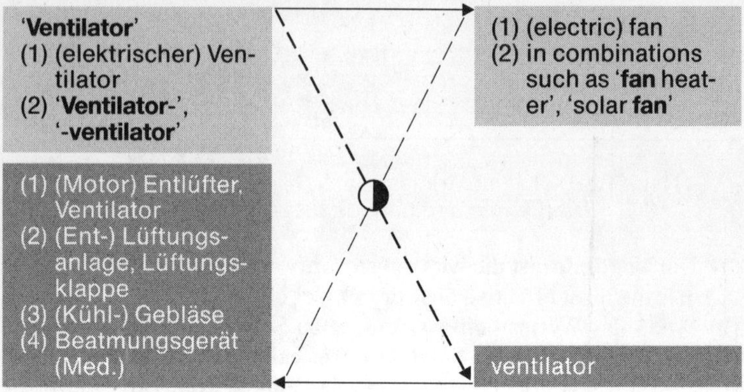

FALSE FRIENDS IN CONTEXT

Golden Days for the Disabled

Social Services Official: This army sergeant has been seriously injured in the latest IRA bomb attack.
Health Services Official: It's a miracle to me how he survived the blast.
Social Services Official: The doctors say he has an iron will and can fight his way back to health.
Health Services Official: He's expected to be kept on a ________ (1) for at least another three days.
Social Services Official: What worries me is he can't breathe without a ________ (2) yet.
Health Services Official: His room is hot and stuffy, so his wife has asked for a ________ (3) to be installed.
Social Services Official: I hope he'll recover soon and I'll say so to the journalists at the reception desk.

SOLUTION

(1) ventilator (2) ventilator (3) fan

VIKAR ≠ vicar

vicar ['vɪkə] .... **VIKAR**

curate ['kjʊərət] ——— (Pfarr**vikar**, Kurat)

VIKAR: (Pfarr**vikar**, Kurat) curate

Note: In der Anglikanischen Kirche ist '**curate**' eine Art Hilfspfarrer, während '**Kurat**' in Deutschland ein katholischer Hilfsgeistlicher mit eigenem Seelsorgebezirk sowie geistlicher Betreuer von katholischen Pfadfindergruppen ist. Einen Kuraten in dieser Funktion gibt es in englischen Pfadfindergruppen nicht.

but: Der Begriff **Vikar** bezeichnet in Deutschland einen katholischen Pfarr**vikar** als Stellvertreter einer Amtsperson oder einen evangelischen Theologen mit 2. theologischer Staatsprüfung, der ein Pfarramt verwaltet, aber noch keine feste Pfarrstelle hat.

Der Bischof von Taunton gab den **Vikaren** Anschauungsunterricht im Predigen, nachdem er eine Gemeinde beim Einschlafen beobachtet hatte.
The Bishop of Taunton gave **curates** lessons in preaching after he saw a congregation sent to sleep.
In dem Prozeß wurde ein Dorfpfarrer beschuldigt, zwei Gemeindemitglieder verführt zu haben, eine davon die Frau seines **Vikars**.
In the trial a village vicar was accused of seducing two parishioners, one of them the wife of his **curate**.

Note: Kurat (bei der Deutschen Pfadfinderschaft St. Georg) = curate
"Most Catholic Scout Troops in Germany have a **curate** for their spiritual needs," added the Scoutmaster.

vicar: (1) Pfarrer
(2) '-**pfarrer**' (in combinations)

Note: The word used in Roman Catholic churches is **priest** or **parish**

priest; the term used in the army, public schools, universities and prisons is **chaplain**. A **vicar** is a clergyman in the Church of England who is fully responsible for his local church.

(1) I went into the library and saw, surprisingly enough, a young man reading Oliver Goldsmith's 'The **Vicar** of Wakefield'.
Ich ging in die Bibliothek und sah zu meiner Überraschung einen Jugendlichen, der gerade Oliver Goldsmiths 'Der **Pfarrer** von Wakefield' las.
(2) "A modern country **vicar** needs a fast car to take eight services in different churches on Sunday," said the bishop.
"Ein moderner Land**pfarrer** braucht ein schnelles Auto, um acht Gottesdienste in verschiedenen Kirchen am Sonntag abzuhalten", sagte der Bischof.

Note: local **vicar** = Orts**pfarrer**
village **vicar** = Dorf**pfarrer**
but: army **chaplain** = Soldaten**pfarrer**
prison **chaplain** = Gefängnis**pfarrer**
school **chaplain** = Schul**pfarrer**
That man had been an army **chaplain** in the Gulf War.
His letter was handed to the MP by the prison **chaplain**.

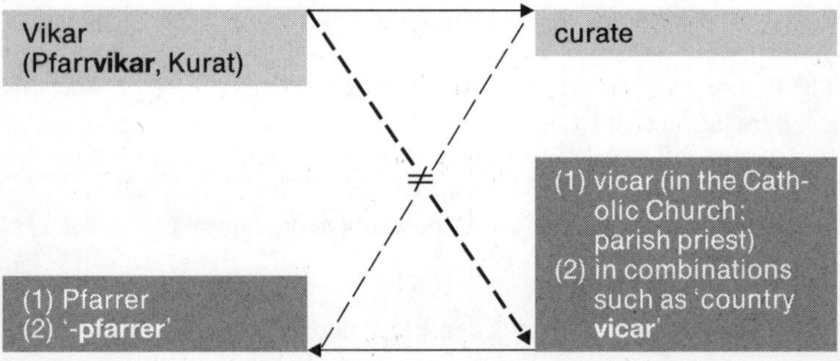

FALSE FRIENDS IN CONTEXT

Pulpit Prattle with a Difference

Report on the First Sermon: A ________ (1) shocked churchgoers by telling them in the middle of his sermon that he was leaving his wife. The ________ (2), the Reverend Trevor Hazelgrove, calmly finished the service before quitting St. Richard's Church in Ham, Surrey. The stunned congregation were told by the ________ (3) he could no longer live with his wife and had to leave the area. For the time being his ________ (4) took over the parish work.
Report on the Second Sermon: A ________ (5) said Mass in a kitchen in memory of Eamonn Andrews, a British TV legend. The ________ (6), Father Barry Murphy, conducted the simple service in the room the former TV star had loved. It was a family tribute of a congregation of five, consisting of his widow, their three children and their housekeeper, remembering the This-is-Your-Life star, a year after he had died in his favourite room.

SOLUTION

(1) vicar (2) vicar (3) vicar (4) curate (5) priest (6) priest

An Ad with a Difference

Last Tuesday I read this advertisement in the local morning paper, "Young Mother's Club. Anyone wanting to become a young mother, contact the ________ (7)."

SOLUTION

(7) vicar

WARENHAUS ≠ warehouse

warehouse

WARENHAUS

department store

WARENHAUS: department store; store

Linda war Packerin in einem **Warenhaus**, bis sie schwanger wurde.
Linda was a packer in a **department store** until she became pregnant.
Der ausländische Besucher konnte kein besseres **Warenhaus** finden; deshalb betrat er Woolworth.
The foreign visitor could not find a better **store**. So he went into Woolworth's.

warehouse: (1) Lager(haus), Lagerhalle
(2) '**Lager**-' (in combinations)
(3) Hafenspeicher
(4) Auslieferungslager

(1) Haven't you seen the old building? Many goods are still stored at the **warehouse**.
Hast du nicht das alte Gebäude gesehen? Viele Güter werden noch immer in das **Lagerhaus** eingelagert.
The old **warehouse** lies on an old industrial estate half a mile from the motorway.
Die alte **Lagerhalle** liegt in einem alten Industriegebiet eine halbe Meile von der Autobahn entfernt.
(2) Das alte Tabak**lager** war zu einem neuen Hotel umgebaut worden.
The old tobacco **warehouse** had been converted into a new hotel.

Note: carpet **warehouse** = Teppich**lager**
factory **warehouse** = Fabrik**lager**
tyre **warehouse** = Reifen**lager**
wood **warehouse** = Holz**lager**
but: ammunition dump (or depot) = Munitions**lager**
refugee **camp** = Flüchtlings**lager**

(3) None of the **warehouses** at the harbour are used any longer.
Keiner der **Hafenspeicher** am Hafen wird noch weiter genutzt.
(4) "I'd like to order this double bed." – "Right you are, sir. I'll ring up our **warehouse** and they'll deliver it to you tomorrow morning, if that's all right with you."
"Ich hätte gerne dieses französische Bett bestellt." – "Ganz wie Sie wünschen, mein Herr. Ich rufe unser **Auslieferungslager** an, und es wird Ihnen morgen vormittag angeliefert, wenn es Ihnen recht ist."

Note: warehouseman = Lagerarbeiter, Lagerhausgehilfe
Warehouseman Neil Barker, 20, was charged with the murder of photographer Dale Campbell.
but: (have) in stock = am **Lager** (haben)
I'm afraid we haven't got these spare parts **in stock**.

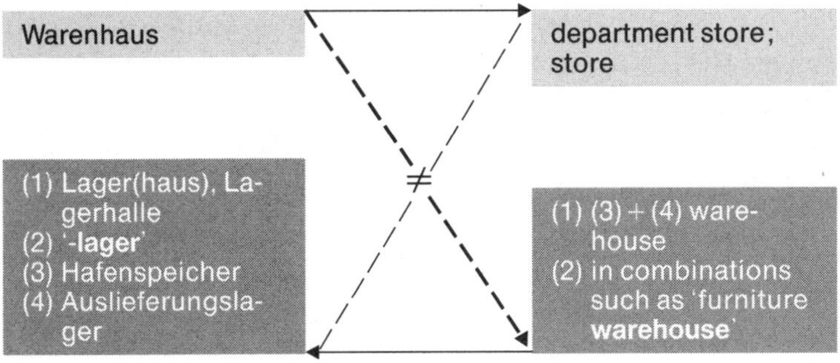

FALSE FRIENDS IN CONTEXT

Reviving Inner Cities

Times Property Reporter: Is it really worth investing £900,000 in an ugly down-market area? What's behind it?
Project Manager: Well, we call it "inner city revival". A particularly good example is South London. "Dirty old Deptford" people used to say. There is lots of land lying unused behind ugly hoardings and buildings. On a grubby corner of the High Street we found an old ________ (1) which had closed down years ago and bought it for a giveaway price together with a forgotten ________ (2) at the back.
Times Property Reporter: How did your project develop?

Project Manager: Then we somehow discovered two rotting ________(3) with views of the Thames and started what is now called Docklands-style ________ (4) conversion. In addition, it stopped those deafening ________ (5) parties causing serious noise and fire risks.
Times Property Reporter: You mean those Acid House Parties with hundreds of teenagers?
Project Manager: Yes. May I show you round the newly developed part of Deptford now?
Times Property Reporter: Certainly, and I'd like to take some pictures to show what the revival of an inner city can look like.

SOLUTION

(1) department store (2) warehouse (3) warehouses (4) **warehouse** conversion (5) **warehouse** parties

ZYLINDER ◑ cylinder

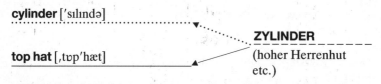

cylinder ['sɪlɪndə]

ZYLINDER
(hoher Herrenhut etc.)

top hat [ˌtɒp'hæt]

ZYLINDER: (hoher Herrenhut etc.) top hat; topper (informal); high hat (AE)

Die beiden Freunde hatten gewettet, die Themse mit **Zylindern** und weißen Handschuhen zu durchschwimmen.
The two friends had made a bet that they could swim across the Thames in **top hats** and white gloves.
Der Gutsverwalter fuhr zu Treibjagden mit **Zylinder** und leistete sich teure Autos – einen aufwendigen Lebensstil, den er nicht aufrechterhalten konnte.
The farm manager rode to hounds in a **top hat** and drove expensive cars – a lavish lifestyle he could not sustain.
“Ich kann es nicht leiden, diesen blöden **Zylinder** tragen zu müssen”, rief Jim aus, “und ich trage ihn nur, um meiner Freundin zu gefallen.”
“I hate having to wear this stupid **topper**,” exclaimed Jim, “and it's only to please my girlfriend.”

Note: **Zylinder** (meist in silbergrauer Seide) = silk hat
(zusammenklappbarer) **Zylinder** = opera hat
zylindertragend, mit **Zylinder** = top-hatted
At Royal Ascot, **top-hatted** gentlemen wrapped tartan travelling rugs round their morning coats to keep off the cold.

but: (kreisrunder) Strohhut, ‘Kreissäge’ = boater
Here was the managing director of New & Lingwood with a **boater** to grace the head of a young Etonian.
‘Melone’ = bowler hat, bowler (BE); derby hat, derby (AE)
Nowadays **bowler hats** are only worn by gentlemen who work in the city.

cylinder: (1) Zylinder (Math., Mech.)
(2) '**Zylinder-**', '**Motor-**' (in combinations)

Note: The adjective is **cylindrical**; the word *cylindric does not exist in English.

(1) A **cylinder** is an object with straight sides and a circular cross-section.
Ein **Zylinder** ist ein Gegenstand mit geraden Mantelflächen und einem kreisrunden Durchmesser.
(2) "There's something wrong near the **cylinder** block," said the mechanic. "But let's check the oil first," he suggested.
"Da ist etwas dicht am **Motor**block nicht in Ordnung", sagte der Monteur. "Aber prüfen wir zunächst das Öl", schlug er vor.
"The new Saab has a trusty four-**cylinder** engine," the car dealer told me.
"Der neue Saab hat einen zuverlässigen Vier-**Zylinder**-Motor", erzählte mir der Autohändler.

Note: be firing on all **cylinders** = in Fahrt kommen, auf Touren kommen
"You ought to be firing on all **cylinders**," our manager described the new developments.
but: oxygen **cylinder** = Sauerstoff-Flasche
During their attempt to find the legendary Lost Cave of Cheddar the two cave divers carried oxygen **cylinders**, radios and food with them.

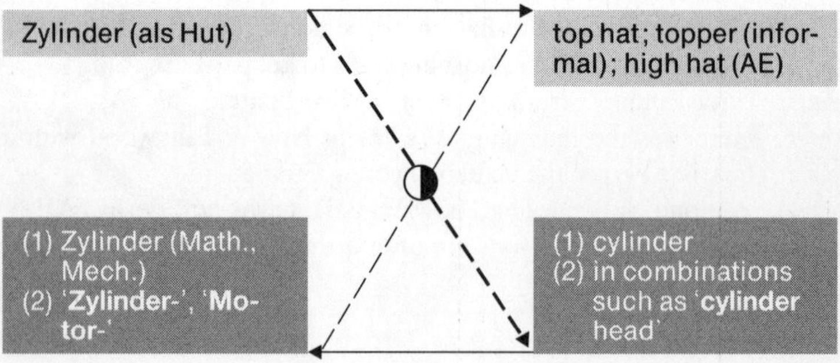

FALSE FRIENDS IN CONTEXT

Recalling Risky Cars

Hundreds of thousands of Vauxhall cars were recalled recently because of faulty brakes. Engineers had discovered that a plastic part on the brake ________ (1) had developed tiny cracks. "The parts will be replaced without charge," the chief executive announced on TV.
Next morning ten private cars arrived at the gates of the Vauxhall works, each of the ten drivers wearing a ________ (2). They claimed their cars had been recalled and demanded to see one of the bosses. They got into their cars again, blocking the entrance to the car factory and waving their ________ (3) to the passing workers. After an hour one of the bosses came to meet them. The drivers' spokesman asked the Vauxhall boss, "What is the best thing to do when the brake ________ (4) of your car gives way?" Before he could answer, one of the bystanders shouted, "Hit something cheap."

SOLUTION

(1) cylinder (2) top hat (3) top hats (4) cylinder

FALSE FRIENDS TRAPS TEST 8

NOT SO EASY FALSE FRIENDS

1.a. Powder skiing is not the best way of improving your ski ________ (**Technik ◑ technique**).
1.b. "I do not believe in modern ________ and never will," the old lady said emphatically (**Technik ◑ technique**).
2.a. They've just opened a new ________ right in the town centre (**Warenhaus ≠ warehouse**). You can even buy genuine caviar there.
2.b. More than fifty people had to be evacuated when a fire broke out in a ________ storing dishwashers and washing machines (**Warenhaus ≠ warehouse**).
3.a. "This is a 1959 Mercedes with a powerful eight- ________ engine," explained the antique car dealer, opening the bonnet (**Zylinder ◑ cylinder**).
3.b. "It's a ________ I want for the wedding," said the bridegroom (**Zylinder ◑ cylinder**). "Have you got one?"
4.a. "Our team is not ________ enough this season to win the competition," the team manager explained (**selbstbewußt ≠ self-conscious**).
4.b. "Tracy has always been a ________ girl, but I'm sure she'll make Tony a good wife," my aunt told her neighbour (**selbstbewußt ≠ self-conscious**).
5.a. "Billions will have to be ________ to protect seaside towns," the Prime Minister announced (**spenden ≠ spend**). "We must learn how to save instead of ________ ," shouted one of the backbenchers (**spenden ≠ spend**).
5.b. "Let's ________ £ 500 to Dr. Barnardo's Homes by washing lorry windscreens," my friend suggested (**spenden ≠ spend**).
6. "You can't back out at this ________ (**Stadium**), John. Hundreds of fans are waiting at the gates of the Arms Park rugby ________ (**Stadion**) in Cardiff," the club manager warned him.
7. Sheila wanted to buy a new electric ________ (**Heizlüfter**) for their seaside apartment, but her husband decided against it.
8. "The ________ (**Vikar**) had refused to pronounce the couple man and wife because he wasn't qualified to do that," wrote the parish magazine.
9. Thousands of dock workers were walking to the city centre carrying ________ (**Transparente**).

10. “After the air disaster I was on a life-support machine for a week and then I was on a ________ (**Beatmungsgerät**),” he told the reporters.

ANSWER SHEET: TRUE FRIENDS TEST 8

NOT SO EASY FALSE FRIENDS

1.a. Powder skiing is not the best way of improving your ski **technique**.
1.b. "I do not believe in modern **technology** and never will," the old lady said emphatically.
2.a. They've just opened a new **department store** right in the town centre. You can even buy genuine caviar there.
2.b. More than fifty people had to be evacuated when a fire broke out in a **warehouse** storing dishwashers and washing machines.
3.a. "This is a 1959 Mercedes with a powerful eight-**cylinder** engine," explained the antique car dealer, opening the bonnet.
3.b. "It's a **top hat** I want for the wedding," said the bridegroom. "Have you got one?"
4.a. "Our team is not **self-confident** enough this season to win the competition," the team manager explained.
4.b. "Tracy has always been a **self-conscious** girl, but I'm sure she'll make Tony a good wife," my aunt told her neighbour.
5.a. "Billions will have to be **spent** to protect seaside towns," the Prime Minister announced. "We must learn how to save instead of **spend**," shouted one of the backbenchers.
5.b. "Let's **donate** £500 **to** Dr. Barnardo's Homes by washing lorry windscreens," my friend suggested.
6. "You can't back out at this **stage**, John. Hundreds of fans are waiting at the gates of the Arms Park rugby stadium in Cardiff," the club manager warned him.
7. Sheila wanted to buy a new electric **fan heater** for their seaside apartment, but her husband decided against it.
8. "The **curate** had refused to pronounce the couple man and wife because he wasn't qualified to do that," wrote the parish magazine.
9. Thousands of dock workers were walking to the city centre carrying **banners**.
10. "After the air disaster I was on a life-support machine for a week and then I was on a **ventilator**," he told the reporters.

FINAL TEST I

FALSE FRIENDS TRAPS

1.a. People should remember that the European climate is dependent on the ________ Stream (**Golf ◑ golf**).
1.b. The definition of a gentleman is a man who can play ________ , but doesn't (**Golf ◑ golf**).
2.a. One of the churches in the Kremlin is a cluster of chapels topped by golden roofs and ________ (**Dom ≠ dome**).
2.b. The exclusive country cottages are situated within three miles of the ________ city of Lincoln (**Dom ≠ dome**).
3.a. "Could you fetch some more ________ from the garden?" my mother asked me. "But don't bring any withered ________ leaves this time." (**Salat ◑ salad**)
3.b. "What are you doing just now?" Laura asked on the phone. – "I'm preparing the ________ for lunch." (**Salat ◑ salad**)
4.a. "These old British ________ lack charm and any kind of comfort," the Canadian soldiers thought (**Baracken ≠ barracks**).
4.b. Thousands of Vietnamese children had to sleep in ________ surrounded by barbed wire in Hongkong (**Baracken ≠ barracks**).
5.a. Teenagers are generally ________ and they are the last to carve their names on trees (**brav ≠ brave**).
5.b. The ________ man in Britain in 1989 saved six people, but was killed in an explosion (**brav ≠ brave**).
6.a. Babies can ________ almost as soon as they are born (**schwimmen ◑ swim**).
6.b. The shipwrecked crew watched their precious stores ________ away in the raging storm in mid-Atlantic (**schwimmen ◑ swim**).
7.a. At many English weddings, the groom and his best man still wear ________ and tails, usually hired from Moss Bros. for the day (**Zylinder ◑ cylinder**).
7.b. Turn the ignition key of the BMW and the six- ________ engine starts immediately (**Zylinder ◑ cylinder**).
8.a. The ________ will pay £ 10 into every school leavers' new account (**Banken ◑ banks**).
8.b. The park was so crowded I couldn't find a ________ to sit on (**Bank ◑ bank**).

9.a. Shortly after the troops surrendered there was a complete collapse of ________ (**Moral ◑ moral**).
9.b. In the last few years public ________ have radically changed in the suburbs of the big American cities (**Moral ◑ moral**).
10.a. Fortunately the new actress is not one of those 'terrible ________' (**Flirt ≠ flirt**).
10.b. Even in later years, Fiona has always enjoyed a little ________ (**Flirt ≠ flirt**).

ANSWER SHEET

FINAL TEST I: TRUE FRIENDS

1.a. People should remember that the European climate is dependent on the **Gulf** Stream.
1.b. The definition of a gentleman is a man who can play **golf**, but doesn't.
2.a. One of the churches in the Kremlin is a cluster of chapels topped by golden roofs and **domes**.
2.b. The exclusive country cottages are situated within three miles of the **cathedral** city of Lincoln.
3.a. "Could you fetch some more **lettuce** from the garden?" my mother asked me. "But don't bring any withered **lettuce** leaves this time."
3.b. "What are you doing just now?" Laura asked on the phone. – "I'm preparing the **salad** for lunch."
4.a. "These old British **barracks** lack charm and any kind of comfort," the Canadian soldiers thought.
4.b. Thousands of Vietnamese children had to sleep in **huts** surrounded by barbed wire in Hongkong.
5.a. Teenagers are generally **well-behaved** and they are the last to carve their names on trees.
5.b. The **bravest** man in Britain in 1989 saved six people, but was killed in an explosion.
6.a. Babies can **swim** almost as soon as they are born.
6.b. The shipwrecked crew watched their precious stores **float** away in the raging storm in mid-Atlantic.
7.a. At many English weddings, the groom and his best man still wear **top hat** and tails, usually hired from Moss Bros. for the day.
7.b. Turn the ignition key of the BMW and the six-**cylinder** engine starts immediately.
8.a. The **banks** will pay £ 10 into every school leavers' new account.
8.b. The park was so crowded I couldn't find a **bench** to sit on.
9.a. Shortly after the troops surrendered there was a complete collapse of **morale**.
9.b. In the last few years public **morals** have radically changed in the suburbs of the big American cities.
10.a. Fortunately the new actress is not one of those 'terrible **flirts**'.
10.b. Even in later years, Fiona has always enjoyed a little **flirtation**.

FINAL TEST II

FALSE FRIENDS TRAPS

1.a. In Britain book ________ are controlled by the publishers (**Preise ◑ prices**).
1.b. A panel of judges will award the first ________ for the best short story (**Preis ◑ price**).
2.a. A strong pound is the best counter-inflationary ________ (**Politik ◑ politics**).
2.b. The influential industrialist had invited old friends from business and ________ to a party at Harrods (**Politik ◑ politics**).
3.a. The new tape is waterproof. It will repair burst water ________ (**Hosen ≠ hoses**).
3.b. Jimmy van Heusen, the American songwriter, would interrupt composing sessions to drop his ________ for vitamin injections (**Hose ≠ hose**).
4.a. You can pay for the hand-painted figurine in three ________ (**Raten ◑ rates**), the advertisement stated.
4.b. Atlanta, the city for the 1996 Olympic Games, has very high hotel ________ (**Raten ◑ rates**).
5.a. Hair loss makes many men feel ________ (**selbstbewußt ≠ self-conscious**), in some cases they even feel depressed.
5.b. All through the yacht race the skipper had looked ________ (**selbstbewußt ≠ self-conscious**). That was one of the reasons why his crew won the race.
6.a. Many British people still eat baked ________ once a week (**Schellfisch ≠ shellfish**).
6.b. ________ consumers in Scotland have claimed there is a risk of poison in ________ nowadays (**Schellfisch ≠ shellfish**).
7.a. Her diet tip was to make your own ________ using the cooking juices (**Sauce ◑ sauce**).
7.b. As always the restaurant offered a variety of ________ such as mushroom ________, onion ________ and cheese ________ (**Sauce ◑ sauce**).
8.a. During the US Open Andre Agassi carries the hopes of the United States on his ________ shoulders (**schmal ≠ small**).
8.b. Every year there's a carnival parade through the ________ streets of Britain's ________ cathedral city, St. David's in Dyfed (**schmal ≠ small**).

9.a. Tony Clynick worked with one of the first projectors to use laser ________ (**Technik ◑ technique**), to produce the famous 3-D effect.
9.b. The tennis camp's aim is to provide an assessment of one's tennis ________ (**Technik ◑ technique**), but also to give tips about match ________ (**Technik ◑ technique**).
10.a. His girlfriend died in hospital from ________ wounds after the accident (**Brust ◑ breast**).
10.b. Unfortunately Mary had ________ cancer and had to be operated on (**Brust ◑ breast**).

ANSWER SHEET

FINAL TEST II: TRUE FRIENDS

1.a. In Britain book **prices** are controlled by the publishers.
1.b. A panel of judges will award the first **prize** for the best short story.
2.a. A strong pound is the best counter-inflationary **policy**.
2.b. The influential industrialist had invited old friends from business and **politics** to a party at Harrods.
3.a. The new tape is waterproof. It will repair burst water **hoses**.
3.b. Jimmy van Heusen, the American songwriter, would interrupt composing sessions to drop his **trousers** for vitamin injections.
4.a. You can pay for the hand-painted figurine in three **instalments**, the advertisement stated.
4.b. Atlanta, the city for the 1996 Olympic Games, has very high hotel **rates**.
5.a. Hair loss makes many men feel **self-conscious**, in some cases they even feel depressed.
5.b. All through the yacht race the skipper had looked **self-confident**. That was one of the reasons why his crew won the race.
6.a. Many British people still eat baked **haddock** once a week.
6.b. **Shellfish** consumers in Scotland have claimed there is a risk of poison in **shellfish** nowadays.
7.a. Her diet tip was to make your own **gravy** using the cooking juices.
7.b. As always the restaurant offered a variety of **sauces** such as mushroom **sauce**, onion **sauce** and cheese **sauce**.
8.a. During the US Open Andre Agassi carries the hopes of the United States on his **slender** shoulders.
8.b. Every year there's a carnival parade through the **narrow** streets of Britain's **smallest** cathedral city, St. David's in Dyfed.
9.a. Tony Clynick worked with one of the first projectors to use laser **technology**, to produce the famous 3-D effect.
9.b. The tennis camp's aim is to provide an assessment of one's tennis **technique**, but also to give tips about match **technique**.
10.a. His girlfriend died in hospital from **chest** wounds after the accident.
10.b. Unfortunately Mary had **breast** cancer and had to be operated on.

FALSE FRIENDS NACH SCHWIERIGKEITSKATEGORIEN

I. GRUNDTYPEN VON FALSE FRIENDS

◑ = halbwahre (partielle) False Friends

EASY FALSE FRIENDS

(= Buch I)

älter	◑	older
Angel	≠	angle
also	≠	also
Bank	◑	bank
Baracke(n)	≠	barracks
bekommen	≠	become
borgen	◑	borrow
Braut	◑	bride
brav	≠	brave
Brust	◑	breast
dick	◑	thick
Engel	≠	angle
Fleisch	◑	flesh
Flur	≠	floor
Fotografie	◑	photography
Fotograf	≠	photograph
Golf	◑	golf
Kanal	◑	canal
Kropf	◑	crop
Mann	◑	man
Mappe	≠	map
Meinung	≠	meaning
Mörder	≠	murder
nächste	◑	next
Perle	◑	pearl
Rente	≠	rent
Sauce	◑	sauce
schmal	≠	small
Schnecke	≠	snake
schwimmen	◑	swim
See	◑	sea
Seite	◑	side
Sender	≠	sender
sparen	≠	spare
Straße	◑	street
Strom	◑	stream
Tablett	≠	tablet
wenn	◑	when
wer	≠	where
wo	≠	who

NOT SO EASY FALSE FRIENDS

(= Buch I)

Achse	◑	axis
Achsel	≠	axle
Akt	◑	act
Akte(n)	≠	act(s)
alarmieren	◑	alarm
Allee	≠	alley
Antenne	◑	antenna
Art	≠	art
ausgesprochen	≠	outspoken
blank	≠	blank
Dom	≠	dome
Fabrik	≠	fabric

familiär	≠ familiar
Flirt	≠ flirt
Gift	≠ gift
Hausmeister	≠ housemaster
Helm	≠ helm
Hose	≠ hose
isoliert	◑ isolated
Major	≠ mayor
Moral	◑ moral
Pension	◑ pension
Physiker	≠ physician
Plastik	◑ plastics
Politik	◑ politics
Preis	◑ price
Prospekt	≠ prospect
Rate	◑ rate
Salat	◑ salad
Schal	≠ shawl
Schatten	◑ shade
Schellfisch	≠ shellfish
selbstbewußt	≠ self-conscious
spenden	≠ spend
Stadium	≠ stadium
Technik	◑ technique
Transparent	≠ transparency
Ventilator	◑ ventilator
Vikar	≠ vicar
Warenhaus	≠ warehouse
Zylinder	◑ cylinder

DIFFICULT FALSE FRIENDS

(= Buch II)

Akkord	≠ accord
Aktion	≠ action
aktuell	≠ actual
Allüren	≠ allure
Ambulanz	◑ ambulance
apart	≠ apart
Artist	≠ artist
Basis	◑ basis
Chef	≠ chef
delikat	◑ delicate
Dessert	≠ desert
dezent	◑ decent
engagiert	◑ engaged
eventuell	≠ eventual
Existenz	◑ existence
famos	≠ famous
fatal	◑ fatal
Fraktion	≠ fraction
genial	≠ genial
graziös	≠ gracious
human	◑ human
Kaution	◑ caution
Konfession	≠ confession
Konkurrenz	≠ concurrence
konsequent	◑ consequent
kontrollieren	◑ control
Konzept	≠ concept
Menü	≠ menu
mondän	≠ mundane
ordinär	◑ ordinary
pathetisch	◑ pathetic
prägnant	≠ pregnant
Prozeß	◑ process
rentabel	≠ rentable
Rezept	≠ receipt
sensibel	≠ sensible
seriös	◑ serious
spendieren	≠ spend
Stipendium	≠ stipend
sympathisch	≠ sympathetic
temperamentvoll	≠ tempera-mental
Trakt	≠ tract
transpirieren	≠ transpire
unsympathisch	≠ unsympath-etic

II. SONDERTYPEN VON FALSE FRIENDS

◑ = halbwahre (partielle) False Friends

PARTICULARLY DIFFICULT FALSE FRIENDS

(= Buch II)

TERRIBLE TWINS

elektrisch	◑	electric
historisch	◑	historic
klassisch	◑	classic
komisch	◑	comic
Kritik	≠	critic
kritisch	≠	(*) critic
magisch	◑	magic
ökonomisch	◑	economic
politisch	≠	politic
zynisch	≠	(*) cynic

TRICKY OVER/UNDER-COMPOUNDS

überblicken	◑	overlook
Überfluß	≠	overflow
überhören	≠	overhear
übernehmen	≠	overtake
überreichen	≠	overreach
überschlafen	≠	oversleep
übersehen	≠	oversee
Übersicht	≠	oversight
überwinden	≠	overwind
Unterarm	≠	underarm
untergehen	≠	undergo
unterliegen	≠	underlie
unternehmen	≠	undertake
Unternehmen	≠	undertaking
Unternehmer	≠	undertaker
unterschreiben	≠	underwrite

CONFUSIBLES

barbarisch	◑	barbaric
definitiv	◑	definitive
desinteressiert	≠	disinterested
intensiv	◑	intensive
kontinuierlich	◑	continual
lose	≠	lose
luxuriös	≠	luxuriant
meisterlich	◑	masterly
momentan	◑	momentary
sinnlich	◑	sensual
stationär	≠	stationery
triumphierend	◑	triumphant
zeremoniell	◑	ceremonial

PSEUDO-ANGLICISMS

Affekt	◑	(*)affect
Bowle	≠	bowl
Chips	≠	chips (BE)
Dressman	≠	*dressman
last not least	≠	*last not least
Oldtimer	◑	(*)old-timer
Shakehands	≠	*shakehands
Showmaster	≠	*showmaster
Slip	≠	(*)slip
Smoking	≠	*smoking
Talkmaster	≠	*talkmaster
die Teens	≠	(*)the teens
Twen	≠	*twen
Verkehrs**rowdy**	≠	traffic ***rowdy**

FALSE FRIENDS: LITERATURHINWEISE

1. Literatur zum False Friends-Phänomen (mit Fehlerbeispielen)

Alfes, Leonhard. “**Falsche** und **halbehrliche** Freunde. Ein Problem der Wortschatzdidaktik”. **Englisch** 20 (1985), 140–145.

Barnickel, Klaus-Dieter. “Trügerische Verwandte: Überlegungen zu einem vergleichenden Fehlerwörterbuch Deutsch–Englisch”. **Erlanger Anglistik und Amerikanistik in Vergangenheit und Gegenwart**, hrsg. von U. Bertram und D. Petzold. **Erlanger Forschungen**, Reihe A, Bd. 52 (Erlangen 1990), 153–174.

Breitkreuz, Hartmut. “Arbeitsformen des differenzierten **Notebook**”. **Englisch** 7 (1972), 120–122.

Breitkreuz, Hartmut. “**False Friends** und ihre unterrichtliche Behandlung”. **Die Neueren Sprachen** 72, 22 N. F. (1973), 70–74.

Breitkreuz, Hartmut. “Pseudo-Anglizismen – Ein Beitrag zur Fehlerforschung”. **Grazer Linguistische Studien** 3 (1976), 5–27.

Breitkreuz, Hartmut und Wiegand, Nicole. “Zur Problematik gemein- und fachsprachlicher **False Friends**”. In: **Fremdsprachenunterricht im Wandel. Lieselotte Weidner zum 65. Geburtstag**. Schriftenreihe zur Lehrerbildung, Lehrerfortbildung und pädagogischen Weiterbildung, Bd. 13 (Heidelberg 1989), 94–110.

Breitkreuz, Hartmut. “Zur Typisierung von **False Friends**”. **Abstracts zur 21. Jahrestagung der Gesellschaft für Angewandte Linguistik** (Bonn 1990), 30.

Fanning, Hiltgunt. “Falsche Freunde in zweisprachiger Erziehung (Englisch/Deutsch)”. **Studien zur Sprachdifferenzierung**. Roland Arnold zum 60. Geburtstag. **Wissenschaftliche Beiträge der Ernst-Moritz-Arndt-Universität Greifswald** (Greifswald 1990), 47–51.

Perl, Matthias, und Winter, Roger. “Zum Problem der **False Friends**”. **Fremdsprachenunterricht** 16 (1972), 183–185.

Siegrist, Ottmar K. “**False Friends** im Bereich Aussprache und ihre unterrichtliche Behandlung". **Erziehungswissenschaft und Beruf** 27 (1979), 93–98.

Siegrist, Ottmar K. "'England' und 'English'. Zwei **False Friends** hinsichtlich ihrer Aussprache?" **Praxis des Neusprachlichen Unterrichts** 31 (1984), 286–288.

Siegrist, Ottmar K. "Idiomatische **False Friends**". **Abstracts zur 21. Jahrestagung der Gesellschaft für Angewandte Linguistik** (Bonn 1990), 173.

Thiemer, Eberhard. "Die 'falschen Freunde' als Erscheinung zwischensprachlicher und innersprachlicher Interferenz". **Fremdsprachen** 23 (1979), 263–271.

Wandruszka, Mario. "Falsche Freunde: Ein linguistisches Problem und seine Lösung". **Lebende Sprachen** 24 (1979), 4–9.

2. Sprachpraktische Literatur und False Friends-Sammlungen

Allen, Edward Frank. **How to Write and Speak Effective English**. New York: Crest, 3rd printing, 1962.

Greenbaum, Sidney, and Whitcut, Janet. **Longman Guide to English Usage**. Harlow: Longman Group, 1988.

Helliwell, Margaret. **Can I Become a Beefsteak? Trügerische Wörter zum Nachschlagen und Üben**. Berlin: COUP, 1989.

Howard, Godfrey. **A Guide to Good English** in the 1980s. London: Pelham, 1985.

Parkes, Geoff, and Cornell, Alan. **German–English False Friends. Reference and Practice**. Book 1. Southampton: England, 1989.

Pascoe, Graham, and Pascoe, Henriette. **Sprachfallen im Englischen. Wörterbuch der falschen Freunde**. München: Hueber, 1985.

Room, Adrian. **Dictionary of Confusing Words and Meanings**. London: Routledge, repr. 1986.

Tennant, John. **A Handbook of English Usage**. London: Longmans, 1964.

Wolfe, Patrick. "Exploiting **False Friends**". **Modern English Teacher** 9 (1981), 14–16.

FALSE FRIENDS INDEX: ENGLISCH A–W

Der englische Index erfaßt die in diesem Buch behandelten False Friends-Paare (vgl. die Übersicht "False Friends nach Schwierigkeitskategorien" auf den Seiten 278–279) und weitgehend die Wortkombinationen (Kollokationen) soweit sie mit den ausgewiesenen False Friends in direkter Verbindung stehen.
Die Seitenzahlen in Fettdruck geben den Haupteintrag des jeweiligen False Friend bzw. True Friend an, die Seitenzahlen in Normaldruck liefern dem Benutzer weitere Beleg-Beispiele an die Hand. In einigen Fällen wie *act(s), bank, canal/channel, pension* wurde aus Gründen der Eindeutigkeit eine Bedeutungszuordnung vorgenommen.

act(s) (1) (Tat, Handlung) **150**, 150, **151**, 151, 152, **153**, 153, 154, 177
act(s) (2) (law) 151, 152, **153**, 153, **154**, 154
acts (3) (Bible) **153**, **154**, 154
aerial **161**, 161, **162**, 162, 163
agree with s. o. **35**, 36, 37; not agree with **35**, 36, 37
alarm **156**, 156, **157**, 157; be alarmed (at) **156**, 156, **157**, 157, 158
alert **156**, 156, **157**, 157, 158, 178
alley **159**, 159, **160**, 177, 178; *alley*way 160; back *alley* 160
also **27**, **28**, 28, 229
angel **56**, 56, **57**, 57, 58; *angels* of death 80; arch*angel* 56; avenging *angel* 56; guardian *angel* 56, 57
angle **24**, **25**, 52, **56**, 56, **57**, 57; acute *angle* 24, obtuse *angle* 24, right *angle* 24; from my *angle* 26, from this *angle* 24, 57
angler 24, 25, 137
angling 24
annuity **95**, 95, 96
antenna **161**, 161, **162**, 163
under the *arm* **147**, 147, **148**, 149, 178
armpit **147**, 147, **148**, 148
art 164, **165**, 165, 177, 178, 249, 254, 255, 256; *art* exhibition 165; *art* collector 165; *art* dealer 165, 166, 254, 255; *art* exhibition 165; *art* gallery 165; *art* historian 165; *art* lover 165; *art* theory 165
aspect **114**, 114, **115**, 116
assassin **87**, 87, **89**
assassination **87**, 88, **89**; character *assassination* 88
avenue **159**, 159, **160**, 160, 178
axis **144**, 144, **145**, 145; *Axis* Powers 144; *axis* of rotation 144; *axis* of symmetry 144; diagonal *axis* 144
axle **144**, 144, **145**, 145, **147**, **148**, 148, 178; *axle* load 144; *axle* suspension 148; *axle* test 148; front *axle* 148; rear *axle* 144

(school) bag **81**, 81, **82**, 148
bank (1) (Geldinstitut) 17, 19, **30**, **31**, 145, 167, 272, 274; *bank* account 171; *bank* robbers 193; bank statement 172
bank (2) (Fluß-, Seeufer) **30**, 30, **31**, 188
bank (3) (Computer: Speicher) **30**, **31**
banner **254**, 254, **255**, 256, 271
barracks 12, 18, **32**, 32, **33**, 33, 274
bay (Golf, Bucht) **68**, 68, **69**; *Bay* of Biscay 68; *Bay* of Bengal 68
bead (Holz-, Glasperle etc.) **92**, 92, **93**, 93; *beads* of perspiration **92**, 92, **93**; glass *beads* 92; wooden *beads* 92, 109
become **36**, **37**, 52, 111, 203, 215, 217, 242, 252, 261; *become* angry 36, *become* famous 36; *become* fat 55, *become* very friendly 36, *become* ill 36, *become* pregnant 262, *become* much reduced 120, *become* rich 37, *become* serious 239; become of **36**, 36, 37
behaviour **164**, 164, **165**

bench **30**, **31**, 52, 274
blank **170**, 170, **171**, 171, 172, 178
borrow 12, **39**, 39, **40**, 40, 51, 52
brave **45**, 45, **46**, 46, 157, 272, 274; be brave 46
breast **47**, 47, **48**, 48, 49, 251, 276, 277; *breast* cancer 48; *breast* enlargement 251; *breast* stroke 48; chicken *breast* 48
bride **42**, 42, **43**, 43, 52; *bride*groom 43, 269, 271; *bride*-to-be 42, 43; jilted *bride* 42; war *bride* 43; would-be *bride* 42
briefcase **81**, 81, **82**, 82
bright **170**, 170, **171**, **172**
brochure 181, **224**, 224, **225**, 225
(be) broke (coll.) **170**, 170, **171**

call (= alarmieren) **156**, 156, **157**, 158
canal (artificial) **71**, 71, **72**, 73; Corinth *Canal* 71; the Kiel *Canal* 72
(woman) caretaker (BE), janitor (AE) **190**, 190, **191**, 191, 214
case **81**, 81, **82**, 82
cathedral 133, **173**, 173, **174**, 174, 175, 183, 274, 275, 277
channel (natural) **71**, 71, **72**, 72, 73; the *Channel* Tunnel 71; Bristol *Channel* 73; the English *Channel* 71; North *Channel* 71; St. George's *Channel* 71
chest **47**, 47, 48, 49, 277; *chest* height 47, 48; *chest* muscle 47
closest **90**, 90, **91**, 140
come true 37, 135
contribute (to) **246**, 246, 247
corpulent **53**, 53, **55**
corridor **62**, 62, **63**, 63, 80
crop (1) (of animals) **74**, 74, **75**, crop (2) (harvest) **74**, 74, **75**, 75; *crop* failures 38; apple *crop* **74**
curate **259**, 259, 260, 261, 271
current (1) (electric current) **127**, 127
current (2) (air, ocean current) **127**, 127, **128**; Humboldt *Current* 127; Peru *Current* 127
curtain (= Gardinen-*schal*) **231**, 231, **232**
cylinder **266**, 266, 267, 269, 272, 274

decided(ly) 12, 13, 14, 15, **167**, 167, **168**, 178
department store **262**, 262, **263**, 263, 271
do s. o. good **35**, 36, **37**
dome **173**, 173, **174**, 174, 175, 177, 178, 272, 274
donate (to) **246**, 246, **247**, 247, 271
drift **106**, 106, 107, 108
can't *drink* sth. **35**, 36, **37**

cant's *eat* sth. **35**, **37**
economize (on) **120**, 120, **121**, 141
elder **22**, 22, **23**, 23, 52; *elder* brother 52; *elder* sister 22; the *elder* of the two 22, 138
extremely (= ausgesprochen) 13, 14, 15, 79, 80, **167**, 167, **168**, 243

fabric **179**, **180**, 180, 181, 213, 214
factory **179**, 179, **180**, 181, 214, 267
fall ill 37, 38
familiar **182**, **183**, 183, 184, 222
(electric) *fan* 18, **257**, 257, **258**, 258; *fan* heater 257, 271
fare **222**, 222; bus *fares* 222
fat 9, **53**, 53, 54, **55**, 55, 80; a big *fat* cigar 54; a *fat* commission 54; *fat* profits 53; a big *fat* salary 54; a *fat* wallet 53
fiancée **42**, 42, 52; jilted *fiancée* 42, 43
file(s) 54, **81**, 81, **153**, 153, **154**, 154, 178; client *files* 153; patient's *files* 154; personal *files* 153; police *files* 154; post-office *files* 82
fishing 31, 112; *fishing*-licence 24, 26; *fishing*-reel 24; fishing-rod **24**, **25**, 26; *fishing*-tackle 24; do some *fishing* 112; go *fishing* 24
flesh **59**, 59, **60**, 61, 79, 80, 85
flirt (noun) **185**, 185, **186**, 186, 213, 214, 273, 274
flirt (with) **185**, 185, 186, 214
flirtation **185**, 185, **186**, 186, 214, 274
float **106**, 106, **107**, 107, 108, 110, 274; *floating* hospital 106; *floating* restaurant 106; '*floating*' tomb 106
floor 19, **62**, 62, **63**, 63, 79, 199; ground *floor* (BE), first *floor* (AE) 63; first *floor* (BE), second *floor* (AE) 63, 199; second floor (BE), third *floor* (AE) 63, 199
folder **81**, 81, **82** 110
fratricide **87**, 87, **88**, 88, **89**

genocide **87**, 88, **89**
get (sth.) **35**, 35, **37**, 52, 109, 110, 123, 131, 140, 141, 177, 178, 209, 242; *get* a bad name **35**, 35; *get* cold feet **35**, 35; *get* dark 37, 125

gift 11, 19, **187**, 187, **188**, 188, 189, 213, 214
go bad 36; *go* from bad to worse 37; *go* blind 36, 38; *go* crazy 37; *go* deaf 37; *go* mad 37; *go* wrong 37
goitre (BE), goiter (AE) **74**, 74, **75**, 75, 80, 239
golf 23, **68**, **69**, 69, 118, 272, 274; *golf* ball 23; *golf* club 69; *golf* course 69; *golf* links 69; *golf* season 69; *golf* swing 69; *golf* title 69; *golf* trousers 41
good (= brav) **45**, 45, **46**
gravy **97**, 97, **98**, 98, **99**, 110, 277; *gravy* stains 97, 99; *gravy* trail 97; *gravy* trips 97
guest-house **209**, 209, **210**, 211
gulf (1) (= Golf als geographische Bezeichnung) **68**, 68, **69**, 70, 202, 260, 274; *Gulf* of Aden 68; *Gulf* coast 68; *Gulf* region 69; *Gulf* of Suez 68; *Gulf* War 70
gulf (2) (= Meeres*busen*) 68; *Gulf* of Bothnia 68; *Gulf* of Finland 68
gulf (3) (= Kluft) 68, 80

haddock 12, 79, 80, **238**, 238, **239**, 239, 241, 242, 277
hall/hallway **62**, 62, **63**, 63, 80
have (= bekommen) **35**, 35, **37**; *have* a baby 35; *have* twins 35; have visitors 35
heading 11
headline 11, 197
heavy 9, 54, 106; *heavy* rush-hour traffic 9; *heavy* drops of rain 54; *heavy* rain 106
helm 19, **194**, 194, 213, 214
helmet **193**, 193, **194**, 194, 214; crash *helmet* 193; safety *helmet* 193; space *helmet* 193
hire purchase **226**, 226, 228
honest **45**, 45, 46
hose **196**, 196, **197**, 197, 198, 214, 275, 277
housemaster/housemistress **190**, 190, **191**, 191
husband 45, 59, 67, **76**, 76, **77**, 77, 80, 95, 99, 101, 137, 140, 141, 156, 171, 197, 214, 234, 269, 271
huts **32**, 32, **33**, **52**, 274; contractor's *huts* 32; corrugated iron *hut* 32; Nissen *hut* 32; Quonset *hut* (AE) 32; wooden *huts* 33

if 23, 38, 49, 51, 62, 75, 79, 80, 96, 118, 122, **132**, 132, **133**, 133, 141, 145, 159, 218, 229, 232, 242, 247, 249, 250, 257
immediate (geogr.) **90**, 90, **91**
informal **182**, 182, 183
isolated (1) be/feel *isolated* 66, **199**, 199, **200**, 200, 213, 214
isolated (2) be *isolated* (from) 145, **199**, 199, **200**
instalment(s) **226**, 226, **228**, 228, 277
insulated **199**, 199, **200**, 200, 214
intimate **182**, 182

killer **87**, 87, 89
kind **164**, 164, **165**, 166, 178

lake 30, 106, 107, **111**, 111, **112**, 112, 113, 141, 147; *Lake* Constance 111; *Lake* District 120; artificial *lake* 111; country *lake* 111; park *lake* 112
landing **62**, 62, **63**
leaflet **224**, 224, **225**, 225, 242
lend 31, **39**, 39, 40, 40, 41, 52
lettuce **229**, 229, 230, 242, 274
loyal **45**, 45, **46**

major **202**, 202, 203, 204
man (1) (allgemein) 42, 45, 46, 47, 63, 64, **76**, 76, **77**, 77, 79, 80, 133, 158, 166, 177, 178, 180, 193, 198, 205, 210, 222, 246, 269, 271, 272, 274, 277; *man* of action 76; *man* of the people 76
man (2) (= der Mensch) 40, 58, **76**, 76
map **81**, 81, **82**, 82, 109, 110; *map* of Britain 82; *maps* of continents 81; *maps* of oceans 81; *maps* of the world 81; road *map* 82; street *map* 82
marked(ly) 13, 14, 15, **167**, 167, **168**
mayor(ess) **202**, **203**, 203, **204**, 204, 205, 214
meaning **84**, 84, **85**, 85, 109, 110; change of *meaning* 85
meat **59**, 59, **60**, 60, 88; *meat* business 60; *meat* dish 60; *meat* importer 59; *meat* prices 80; *meat* selling chain 60
mezzanine 63
(paper etc.) mill **179**, 179, 180
mind **84**, 84, **85**, 85
moral (1) (noun) **206**, **207**, 207, 208, 272
moral (2) (adj.) **207**, 207, 208
morale **206**, 206, **207**, 208, 214, 274
morals **206**, 206, **207**, 273, 274
murder **87**, 88, **89**, 263; *murder* attempt 89; *murder* case 62, 159;

murder gang 89; *murder* suspect 88; murder victim 89; child *murder* 89, 150
murderer/murderess **87**, 87, **89**, 89, 110, 210, 252; child *murderer* 87, 89

narrow **100**, 100, **101**, 125, 160, 277; *narrow* path 100; *narrow* road 125
nature **164**, 164, **165**
nearest **90**, 90, **91**, 91, 110, 201
next **90**, 90, **91**, 91, 107, 109, 110, 120, 150, 162, 216, 224, 225
(painting from the) nude **150**, 150, **151**, 178, 249; *nude* model 150, 151, 152, 166; *nude* painting 150, 249; *nude* photographs 150

obtain (sth.) **35**, 35, **37**
older **22**, 22, **23**, 23, 191
opinion **84**, 84, **85**, 85, 208, 217; *opinion* poll 84, 208; change of *opinion* 84, 85; public *opinion* 208; shade of *opinion* 84
outspoken 12, 13, 14, 15, 16, **167**, 167, **168**, 168, 169

page **114**, 114, **115**, 116, 141, 170
pants **196**, 196, 197
partial (= befangen jur.) 9, 244
party (fig.) **114**, 114, **115**
pearl (= echte Perle) **92**, 92, **93**, 93, 94; *pearl* diver 92; mother of *pearl* 93
(be) penniless **170**, 170, **171**, 172
pension (1) ('penʃn) (= Rente, Pension) **95**, 95, **96**, 96, 109, 110, **209**, 209, **210**, 210, 211,
pension (2) ('pã:ŋsıɔ̃:ŋ) (= small hotel, especially on the Continent) **209**, 209, **210**
personal **182**, 182, 183, 184, 214
pew 17, **30**, **31**, 52
phase **248**, 248, **249**
photo 42, 51, 52, **64**, 64, **65**, 65, **66**, 66; *photo*copier 67; *photo*copy 89; *photo*fit (picture) 67; *photo*montage 67; *photo* session 67; wedding *photos* 66
photograph 56, **64**, 64, **65**, 65, **66**, 66, **67**, 67, 79, 80; nude *photograph* 150
photographer (als Beruf) **66**, 66, **67**, 67, 80, 109, 110; amateur *photographer* 66; fashion *photographer* 67; press *photographer* 66; society *photographer* 66
photographic (= *Foto-*) **64**, **65**; *photographic* equipment 64; *photographic* magazine 64; *photographic* safari 65; *photographic* supplier 64
photography **64**, 64, **65**, 65; colour *photography* 64, 80; trick *photography* 65
physician **215**, 215, **216**, 216; honorary *physician* 216
physicist **215**, 215, **216**, 216, 242; astro*physicist* 216; nuclear *physicist* 215
(chemical etc.) plant **179**, 179, 180
plastic (adj.) **217**, 217, **218**, 218, 267; *plastic* oars 217; plastic bags 217
plastic (noun) **217**, 217, **218**, 218, 267
point (fig.) **114**, 114, **115**, 116
poison **187**, 187, **188**, 189, 214, 277
poisoner **87**, 87, **89**
polish(sth.) **170**, 170, **171**, 217
policy **219**, 219, **220**, 220, 242, 277; company *policy* 220; home *policy* 220
politics **219**, 219, **220**, 220, 241, 242, 275, 277; party *politics* 219, 220
portly **53**, 53, 55
prejudiced 9, 244
price 145, 181, 189, **221**, 221, **222**, 222, 230, 241, 242, 256, 275, 277; *price* freeze 221; *price* lists 181; *price* tag 222
prize 140, 141, 178, **221**, 221, **222**, 242, 277; *prize* draw 221; *prize* money 221; consolation *prize* 221; runners-up *prizes* 140, 141; Nobel Peace *Prize* 193; Turner *Prize* 178
pronounced 13, 14, 15, **167**, 167, 168, 169
prospect **224**, 224, **225**, 225, 241, 242
prospectus **224**, 224, **225**

rate 19, 116, **226**, 226, 227, **228**, 228, 242, 252, 275, 277
real 53; a *real* surprise 53
receive (sth.) **35**, 35, **37**
record(s) **153**, 153, **154**, 154, 210; *records* of the trial 153; patient's *records* 154
relaxed **182**, 182, 183, 184
rent **95**, 95, **96**, 96, 109, 110; *rent* arrears 96; *rent* debt 96
right by **90**, 90, **91**
river 107, 109, 110, **127**, 127, **128**, 129, 141, 188
road 33, 114, **123**, 123, 124, **125**, 125, 141, 162,

201; *road* atlas 123; *road* block 125; *road* hump 123; *road* safety offensive 141; coast *road* 125; country *road* 123; feeder *road* 124; cross*roads* 56; slip*road* 124; trunk *road* 123
rod **24**, 25, 26; *rod* tip 24

salad 19, **229**, 229, **230**, 230, 241, 272, 274; cucumber *salad* 229; endive *salad* 229; ham *salad* 229; 242; lobster *salad* 229; side *salad* 230
(silver) salver **130**, 130, **131**, 131, 141
sauce **97**, 97, **98**, 98, 238, 277; cheese *sauce*, 98; chocolate *sauce* 97; custard *sauce* 98; mushroom *sauce* 97; onion *sauce* 97; heavy *sauces* 97; savoury *sauces* 97, 98; sweet *sauces* 97, 98
save (up) **120**, 120, **121**, 121, 122, 269, 271
scarf (pl. scarves) **231**, 231, **232**, 232, 233, 242
scrimp and save (for) **120**, 120, **121**
sculpture **217**, 217, **218**, 218, 242; animal *sculptures* 217; bronze *sculptures* 217
sea 26, 108, **111**, 111, **112**, 113, 141, 239; *sea*food 112; *sea*gull 111, 112; *sea* level 111; *sea*side towns 38, 269, 271; *sea* wall 111, 137; *sea* of colours 112; *sea* of flowers 112; *sea* of spectators 112; Black *Sea* 112; North *Sea* 111, 112; Red *Sea* 68, 112
self-assertive 9, **243**, 243, 244
self-assured 9, **243**, 243, 244
self-confident 9, **243**, 243, **244**, 244, 245, 271, 277
self-conscious 9, 11, **243**, 243, **244**, 244, 245, 271, 275, 277
sender **117**, 117, **118**, 118, 141, 221
serpent 104
shacks **32**, 32, **33**, 33
shade 181, **234**, 234, 235, **236**, 236, 242
shadow **234**, 234, **236**, 236
shanty **32**, 33; *shanty* town 32
shawl **231**, 231, **232**, 232, 233
shed(s) **32**, 32, **33**, 33; tool *shed* 32
shellfish 12, **238**, 238; **239**, 239, 241, 242, 275, 277
shining **170**, 170, 171
shiny **170**, 170, **171**
shorts **196**, **197**, 197, 232
shoulder-straps **147**, 147, **148**, 148
side 67, **114**, 114, **115**, 115, 116, 160, 174, 177, 178, 266; *side* effect 115; *side* entrance 115
slender **100**, 100, **101**, 101, 277; *slender* hands 100, 101
slight **100**, 100, **101**; a *slight* profit 101
slug (without shell) **103**, 103, **104**
small **100**, **101**, 101, 109, 110, 209, 221, 275, 277; a *small* bump 101; a *small* club 100; the *small* crowds 100; a *small* holiday budget 101; a *small* income 101; a *small* inheritance 101; a *small* membership fee 100; (in) the *small* print 101
snail (with shell) **103**, 103, **104**, 105, 110, 162; at a *snail*'s pace 103
snake 18, **103**, 103, **104**, 104, 148; *snake*bites **104**, 105; *snake* charmer 103, 104, 149; *snake* dancer 103; grass *snake* 18, 104; poisonous *snake* 104; rattle*snake* 104, 105; smooth *snake* 104
so **27**, **28**, 28, 41, 46
sort **164**, 164, **165**, 166
spare **120**, **121**, 121, 141; *spare* parts 263
spend (on) **246**, 246, **247** 247, 248, 271
spiritless **45**, **46**, 46
stadium **248**, 248, **249**, 249, 250, 269, 271; *stadium* events 248; *stadium* paper 249; football *stadium* (AE) 249; Olympic *stadium* 248, 249; sports *stadium* 250
stage **248**, 248, **249**, 249, 269; at an early *stage* 248; at this *stage* 248, 249
(broadcasting, TV) station **117**, 117, **118**, 118, 141; pop *station* 117; radio *station* 117, 118
stint oneself (for) **120**, 120, **121**
store 135, **262**, 262, **263**
stout **53**, 53, **55**
strait(s) **123**, 124, **125**; the *Straits* of Dover 124; the *Straits* of Florida 124; the *Strait* of Hormuz 124; the *Strait(s)* of Sicily 124
stream **127**, 127, **128**, 129, 141, 272, 274; *stream* of complaints 128; *stream* of lava 128; *stream* of letters 128; *stream* of people 128, 129; *stream* of refugees 128
street 33, 123, **124**, 124, **125**, 125, 126, 140, 141, 160, 174, 175, 225; *street* lamp 124; *street* party 124; High *Street*

(mainly BE), Main *Street* (mainly AE) 124, 181, 263; village *street* 124; village High *Street* 124, 129
suicide **87**, 88, **89**
swim **106**, 106, **107**, 107, 108, 109, 110, 113, 129, 272, 274

tablet (1) (Tablette) **130**, 130, **131**, 131; painkilling *tablets* 131; vitamin *tablet* 130, 131
tablet (2) (Tafel, Gedenkplatte) **130**, 130, **131**, 131; clay *tablet* 130, **131**; marble *tablet* **131**; memorial tablet **131**, 131
technique 12, 85, 86, 238, 249, **251**, 251, **252**, 252, 269, 271, 276, 277; construction *technique* 251; fish-farming *technique* 238; match *technique* 277; relaxation *technique* 251; ski *technique* 271; teaching *technique* 251; tennis *technique* 277
technology **251**, 251, **252**, 252, 271, 277; computer *technology* 251; laser *technology* 277
then **27**, **28**, 28, 46, 52, 96, 198, 204, 211
therefore **27**, **28**, 28
thick 9, 19, **53**, **54**, 54, **55**, 55, 79, 80; *thick* eyebrows 80; *thick* fog 9, 54; *thick* hair 54; *thick* hedge 54; *thick* paint 9; *thick* smoke 54; a *thick* voice 9, 54
thin **100**, 100, **101**, 110; *thin* in the face 101
toothless **45**, 45, **46**
top hat (BE), high hat (AE) **265**, 265, **266**, 267, 271, 274
topper (informal) **265**, 265, **266**, 271
toxic **187**, 187, **188**, 189
transmitter **117**, 117, **118**, 118, 161
transparency **254**, 254, **255**, 255, 256
tray **130**, 130, **131**, 131
trousers **196**, 196, **197**, 198, 214, 277
turn pale 37, 91
type **164**, 164, **165**, 166, 198, 219, 242

uninspired **45**, 45, **46**
unless **132**, 132, **133**, 133

venom **187**, 187, 188
ventilator **257**, 257, **258**, 258, 271
vicar 19, 41, 147, **259**, **260**, 260, 261
view **84**, 84, **85**, 85, 108

warehouse **262**, 262, **263**, 263, 264, 269, 271; *warehouse* conversion 264; *warehouse* parties 264; carpet *warehouse* 262; factory *warehouse* 262; furniture *warehouse* 263; tobacco *warehouse* 262; tyre *warehouse* 262
way (= Art) 125, 135, **164**, 164, **165**, 166, 208, 252, 269, 271
wedding 133, 269, 271, 272, 274; *wedding*-dress 42; *wedding* day 43; *wedding*-guests 42; *wedding* photos 66
well-behaved **45**, 45, **46**, 52, 274
when 23, 26, 40, 43, 49, 51, 125, **132**, 132, **133**, 133, **137**, 137, **138**, 138, 150, 186, 222, 228, 231, 244, 256
where 16, 31, 33, 41, **134**, 134, **135**, 135, **137**, 137, **138**, 138, 141, 168, 181, 204, 225
which (1) which ... in/in which **137**, 137, **138**
which (2) which ...from/from which **137**, 137, 138
which (3) which of **134**, 134, **135**, 141
who 40, 63, **134**, 134, **135**, 135, **137**, 137, **138**, 138, 186, 204, 236
works (= Fabrik, Werk) **179**, 179, **180**, 267

FALSE FRIENDS INDEX: DEUTSCH A–Z

Der deutsche Index konzentriert sich im wesentlichen auf die behandelten False Friends-Paare und berücksichtigt weitgehend die eingebrachten Wortkombinationen (Kollokationen).
Fettgedruckte Seitenzahlen weisen die Haupteinträge der False Friends aus, normalgedruckte Seitenzahlen liefern weitere Belegstellen. In bestimmten Fällen wie *Akt*, *Bank*, *Fleisch*, *Schattten*, *See*, *Strom* erfolgte eine Bedeutungsdifferenzierung, um das Auffinden des englischen Begriffs zu erleichtern.

abgelegen 67, **199**, **200**, 200
Absender **117**, 117, **118**
absparen (1) sich etwas absparen **120**, 120, **121** (2) sich etwas vom Munde absparen **120**, 120, **121**
Achse **144**, 144, **145**, **147**, **148**, 148, 177; *Achsen*mächte 144; *Achs*test 148; *Achs*federung 148; Diagonal*achse* 144; Hinter*achse* 144; Rotations*achse* 144; Symmetrie*achse* 144
Achsel **147**, 147, **148**, 177; *Achsel*geruch 147; *Achsel*träger 147
älter (-e, -es, -er) **22**, 22, **23**, 51
Akt (1) (in der Malerei etc.) **150**, 150, **151**, 151, 177; *Akt*fotos 151; *Akt*gemälde 150 (2) (im Drama) **150**, **151**, 151 (3) (= Tat, Handlung) **150**, 150, **151**; *Akt* der Menschlichkeit 150
Akten(n) **153**, 153, 154, 177; *Akten*schrank 153; *Akten*tasche 81, 82; *Akten*zeichen 153; Personal*akten* 153; Prozeß*akten* 153
alarmieren **156**, 156, **157**, 177
Allee **159**, 159, **160**, 177
als **132**, 132, **133**, 150
also **27**, **28**, 28, 51
'*Alters*-': *Alters*rente 95; *Alters*ruhegeld 95
Angel **24**, **25**; *Angel*gerät 24; *Angel*rolle 24; *Angel*schein 24; *Angel*spitze 24
Apostelgeschichte (Bibel) 154
Antenne **161**, 161, 162; Motor-*Antenne* 161
Art **164**, 164, **165**, 177
artig 45, 46
Arzt / Ärztin **215**, 215, **216**
Aspekt **24**, **25**, **56**, **57**, 57
auch **27**, **28**, 229
Aufnahme **66**, 66, **67**, 67
ausdruckslos **170**, **171**, 177
ausgeben (für) **246**, 246, **247**
ausgesprochen 12, 13, 14, 15, **167**, 167, 168, 177, 243; *ausgesprochene* Abgeneigtheit 13, 14, 167; *ausgesprochener* Akzent 13, 14, 167; *ausgesprochen* gedrückt 13, 14, 167; *ausgesprochen* gehemmt 243; *ausgesprochen* gemischte Gefühle **13**, 13, 167, *ausgesprochen* schlechtes Wetter 13, 14, 167; *ausgesprochene* Vorliebe 13, 14, 167
Auslieferungslager **262**, **263**, 263
Aussicht **224**, 224, **225**
außerdem **27**, **28**, 28

Bach **127**, 127, **128**, 128
Bank (1) (Geldinstitut) 17, 19, **30**, **31**, 167, 272, 274 (2) (Sitz*bank*) 30, 31, 51, 272, 274 (3) (Kirchen*bank*) 30, 31, 51
Baracke(n) 12, 18, **32**, 32, **33**, 33, 51, 52, 272; *Baracken*-Vorstadt 32; Bau*baracke* 32; Elends*baracke* **32**, **33**; Wellblech-*Baracke* 32; Werkzeug-*Baracke* 32
Bausubstanz **180**, 180
Beatmungsgerät (Med.) **257**, **258**, 258, 270
Bedeutung **84**, **85**, 85; *Bedeutungs*änderung 85
befangen 9, 243, **244**, 244
befreien (von) **120**, **121**, 121
(wohl-)bekannt **182**, **183**, 183
bekommen **35**, **37**, 51, 123, 191, 209; jdm. (gut) *bekommen* **35**, 36, **37**; jdm. nicht *be*-

kommen **35**, 36, 37; Gänsehaut *bekommen* 60
belegt: eine *belegte* Stimme 9, 54
beleihen 39
bescheiden **100**, **101**, 101; ein *bescheidenes* Einkommen 101; ein *bescheidenes* Vermögen 101
(jdn.) beunruhigen **156**, **157**, 157; beunruhigt sein (über) **156**, **157**, 157
Bezahlung **226**, 227, **228**, 241
'ohne *Biß*' (sein) 45, 46
blank **170**, 170, **171**, 217; *blanke* Augen 170; *blankes* Eis 170; *blanker* Hohn 170; die *blanke* Oberfläche des Spiegels 170; *blanker* Unsinn 170; *blank* putzen **170**, 170, **171**, '*blank*' sein (koll.) **170**, 170, **171**
Blickwinkel **24**, **25**, **56**, **57**, 57
'blöd' **54**, **55**
(Fuß-)Boden **62**, 62, **63**, 63
borgen 12, **39**, 39, **40**, 40, 51
Braut **42**, 42, **43**, 43, 51; *Braut*kleid 42; *Braut*paar 42; angebliche *Braut* 42; versetzte *Braut* (am Hochzeitstag) 43; versetzte *Braut* (als Verlobte) 42; zukünftige *Braut* 42
brav **45**, 45, **46**, 46, 51, 272; *brav* halten zu 45; *brav* sein 45; eine *brave* Vorstellung (einer Mannschaft) 45
Brust **47**, 47, **48**, 48, 51, 251, 276; *Brust*beschwerden 47; *Brust*höhe 47; *Brust*kasten 47; *Brust*korb 47; *Brust*krebs 48; *Brust*schwimmen 48; Gänse*brust* 48; Hühner*brust* 48
(Meeres-)Bucht 68
Bürgermeister(in) **203**, 203, **204**, 205, 213
Bürstenschnitt 75
Busen (1) (Frauen*busen*) **47**, 47, **48**
(2) (Meer*busen*) Bottnischer Meer*busen* 68; Finnischer Meer*busen* 68

Chance **224**, 224, **225**
Container für Altglas 30
Courmacher **185**, 185, **186**

daneben **27**, **28**
der, die etc. (in Relativsätzen) **137**, **138**, 138
Diapositiv (ohne Rahmen) **254**, 254, **255**; Dia (mit Rahmen) 254, 255
dicht **54**, 54, **55**, **56**; *dicht* auffahren 56; *dichtes* Haar 9, 54; *dichte* Hekke 54; *dichter* Nebel 9, 54, **55**; *dichter* Rauch 54
dick 9, 19, **53**, 53, 54, **55**, 79; eine *dicke* Brieftasche 53; *dicke* Eiche 9; im *dicksten* Feierabendverkehr 9, 53; *dicker* Fehler 9, 54; ein *dickes* Gehalt 54; ein *dicker* Gewinn 53; ein *dicker* Knöchel 54; ein *dickes* Lob 54; eine *dicke* Provision 54; eine *dicke* Rechnung 54; *dicke* Regentropfen 54; ein *dicker* Wagen 54; eine *dicke* Zigarre 54
Dom **173**, 173, 174, 177, 183, 272; *Dom*reparaturen 173; *Dom*stadt 173

ebenfalls **27**, **28**
ehrlich 45, 46
Einsender **117**, 117, **118**
Engel **56**, **57**, 57, 58; Erz*engel* 56; Rache*engel* 56; rettender *Engel* 56; Schutz*engel* 56; Todes*engel* 79
entwickeln: sich entwikkeln zu **36**, **37**
erübrigen **120**, **121**, 121
Ernte **74**, 74; Apfel*ernte* **74**
Etage **62**, 62, **63**

Fabrik **179**, 179, 180, 213
Fahrpreis **222**, 222
familiär **182**, 182, 183
Farbton **234**, 235, **236**
Fingerspitzengefühl (fig.) **161**, 161, 162
Flanke **114**, **115**, 115
Fleisch (1) (zum Essen zubereitetes Fleisch) **59**, 59, **60**, 79; *Fleisch*gericht **59**, **60**; *Fleisch*importeur 59
(2) (rohes, lebendes Fleisch) **59**, 59, **60**, 60, 79; wildes *Fleisch* 60; sein eigenes *Fleisch* und Blut 59;
(3) (Frucht*fleisch*) 60
Flirt **185**, 185, 186, 213, 273; Telefon*flirt* 185
flirten (mit) **185**, 185, **186**
Flittchen **185**, 185, **186**
Flugwinkel 24, 25
Flur 19, **62**, **63**, 63, 79; oberer Treppen*flur* 62
Flut (fig.) **127**, **128**, 128; eine *Flut* von Beschwerden 128
Folie **254**, 254, **255**; Folie (für Overhead-Projektor) **254**, 254; Alu*folie* 255; Back*folie* 255; Haushalts*folie* 255; Plastik*folie* 255
Foto 42, 57, **64**, 64, **66**, **67**; *Foto*apparat 67; *Foto*ausrüstung 64; *Foto*handel 64; *Foto*-Sit-

zung 67; Akt*fotos* 150; Hochzeits*fotos* 66
Fotografie **64**, 64, 79
(das) Fotografieren **64**, 64, **65**, 65
freimütig 14, 15, **167**, **168**, 168
freundschaftlich **182**, **183**, 183
Fühler (bei Insekten etc.) **161**, 161, **162**
fürchten: sich *fürchten* (vor) **156**, 156, **157**

Gasse: (kleine) Gasse **159**, 159, 160; Gäßchen **159**, **160**; Hinter*gäßchen* 160, Sack*gasse* 160
Gebläse: (Kühl-)Gebläse **257**, 257, 258
Gebühr **226**, 227, **228**
Gedächtnisspeicher 30
geflügelt **182**, **183**, 183; *geflügeltes* Wort 183
gehemmt **243**, 243, **244**
Gefüge: Gesellschafts*gefüge* **180**, 180
gehemmt 9, **243**, 243, **244**
gering **100**, 100, **101**; ein *geringer* Mitgliedsbeitrag 100
Geschoß: Erd*geschoß* 63; Zwischen*geschoß* 63
Gesetz(e) **150**, 150, **151**, **153**, 153, **154**, 154
Gesichtspunkt **24**, 25, **56**, **57**, 57
Gespür **161**, **162**
Gewebe **180**, 180, 181
Gewölbe **173**, 173, **174**
Gift 11, 19, **187**, 187, **188**, 213; *Gift*müll 187
Glatze **173**, **174**, 174
Golf (1) (als Sportart) **69**, 69, 272; *Golf*anlage 69; *Golf*klub 69; *Golf*platz 69; *Golf*saison 69; *Golf*titel 69; Mini-*Golf* 69
(2) (als geographische Bezeichnung) **68**, 68, **69**, 202, 272; *Golf* von Aden 68; *Golf* von Biscaya 68; *Golf* von Mexiko 68; *Golf* von Suez 68; mexikanische *Golf*küste 68

Hafenspeicher **262**, **263**, 263
Handlung(en) **150**, 150, **153**, 153, **154**
Hausleiter(in) **190**, 190, **191**
Hausmeister(in) **190**, 190, **191**, 213
Heizlüfter 257, 269
Helm 19, **193**, 193, **194**, 213; Astronauten-*Helm* 193; Blau*helme* 193; Sicherheits*helm* 193; Sturz*helm* 193; Tropen*helm* 193
Hose **196**, 196, 197, 213, 275; Freizeit-*Hose* **196**, 196, **197**; Kord*hose* 196; Strumpf*hose* 196; Wind*hose* 196; die *Hosen* anhaben 196

isoliert **199**, 199, **200**, 200, 214; sich *isoliert* fühlen **199**, 199, **200**; *isoliert* sein **199**, 199, **200**, 200; isoliert werden (von) **199**, 199, **200**

Kanal (1) (natürlich) **71**, 71, **72**, 72; Ärmel*kanal* 71; Nord-*Kanal* 71; St. Georgs-*Kanal* 71; *Kanal*tunnel 71
(2) (künstlich) **71**, 71, **72**, 72, 73; Nord-Ostsee-*Kanal* 72
(3) (diplomatische *Kanäle*) **71**, 71, **72**, 79
(4) (TV, Radio) **71**, 71, **72**
Kandidat: (aussichtsreicher) Kandidat (Sport) **224**, 224, **225**
'schwer von *kapee*' **54**, 54, **55**
Karte: (Land- etc. Karte) **81**, 81; *Karten* der Erdteile 81; *Karten* der Ozeane 81; Welt*karten* 81
Kaserne **32**, **33**
klein **100**, 100, **101**, 209, 221
Kluft (fig.) 68, 79
Kokette **185**, 185, **186**
kokettieren (mit) **185**, 185, **186**
Kropf (1) (beim Menschen) **74**, 74, 79
(2) (Verdauungsorgan bei Tieren) **74**, 74, 75
Kunst **165**, 165, 255; *Kunst*ausstellung 165; *Kunst*fahrer 165; *Kunst*freund 165; *Kunst*galerie 165; *Kunst*genuß 165; *Kunst*händler 165; *Kunst*historiker 165; *Kunst*leder 165; *Kunst*pause 165; *Kunst*seide 165; *Kunst*stoff **217**, 217, **218**
Kuppel **173**, 173, **174**; *Kuppel*gebäude **173**, 173, 174; Plastik-*Kuppel*gebäude 173

Lager: *Lager*arbeiter 263; *Lager*halle **262**, 262, **263**; *Lager*(haus) **262**, 262, **263**; *Lager*hausgehilfe 263; Auslieferungs*lager* **262**, 262, **263**, 263; Fabrik*lager* 262; Flüchtlings*lager* 262; Holz*lager* 266; Munitions*lager* 262; Reifen*lager* 262; Tabak*lager* 262; Teppich*lager* 262
leer **170**, **171**, 171
leibhaftig 60
leihen **39**, 39; aus*leihen* **39**, 39, **40**, 40; (sich) etwas *leihen* **39**, 39, **40**
liebäugeln (mit) **185**, 185, **186**
(Ent-)Lüftungsanlage

257, 258; Lüftungsklappe 257, 257, 258

Major(in) 202, 202, 203, 204; '*Major* zur See' 202, 202, 204; Armee-*Major* 202; Heilsarmee-*Major*(*in*) 202, 202, 204; Luftwaffen-*Major* 202, 202, 203; Marine-*Major* 202, 204; Tambour-*Major*(*in*) 202, 202, 204
Mann (1) Mann 42, 45, 47, 76, 76, 77, 77, 79; *Mann* in den besten Jahren 76; *Mann* des Volkes 76; *Mann* der Tat 76
(2) Ehe*mann* 45, 59, 76, 76, 77, 79, 95, 137, 171
Mannschaft (Sport) 114, 115, 115
Mappe 81, 81, 82, 109; Akten*mappe* 81, 82
Mediziner(in) 215, 215, 216
Meer (1) (allgemein oder als Bezeichnung) 111, 112, 112; Rotes *Meer* 68, 112; Weißes *Meer* 112
(2) (fig.) Blumen*meer* 112; Farben*meer* 112; Zuschauer*meer* 112
(eßbare) Meeresfrüchte 238, 238, 239, 239
Meinung 84, 84, 85, 109, 217; *Meinungs*änderung 84; *Meinungs*befragung 84; *Meinungs*schattierung 84; *Meinungs*umschwung 84; *Meinungs*verschiedenheiten 84
Mensch(en) 76, 76, 77, 137
Miete 95, 95, 96; *Miet*rückstände 96; *Miet*zins 95, 95, 96
Mitbewerber (im Sport) 224, 225
Mörder(in) 87, 87, 89, 109; Bruder*mörder* 87, 87, 88, 89; Gift*mörder* 87, 87; Kinder*mörder* 87; Mutter*mörder* 88; politischer *Mörder* 87, 87, 89; Vater*mörder* 88; vorsätzlicher *Mörder* 88; Selbst*mörder* 88
Moral (1) (innere Einstellung) 206, 206, 213, 272
(2) ('Lehre') 206, 207, 273
Mord 87, 88, 89; *Mord*fall 62, 153; *Mord*verdächtiger 88; Bruder*mord* 88; Mutter*mord* 88; Ruf*mord* 88; Selbst*mord* 88; Vater*mord* 88; Völker*mord* 88; vorsätzlicher *Mord* 88
mutig 45, 46, 46; *mutig* sein 46

nächste (1) (in der Reihenfolge) 90, 90, 91, 91, 109, 120, 151
(2) (räumlich) 90, 90, 91, 109
'*Neben-*' (etc.): 114, 115, 115; *Neben*effekt 115; *Neben*eingang 115
Nuance 234, 235, 236
Nummer (im Zirkus etc.) 150, 151, 151; Zirkus*nummern* 151

offen 14, 15, 167, 167, 168, 168

Pacht(geld) 95, 96, 96
Parkett 62, 63
Pension (1) (Gästehaus, kleines Privathotel) 209, 209, 210
(2) (Rente) 209, 210, 210
Perle (1) (echt, natürlich) 92, 92, 93; *Perl*mutt 93; *Perlen*taucher 92; echte *Perlen* 92
(2) (aus Glas, Holz etc.) 92, 92, 93; Glas-*Perlen*kette 92; Holz-*Perlen*kette 92, 109; Schweiß*perle* 92, 92, 93, 93
Pfarrer 147, 259, 260, 260
Pflanzen 74, 74, 75
Phantombild 67
Physiker(in) 215, 215, 216, 241; Atom*physiker* 215
Plastik (1) (als Kunstgegenstand) 217, 217, 218, 241; Bronze-*Plastiken* 217; Tier*plastiken* 217
(2) (als Kunststoff) 217, 217, 218, 218; *Plastik*flaschen 217; *Plastik*folie 218; *Plastik*ruder 218; *Plastik*tüten 217; *Plastik*zitronen 217
(Gedenk-)Platte 130, 131, 131
Politik (1) (praktisch, konkret) 219, 219, 220, 241, 275; Außen*politik* 219; Wirtschafts*politik* 219; Umwelt*politik* 219
(2) (allgemein, theoretisch) 219, 219, 220, 241, 275; Partei*politik* 220
Preis (1) (Gewinn-, Sieges*preis*) 221, 221, 222, 241, 275; *Preis*geld 221; *Preis*richter 221; *Preis*skat 221; Friedens-Nobel*preis* 193; Trost*preis* 221
(2) (Laden-, Verkaufs*preis*) 221, 221, 222, 222, 241, 262, 275; *Preis*lage 221; *Preis*schlager 222; *Preis*senkung 222; *Preis*stopp 221; *Preis*sturz 222; Billig*preis*-Flüge 221; Selbstkosten*preis* 222
Prospekt 224, 224, 225, 241; Informations*pro-*

spekt 224; Reise*prospekt* 224

Quote **226**, 226, **228**; Ausfall*quote* 226; Erfolgs*quote* 226

Rate 19, **226**, 226, 227, **228**, 228, 275; auf *Raten* 226; Heirats*rate* 227; Inflations*rate* 227; Scheidungs*rate* 227
Rente **95**, 95, **96**, 96, 109; Alters*rente* **95**, 95, **96**; Invaliditäts*rente* 95; Kriegswitwen*rente* 95; Leib*rente* **95**, 95, 96; Witwen*rente* 95
Ruder (fig.) **194**, 194

Salat (1) (Natur*salat*) 19, **229**, 229, **230**, 241, 272; Iceberg-*Salat* 229
(2) (zubereiteter *Salat*) 19, **229**, 229, **230**, 230, 241, 272; *Salat* (als Beilage) 230; *Salat*sauce 229; Endivien*salat* 229; Gurken*salat* 229; Hummer*salat* 229; Kartoffel*salat* 229; Schinken*salat* 229; Tomaten*salat* 229
(geldlicher) Satz **226**, **228**, 241
Sauce (1) (Braten*sauce*) **97**, 97, **98**, 98, 109, 275
(2) (süße oder pikante *Sauce*) **97**, **98**, 98, 275; Käse-*Sauce* 98; Pils*sauce* 97; Vanille*sauce* 97; Zwiebel*sauce* 97
Schäker(in) **185**, 185, **186**
Schal (1) (Umlege*schal*) **231**, 231, 232, 241
(2) (Gardinen*schal*) **231**, 231, 232
Schatten (1) (*Schatten*bild-, umriß) **234**, 234, **236**
(2) (*Schatten* als Schutz vor der Sonne) **234**, 235, **236**, 241
(3) (*Schatten* fig.) **234**, 235, **236**
Schattierung **234**, 235, **236**
Schellfisch 12, **238**, 238, **239**, 241, 275
Schlagzeile 11
Schlange 18, **103**, 103, **104**, 104; *Schlangen*beschwörer 103; *Schlangen*biß 104; *Schlangen*tänzer 103; *Gift*schlange 104; Klapper*schlange* 105
(Wasser- etc.) Schlauch **197**, 197, 198, 213
schmal **100**, 100, **101**, 101, 275; *schmal* im Gesicht 100, 109; ein *schmaler* Gewinn 100; *schmale* Hände 100; ein *schmaler* Pfad 100
Schnecke (1) (Gehäuse*schnecke*) **103**, 103, **104**, 109
(2) (Nackt*schnecke*) **103**, 103, **104**
Schultasche 81, 82
schwimmen (1) (aktiv) **106**, 106, **107**, 107, 109, 272
(2) (passiv) **106**, 106, **107**, 272; *schwimmendes* Hospital 106; *schwimmendes* Restaurant 106; '*schwimmender* Sarg' 106
'ohne *Schwung*' 45, 46
See (1) (*der* See) 107, **111**, 111, **112**, **147**; Binnen*see* 111; Boden*see* 111; Land*see* 111; künstlicher *See* 111
(2) (*die* See) **111**, 111, **112**, 112, 140; Barent*see* 112; Irische *See* 112; Nord*see* 111; Ost*see* 112
(3) (bestimmte Meerestiere, -fische und Seevögel) *See*hund 112; *See*möwe 111; *See*stern 112; *See*zunge 112
Seite **114**, 114, **115**, 116, 140, 266
selbstbewußt 9, 11, **243**, 243, 244, 269, 275
Sender **117**, 117, **118**, 140
Silbertablett **130**, 130, 131
Sinn **84**, **85**, 85
sparen (für/an) **120**, 120, **121**, 140
spenden **246**, 246, **247**, 269
Stadion (1) (Sport-*Stadion*) **248**, 248, **249**, 249
(2) (überdachtes *Stadion*) **173**, **174**, 174
Stadium **248**, 248, **249**, 269
Stadtplan **81**, **82**, 82
Steuer (auf dem Schiff) **194**, 194
(lokale) Steuer **226**, 227, **228**
Stock(werk) **62**, 62, **63**, 63; erster *Stock* 63; fünfter *Stock* 62; zweiter *Stock* 62, 63
Stoff **180**, 180, 181
Straße (1) (inner- und außerhalb von Ortschaften) **123**, 123, **124**, 124, **125**, 125, 140; *Straßen*atlas 123; *Straßen*fest 124; *Straßen*karte **81**, 81; *Straßen*kreuzung 56; *Straßen*laterne 124; *Straßen*schwelle 123; Dorf*straße* 124; Fern*straße* 123; Haupt*straße* 124; Land*straße* 123; Zubringer*straße* 124; Zufahrts*straße* 124
(2) (Meeres*straße*) **123**, 124, **125**; *Straße* von Dover 124; *Straße* von Florida 124; *Straße* von Hormus 124; *Straße* von Sizilien 124
Strom (1) (elektrischer *Strom*) **127**, 127, **128**, 128

(2) (großer Fluß, *Strom*) **127**, 127, **128**, **129**, 140
(3) (Luft-, Meeres*strom*) **127**, 127, **128**; Golf*strom* 128
(4) (*Strom* fig.) **127**, **128**, 128; ein *Strom* von Menschen 128; der *Strom* der Zeit 128; Bewußtseins*strom* 128

Tablett 12, **130**, 130, **131**, 140
Tablette **130**, 130, **131**, 131; Schlaf*tabletten* 131; Vitamin*tabletten* 130
(Marmor-, Ton- etc.) Tafel **130**, **131**, 131
Tanzfläche **62**, **63**, 63
tapfer **45**, 45, **46**
Tat(en) **150**, 150, **151**, **153**, 153, 154; Gewalt*taten* 153; Mann der *Tat* 76
Technik (1) (allgemein) 12, **251**, 251, **252**, 276; das Zeitalter der *Technik* 251; die neue Druck*technik* 251
(2) (speziell) 12, **251**, 251, 252, 269, 276; Bau*technik* 251; Entspannungs*technik* 251
Tempo **226**, 226, **228**
Transparent **254**, 254, **255**, 269
treu 45, 46

Überschrift 11
übrig **120**, 121, 121; *übrig* haben 120, **121**, 121
unausgefüllt 170, **171**, 171
ungeschminkt 14, 15, **167**, **168**, 168
unverblümt 14, 15, **167**, **168**, 168

Ventilator 18, **257**, 257, **258**
verblüfft **170**, **171**, 171
verbringen **246**, 246, **247**
verlegen 9, **243**, **244**, 244
verschonen **120**, **121**
verständnislos **170**, **171**, 171, 177
(plump-)vertraulich **182**, **183**, 183
(wohl-)vertraut **182**, **183**, 183
Vikar 19, **259**, 259, **260**, 269

wann (in Fragen) **132**, 132, **133**
Warenhaus **262**, 262, **263**, 269
(jdn.) warnen **156**, 156, **157**
wem, wen **137**, 137, **138**
wenn **132**, 132, **133**, 140, 229; wenn nicht **132**, 132, **133**, 133
wer **134**, 134, 135, **137**, 137, **138**, 140
werden (1) (beruflich etc. etwas *werden*) **36**, **37**, 203, 215; *werden* aus **36**, **37**
(2) (in bestimmten Verbindungen) bleich *werden* 91; dunkel *werden* 37, 125; knapp *werden* 120; krank *werden* 91; lebenswichtig *werden* 130; reich *werden* 36; verrückt *werden* 37; wahr *werden* 37; schwanger *werden* 262
Winkel (Math.) **24**, 51, **56**, **57**; rechter *Winkel* 24; spitzer *Winkel* 24; stumpfer *Winkel* 24
wo **134**, 134, 135, **137**, 137, **138**, 140
woher **134**, 134, **135**, 135, 137
wohin **134**, 134, **135**

zaghaft 45, 46
Ziffer **226**, 227, **228**; Geburten*ziffer* 227
zusätzlich **120**, **121**, 121
Zylinder (1) (als Herrenhut) **265**, 265, **266**, 269, 272
(2) (Math., Mech.) **266**, 266, 269, 272
Zahl **226**, 227, **228**; Puls*zahl* 227
Zinssatz **226**, 227, **228**

rororo sprachen

Herausgegeben von Ludwig Moos

Gunther Bischoff
Speak you English?
Programmierte Übung zum Verlernen typisch deutscher Englischfehler (6857)
Managing Manager English
Gekonnt verhandeln lernen durch Üben an Fallstudien (7129)
Better times
Programm zum Gebrauch der englischen Zeiten (7987)

René Bosewitz/Robert Kleinschroth
Joke Your Way Through English Grammar
Wichtige Regeln zum Anlachen (8527)

René Bosewitz/Hartmut Breitkreuz
Do up your Phrasals
Fünfhundert Wendungen wichtiger Verben (8344)

Claire Bretécher/Isabelle Jue/Nicole Zimmermann
Le Français avec les Frustrés
Ein Comic-Sprachhelfer (8423)

Ahmed Haddedou
Questions Grammaticales de A à Z
Tout ce que vous avez toujours voulu savoir sur la grammaire sans jamais oser le demander (8445)

Hans-Georg Heuber/Marie-Thérèse Pignolo
Ne mâche pas tes mots
Nimm kein Blatt vor den Mund!
Französische Redewendungen und ihre deutschen Pendants (7472)

C 2199/6

Hans-Georg Heuber
Talk one's head off
Ein Loch in den Bauch reden
Englische Redewendungen und ihre deutschen «opposite numbers» (7653)

Emer O'Sullivan/Dietmar Rösler
Modern Talking
Englisches Quasselbuch mit Sprüchen und Widersprüchen (8427)

Mario Parisi/Liborio Pepi
Parole Espresse
Italienisches Quasselbuch mit Sprüchen und Widersprüchen (8434)

Ernest Pasakarnis
Grammar Questions from A – Z
Everything you always wanted to know about Grammar but were afraid to ask (8359)
The Word Lover's Guide to How Words Work
Ein moderner Vokabeltrainer (8426)
Master your Idioms
Der Schlüssel zu den englischen Redewendungen (8491)

Senzaparole
Finalmente in Italia
Italienischkurs für wenig und weiter Fortgeschrittene (8471)

Jacques Soussan
Pouvez-vous Français?
Programmierte Übung zum Verlernen typisch deutscher Französischfehler (6940)

A·N·D·E·R·S·R·E·I·S·E·N

STÄDTE

Roland Günter
Amsterdam (7506)

zitty-Illustrierte Stadtzeitung
Berlin (9061)

Manfred Waffender/Jonathan Walters
London (7502)

Werner W. Wille
New York (7512)

Günter Liehr
Paris (7509)

Peter Kammerer/Henning Klüver
Rom (7514)

Manfred Waffender
San Francisco (7507)

Frida Bordon
Venedig mit Venetien (7570)

Herausgegeben von Falter
Wien (7563)

Herausgegeben
von
Ludwig Moos

rororo SACHBUCH

C 2400/1

A·N·D·E·R·S·R·E·I·S·E·N

Herausgegeben
von
Ludwig Moos

LÄNDER

Christof Kehr
Andalusien (7575)

Dirk Wegner
Australien (7598)

Roland Motz
Balearen/Barcelona (7579)

Petra Schaeber/Martin Wilke
Brasilien (7594) Oktober '91

Hartiwg Bögeholz
China (7580)

Per Ketman/Andreas Wißmach
DDR (7568)

Dagmar Beckmann/Ulrike Strauch
Elsaß (7585)

Günter Liehr
Frankreich (7519)
Südfrankreich (7582)

Ingrid Backes/Gabriela Daum
Griechenland (7508)

Michael Kadereit
Großbritannien (7530)

Christoph Potting/Annette Weweler
Irland (7525)

SACHBUCH rororo

C 2400/1 a

A·N·D·E·R·S·R·E·I·S·E·N

Herausgegeben von Ludwig Moos

PRAKTISCHE REISEBÜCHER

Ingrid Backes
Das FrauenReiseBuch
(7572)

Hartwig Bögeholz/Werner Radasewsky
Almanach 90/91
Adressen, Infos & Ideen
Der Kompaß durch den Reisedschungel
(7587)

Helmut Hermann
Das ReiseFotoBuch
Ausrüstung, Technik, Praxis und Gespür (7589)

Isabelle Jue/Nicole Zimmermann
Sprachbuch Frankreich
(7520)

Christoph Kehr/Ana Rodriguez Lebrón
Sprachbuch Spanien
(7588)

Johannes Müller/Peter Müller
Gesund unterwegs
Medizinisches Reisehandbuch
(7583)

Emer O'Sullivan/Dietmar Rösler
Sprachbuch Großbritannien / Irland
(7564)

Sprachkollektiv Senzaparole
Sprachbuch Italien
(7571)

SACHBUCH rororo

C 2400/1 c

Hobby und Freizeit

Eine Auswahl

Norbert Golluch/Eckhard Klötzer
Das Sperrmüll-Buch
(8757)

Eva C. Huvos
Im Notfall Petersilie
Tips und Tricks einer chaotischen Hausfrau (8366)

Hans-Eberhard Lessing
Das Fahrradbuch
Radfahren mit Know-how (8339)

Raimund Pousset (Hg.)
Der erste Urlaubskoffer
222 Ferienspiele: Rätselhaftes, Witziges, Spannendes und Kriminalistisches für jung und alt (7914)
Der zweite Urlaubskoffer
Das große Schmöker- und Spiele-Buch (7990)

Jürgen Stark/Klaus Farin
Das Fußball Lesebuch
(8596)

Kristine Steinhilber/Cornelius Siegel
Danke, ich schaff's alleine!
Das Autobuch für Frauen (7423)

Helmut Steuer/Claus Voigt
Das neue rororo Spielbuch
(handbuch 6270)

G.J.F. van Tuil/E.R.A. van Heerde
Wünschelruten-Gehen
Eine neue Einführung in eine alte Technik (8751)